"Missional pneumatologies are rare enough, ~~and when~~ Gary Tyra ~~fills~~ this serious theological vacuum with this truly excellent exploration of the role of the Spirit in mission, we can only be grateful. This is an addition to the missional conversation we have been waiting for."

Alan Hirsch, founder of Forge Mission Training Network and author of *The Forgotten Ways*

"Tyra's sensitive scholarship and pastoral experience have helped him to come up with a sound, balanced and readable volume—a welcome contribution of immense value to the health of the global church. Although Tyra's views are significantly shaped by his Pentecostal roots, the case he presents is consonant with evangelical essentials and should provoke interest and response from a wide spectrum of Christians who warmly and reverently welcome the work of the Holy Spirit in the life of the church today. This book is an essential addition to every theological library!"

Ivan Satyavrata, senior pastor and chairman, The Assembly of God Church and Mission, Kolkata, India, and International Deputy Director, South Asia, The Lausanne Movement

"Gary Tyra has succeeded in translating and interpreting the 'tongues' of Pentecostal missiology into evangelical idiom! Students will be immersed into the salvation-missional history of the Bible and introduced to the most vital streams in contemporary mission theology. A must-read for missiologists and anyone else seeking to fulfill the Great Commission."

Amos Yong, professor, Regent University School of Divinity, and coeditor of *Pneuma*

"Among the many recent 'turns' in the doctrine and spirituality of the Holy Spirit, the turn to mission might well be the most significant one! A fresh, inspiring and prophetic missional pneumatology outlined and developed in this work, in close conversation with missional ecclesiology, provides the kind of biblical, practical and theological impetus evangelicals have been waiting for. The reader will be faced with a simple and profound challenge: The missionary Spirit of the missionary God is ready for the world—what about you and your church?"

Veli-Matti Kärkkäinen, professor of systematic theology, Fuller Theological Seminary

"Outside of the West, the church is exploding in rapid growth and influence, and leading experts tell us that much of it is due to supernatural manifestations of the Holy Spirit. What has been needed is a biblically and theologically savvy defense of this role of the Spirit in the church's mission. Tyra's excellent book more than adequately fills that need. His treatment of the importance of the prophetic is alone worth the price of the book."

J. P. Moreland, Distinguished Professor of Philosophy, Talbot School of Theology, Biola University, and coauthor of *In Search of a Confident Faith*

"It's ironic that it's taken a century for this book to be written. Gary Tyra helps Pentecostals and non-Pentecostals see that we all are charismatic, each of us embodying the Spirit who is missional. Regardless of one's experience, all are called to hear his promptings and, in obedience, see the many ways his power is manifested. The Spirit conspires to do the will of the Father. Each member of the people of God has all that's needed to function in fullness as his missional witness. Tyra has provided a very readable, biblically informed and anecdotal manuscript showing how the Spirit is missional. A complete and deeply helpful book for one's devotional and ministry life."

Brian C. Stiller, global ambassador, The World Evangelical Alliance, and president emeritus, Tyndale University College and Seminary

"I applaud Gary Tyra's bridge-building efforts on this most practical and pivotal arena of our joint witness throughout the body of Christ."

Jack W. Hayford, president, The King's University

"This book marks a new frontier in evangelical missiology, the gift being a new breed of Pentecostal pastor who blends evangelical learning with Pentecostal experience of the Spirit into a rare but emerging genre: missiological pneumatology."

Russ Spittler, professor emeritus of New Testament and provost emeritus, Fuller Theological Seminary

"For more than a decade, in dialogue with the missional and emerging movements, I have awaited this book. Thank God for Gary Tyra's insights regarding how the church's ongoing conversational relationship with the Holy Spirit informs engagement with culture and empowers Christian mission. Best I've seen by a wide margin."

Todd Hunter, missionary bishop, The Anglican Mission, and author of *Christianity Beyond Belief*

"Gary Tyra offers a sweeping panoramic view of the Spirit in mission. This academically critical and yet extremely reader-friendly study serves well as a prophetic call for all Christian communities to be Spirit-empowered witnesses following God's trajectory in mission."

Wonsuk Ma, Ph.D., executive director, Oxford Centre for Mission Studies

"The title of this book states clearly the focus of Tyra's work. The Holy Spirit and mission are neither isolated themes nor disconnected activities, but are clearly connected to a missionary God whose redemptive impetus is centered in the continuing mission of Jesus, empowered by the Spirit. Tyra moves beyond the defining parameters of his own faith tradition and speaks clearly about what should be the heartbeat of every follower of Jesus who realizes that the redemptive mission of Jesus is the organizer for our meaning and purpose in life."

Byron D. Klaus, president, Assemblies of God Theological Seminary, Springfield, Missouri

"*The Holy Spirit in Mission* breaks fresh ground in connecting the dots between a missional pneumatology and a missional ecclesiology. . . . This book is a must-read—and a very engaging read—for church ministers, rank-and-file church members, denominational leaders, college students and seminarians, and theological educators. I highly recommend it."

Murray W. Dempster, Distinguished Professor of Social Ethics, Southeastern University

"*The Holy Spirit in Mission* by Gary Tyra challenges the evangelical church in post-Christian America to live and serve by the dynamic of a missional pneumatology. Tyra's presupposition is that being missional is the heartbeat of the Holy Spirit. His message is timely, provocative and compelling, and it captures the spirit of missions. Christian leaders might want to buy this book by the dozen and share it with their leadership teams. Those who have ears to hear need to hear what this prophetic book says to evangelical Christians about prophetic speech and action in Christian witness."

Roger Stronstad, Biblical Theology Director, Summit Pacific College

"This book makes an important contribution to the growing literature on the missional church movement by focusing on the Holy Spirit and the role of prophetic activity. Tyra's view of prophetic activity is supported with a careful analysis that draws out implications for a renewed ministry focus on engaging Western culture. I highly recommend it."

Michael Wilkinson, Trinity Western University

"Prophecy is a much-misunderstood gift of grace that has been lost to much of the contemporary American church. Gary Tyra has provided a biblically informed and practical book to guide church leaders in the restoration of prophetic speech and action for Christian witness and service."

Margaret M. Poloma, professor emeritus of sociology, The University of Akron

"Gary Tyra's emphasis on prophetic speech and action as critical elements of Spirit empowerment in the life of a believer are a theme that has been underrepresented in the theological literature and underutilized in concrete practice. This book inspires pastors and laypeople to obey the Spirit's divine promptings to act in a manner that will indeed change the lives of hurting people."

Doug Petersen, associate editor, *Pneuma,* and professor, Vanguard University

"I warmly recommend this practical theology of the Spirit to my fellow ministers. In a time in which newly acquired knowledge outpaces experience and wisdom, and theory is preached in isolation from the practice of ministry, Tyra argues for a more dialectical approach in presenting the whole-life transformation of the prophetic mission of the Holy Spirit in the life of the church in America."

Jesse Miranda, executive presbyter, General Council of Assemblies of God, and CEO, National Hispanic Christian Leadership Conference

"Gary Tyra suggests that the renewal of evangelical witness in a post-Christian era will involve a rediscovery of the Spirit's guidance in all aspects of serving God's kingdom purposes in the world. The result is a missional pneumatology that calls churches to discern and embody ever anew the Spirit's ongoing witness to the word of the living God. Tyra's vision is timely not only for Pentecostals and evangelicals but for Christians of all confessional families."

Frank D. Macchia, author of *Baptized in the Spirit: A Global Pentecostal Theology*

"*The Holy Spirit in Mission* is a fresh call to the church to intentionally participate with the Holy Spirit in what God is doing in the church and in the world. It engages the best of missional scholarship while giving very practical examples of how we can all be involved with the Spirit in God's mission. I highly recommend it to all church leaders."

Berten A. Waggoner, national director, Vineyard USA

"This important book repairs the disconnect between big-picture 'missional' depictions of the Spirit's work in renewing the creation and those who are calling us to engage in prophetic speaking and acting in the power of the Spirit. Gary Tyra not only makes his biblical-theological argument in a convincing manner, but he reinforces his case with powerful real-life accounts of the Spirit's prophetic leadings."

Richard J. Mouw, president and professor of Christian philosophy, Fuller Theological Seminary

THE

HOLY SPIRIT

IN MISSION

PROPHETIC SPEECH AND ACTION
IN CHRISTIAN WITNESS

GARY TYRA

IVP Academic

An imprint of InterVarsity Press
Downers Grove, Illinois

InterVarsity Press
P.O. Box 1400, Downers Grove, IL 60515-1426
World Wide Web: www.ivpress.com
E-mail: email@ivpress.com

*InterVarsity Press® is the book-publishing division of InterVarsity Christian Fellowship/USA®, a movement of
students and faculty active on campus at hundreds of universities, colleges and schools of nursing in the United States
of America, and a member movement of the International Fellowship of Evangelical Students. For information
about local and regional activities, write Public Relations Dept., InterVarsity Christian Fellowship/USA, 6400
Schroeder Rd., P.O. Box 7895, Madison, WI 53707-7895, or visit the IVCF website at <www.intervarsity.org>.*

All Scripture quotations, unless otherwise indicated, are taken from the Holy Bible, New International Version®.
NIV®. *Copyright ©1973, 1978, 1984 by International Bible Society. Used by permission of Zondervan Publishing
House. All rights reserved.*

*While all stories in this book are true, some names and identifying information in this book have been changed to
protect the privacy of the individuals involved.*

Design: Cindy Kiple
*Images: The Dove of the Holy Spirit by Sebastiano Bombelli at Palazzo Ducale, Venice, Italy. Cameraphoto Arte
        Venezia/The Bridgeman Art Library.*

ISBN 978-0-8308-3949-0

Printed in the United States of America ∞

Library of Congress Cataloging-in-Publication Data

Tyra, Gary, 1955-
  The Holy Spirit in mission: prophetic speech and action in
Christian witness/Gary Tyra.
      p. cm.
  Includes bibliographical references and indexes.
  ISBN 978-0-8308-3949-0 (pbk.: alk. paper)
  1. Holy Spirit. 2. Missions. 3. Prophecy—Christianity. I. Title.
  BT121.3.T97 2011
  231'.3—dc23

2011023123

P	20	19	18	17	16	15	14	13	12	11	10	9	8	7	6	5
Y	28	27	26	25	24	23	22	21	20	19						

This book is dedicated to Dr. Russell P. Spittler,
a consummate evangelical-Pentecostal scholar
and statesman whose example, counsel and friendship
have meant a great deal to me over the years.

CONTENTS

ACKNOWLEDGMENTS

Having produced three books prior, one thing I've learned is that the publication process is a long and involved one. I want to briefly acknowledge here my indebtedness to several groups of people whose help was crucial to this book's realization.

First, I want to express gratitude to all of my colleagues in the religion department at Vanguard University who, in various ways, provided support for this project. In particular, I want to thank Ed Rybarczyk, who read over an early version of the manuscript, offering some constructive suggestions in response; Greg Austring and Doug Petersen who, as veteran missionaries possessing insightful field experience related to the book's topic, consented to be interviewed and have their thoughts included in this work; Frank Macchia, for allowing me to cite his own pneumatological work so extensively; and Rich Israel, Roger Heuser, Jerry Camery-Hoggatt, Bill Dogterom, April Westbrook, Diana Wahlstedt, Markita Roberson and Angel McGee, for their timely words of encouragement. An additional word of thanks is owed to Doug Petersen for his gracious and eager assistance in wrangling together a top-notch group of endorsers for the book.

Second, I really must go on to indicate my sincere appreciation for the gracious manner in which the library staff at Vanguard University (Alison English, Mel Covetta, Mary Wilson, Pam Crenshaw, Elena Nipper and Jack Morgan) facilitated my research. You are a wonderful group of academic professionals with whom it is a pleasure to work.

Third, I want to thank all the folks at IVP who labored to make this book a reality. I owe a special debt of gratitude to Dr. Gary Deddo, senior editor at IVP Academic, for believing in this project and serving as a wise, insightful and patient partner with me in this publishing endeavor. Though I will be careful to issue the obligatory disclaimer that at the end of the day I alone am responsible for whatever flaws this scholarly work possesses, I want to express my deep appreciation for the keen theological contribution Gary made to this work along the way. This is a much better book because of Gary's involvement with it!

Fourth, I offer sincere thanks to those members of the Evangelical Theological Society and Society for Pentecostal Studies who heard me present academic papers based upon this work, and who offered both constructive and affirming comments in response. They too made this a better book.

Fifth, it's hard to state sufficiently how important it was during the long composition process for me to have interactions with evangelical church leaders, church members and students, some Pentecostal-charismatic and some not, whose eyes lit up when I described for them the thesis of this work. It was your excited, passionate, affirming responses that kept me thinking that I was on to something that just might make a difference in the way we evangelicals engage in missional ministry in our post-Christian context. You know who you are: many thanks to all of you for your generosity of mind and spirit.

Finally, though my adult children Brandon and Megan are out of the house these days and less affected by my writing process, my dear wife (and sometimes writing partner), Patti, continues to demonstrate what genuine marital love looks like by her willingness to allow me to spend so much time in my corner of the den, hunched over my laptop computer amid multiple stacks of books. Thank you, Patti, for being so patient with me. I love you more and more as the days go by. I'm a better man because of you!

Introduction

ONE OF THE ARTICLES OF FAITH included in the Cape Town Commitment—the document created at Cape Town 2010: The Third Lausanne Congress on World Evangelization—emphasizes the importance of the Holy Spirit to the mission of the church. This particular article says:

> We love the Holy Spirit within the unity of the Trinity, along with God the Father and God the Son. He is the missionary Spirit sent by the missionary Father and the missionary Son, breathing life and power into God's missionary Church. We love and pray for the presence of the Holy Spirit because without the witness of the Spirit to Christ, our own witness is futile. Without the convicting work of the Spirit, our preaching is in vain. Without the gifts, guidance and power of the Spirit, our mission is mere human effort. And without the fruit of the Spirit, our unattractive lives cannot reflect the beauty of the gospel.[1]

I am especially struck by the assertion: "He is the missionary Spirit of the missionary Father and the missionary Son, breathing life and power into God's missionary church." Fully convinced of the veracity of this statement, I have written *The Holy Spirit in Mission: Prophetic Speech and Action in Christian Witness* in the hope that it might serve as a practical biblical theology of the Spirit that can aid in the formation of

---

[1]"The Cape Town Commitment" 1.5, March 27, 2011, www.lausanne.org/ctcommitment. See also the chapter titled "Our God Is a Missionary God," in John Stott, *The Contemporary Christian* (Downers Grove, Ill.: InterVarsity Press, 1992), pp. 321-26, as cited in Christopher J. H. Wright, *The Mission of God: Unlocking the Bible's Grand Narrative* (Downers Grove, Ill.: InterVarsity Press, 2006), p. 24, n. 2.

biblically informed, Spirit-empowered, missionally faithful Christians and churches.[2]

This book is grounded in an observation I made while surveying what the Bible as a whole has to say about the Holy Spirit in mission: *God's Spirit has a penchant for using God's people to accomplish God's purposes.* Furthermore, a primary way the Holy Spirit does this is by prompting Christ's followers to speak and act toward others on behalf of him, in ways designed to evangelize, edify and equip. What follows is a true story designed to illustrate the kind of missional faithfulness and hopefulness I sincerely believe the missionary Spirit wants to produce in our lives.[3]

I begin most days with a two-mile prayer walk. Though the goal of these spiritual strolls is ideally to initiate a day-long experience of spiritual communion with the risen Christ, I will often stop and converse with fellow pedestrians I have become acquainted with over the years. Recently (at the time of this writing) I was chatting with a dear woman who up to that time had given every indication of being unchurched. During our brief exchange I felt impressed by the Holy Spirit to ask her to remember my daughter in prayer, as she was about to undergo some serious medical tests. I obeyed this prompting, knowing full well that the woman had never given me any reason to believe that she was a believer in anything supernatural. I remember thinking to myself that perhaps it was the Holy Spirit's desire to, in this manner, instill within this woman's mind and heart a gentle reminder of the possibility that the world around her might entail a spiritual dimension after all—a dimension she may have been guilty of neglecting.

---

[2]Ed Stetzer and David Putnam speak of the need for missional churches to be both Spirit-empowered and biblically informed (Ed Stetzer and David Putnam, *Breaking the Missional Code: Your Church Can Become a Missionary in Your Community* [Nashville: Broadman & Holman, 2006], pp. 39-42, 53-58, 190).

[3]James Davison Hunter offers a thoughtful response to the missional query: "What does it mean for the believer to be faithful in this generation?" (James Davison Hunter, *To Change the World: The Irony, Tragedy, and Possibility of Christianity in the Late Modern World* [New York: Oxford University Press, 2010], p. 224). Hunter goes on to advocate for something he refers to as a "faithful presence" that calls for believers to be faithful (lovingly present as an agent of *shalom*) to God himself, to one another, to their tasks and within their spheres of influence (ibid., pp. 243-48). Though not exactly the same, there are nevertheless some great affinities between Hunter's advocacy for a faithful presence and this book's call for a missional faithfulness.

It was a few days later that our paths crossed once again. The first words from my friend's mouth took the form of a question: "How did your daughter's medical tests turn out?" Both the eagerness with which she posed this query and the visible sense of relief she displayed when my response indicated that all was well evidenced her genuine concern for my daughter and for me. But, more than that, she seemed somewhat determined to let me know that she had been "thinking" of my daughter (not praying), and that she had "given up on religion" and "stopped going to church" a long time ago. We had never discussed spiritual matters before that time. It was obvious that we were doing so now *because of my having obeyed the Spirit's prompting to ask her to say a prayer for something I was anxious over.* At that point, a brief but significant street-side ministry conversation ensued, during which I was able to make a distinction for my friend between religion and relationship, between what we imperfect human beings have done over the years in the name of Christ, and the teachings of Jesus themselves. Before the conversation had concluded, she had identified the need for a physical healing in her own life and eagerly received my promise to be praying for her.

Where will this new turn in our relationship lead? On the one hand, I don't know for sure (though I can report that our interactions since then have indicated that our friendship has moved to a new level of interpersonal trust and vulnerability that makes possible a much wider range of conversational topics, including matters of the heart and of the soul). On the other hand, it is also true that it is not my responsibility to actually be effective in my ministry interactions with others, just to be faithful, presuming that the Holy Spirit knows what he is doing when he graciously allows us to participate in his missional ministry toward the world he helped create.

Has this ever happened to you? Have you ever felt "led," "prompted" or "impressed" to speak or act toward another person or group of pesons on God's behalf, whether to evangelize or edify or equip? Have you ever, like the disciple Ananias (of Damascus) referred to in Acts 9:10-20, had your day interrupted as God called you to speak or act into someone's life in his name? Do you believe that it is possible for Christ's followers to have the Spirit of God speak to them, providing them with ministry assignments designed to further the kingdom cause in specific ways? To what degree do you believe that God's Spirit has a penchant for using God's people to achieve God's purposes in the world?

THE NEED FOR A NEW PNEUMATOLOGY

Many missiologists (theologians who focus on the topic of mission) are convinced that these are some very important questions we evangelicals in the West (Europe and North America) need to be asking ourselves since we are living in societies that are becoming increasingly post-Christian (i.e., more and more people around us are indicating in various ways that they are "over" Christianity and "done" with the church).

For example, in the widely read *Missional Church: A Vision for the Sending of the Church in North America* we find the following ironic observation being made:

> On the one hand, during the twentieth century Christianity has become a truly worldwide movement, with churches established on every continent and among every major cultural group. The great modern missionary movement has been, despite all the controversy and debate, a truly successful enterprise. On the other hand, while modern missions have led to an expansion of world Christianity, Christianity in North America has moved (or been moved) away from its position of dominance as it has experienced the loss not only of numbers but of power and influence within society.[4]

Just how post-Christian has America become? By some accounts the numbers are astounding. In their book *Lost in America* Tom Clegg and Warren Bird report that

> the unchurched population in the United States is so extensive that, if it were a nation, it would be the fifth most populated nation on the planet,

---

[4]See Darrell Guder, ed., *Missional Church: A Vision for the Sending of the Church in North America* (Grand Rapids: Eerdmans, 1998), pp. 1-7. Please note that while the brief allusion to the worldwide growth of Christianity presented in this quote is necessarily vague and imprecise, in chap. 3 of this book I will explore more deeply some of the reasons where, how and why the Christian gospel has taken root globally.

after China, the former Soviet Union, India and Brazil. Thus, our un-churched population is the largest mission field in the English-speaking world and the fifth largest globally.[5]

This staggering statistic explains why more and more missiological works are encouraging evangelicals to approach North America and Europe as bona fide mission fields.[6] It is with that precise message in mind that Alan Roxburgh and Scott Boren, authors of *Introducing the Missional Church*, write:

> Wherever we travel we meet more and more Christians who have walked away from church life in practically all its forms. Whether it is traditional, seeker, emergent, or whatever it is no longer the point for a growing number of people. They sense we are living in a different world and that their church experiences don't connect with the huge issues of life that they face.[7]

Sadly, the same kind of post-Christian dynamic taking place in North America is present also in the countries that make up Western Europe.[8] A particularly haunting depiction of the declining influence of the church everywhere in the West, but especially in Europe, is one provided by missiologist Gailyn Van Rheenen:

> The church has become one of many options in an increasingly complex world in which world religions, new spiritualities, and secular therapies compete in a multicultural market place. The cathedrals and church

---

[5]Tom Clegg and Warren Bird, *Lost in America: How You and Your Church Can Impact the World Next Door* (Loveland, Colo.: Group, 2001), p. 25.

[6]Six principal works in this regard are Lesslie Newbigin, *Foolishness to the Greeks: The Gospel and Western Culture* (Grand Rapids: Eerdmans, 1986); Newbigin, *The Gospel in a Pluralist Society* (Grand Rapids, Eerdmans, 1989); George R. Hunsberger and Craig Van Gelder, *The Church between Gospel and Culture* (Grand Rapids, Eerdmans, 1998); Guder, *Missional Church*); Craig Van Gelder, ed., *Confident Witness—Changing World: Rediscovering the Gospel in North America* (Grand Rapids: Eerdmans, 1999); and Alan J. Roxburgh and M. Scott Boren, *Introducing the Missional Church: Why It Matters, How to Become One* (Grand Rapids: Baker, 2009).

[7]Roxburgh and Boren, *Introducing the Missional Church*, p. 75.

[8]For more statistical evidence of the increase of unchurched people in the United States in recent years, see Ed Stetzer and David Putnam, *Breaking the Missional Code*, pp. 8-9, 89-91. On Western Europe see, for example, Philip Jenkins, *God's Continent: Christianity, Islam, and Europe's Religious Crisis* (New York: Oxford University Press, 2007), pp. 1-2, 27-28; Michael Frost and Alan Hirsch, *The Shaping of Things to Come: Innovation and Mission for the 21st-Century Church* (Peabody, Mass.: Hendrickson, 2003), pp. 14-15; and Roxburgh and Boren, *Introducing the Missional Church*, p. 68.

buildings are considered by some, especially in Europe, to be relics of the past.[9]

Both inspired and challenged by the prolific growth of Christianity in the global South, many Western evangelicals are rightly concerned about the vitality of the mission in their own locale.[10] And it is not simply a downward slide in terms of church attendance that is causing alarm; it is also the growing acceptance in these societies of religious relativism—the idea that all religions are equally effective at helping people connect with God, and that no one religion is more true or salvific than any other. According to a 2007 survey conducted by the Pew Forum on Religion and Public Life, 70 percent of Americans who affiliate themselves with a particular religious tradition nevertheless believe that many religions can lead to eternal life.[11] The research conducted by Ed Stetzer, Richie Stanley and Jason Hayes and reported in their book *Lost and Found* indicates that 58 percent of American adults aged twenty to twenty-nine, and 67 percent of American adults thirty years or older believe that the God of the Bible is no different from the gods or spiritual beings depicted by world religions such as Islam, Hinduism and Buddhism.[12]

Historically, evangelicals have affirmed the idea that "Jesus is Lord" (see Rom 10:9; 1 Cor 12:3; Phil 2:11), and that he is not simply *a* way to God but *the* way (see Jn 14:6; Acts 4:12; 1 Tim 2:5-6). Astoundingly, the Pew Forum on Religion and Public Life survey cited earlier indicated that more than half (57 percent) of evangelical Protestant church members said they agreed with idea that many religions can lead to eternal life.[13] This statistic in particular serves as bad news in at least two ways: First, the fact that so many evangelical church members have

---

[9]Gailyn Van Rheenen, "Changing Motivations for Missions," in *The Changing Face of World Missions: Engaging Contemporary Issues and Trends*, ed. Michael Pocock, Gailyn Van Rheenen, and C. Douglas McConnell (Grand Rapids: Baker Academic, 2005), p. 168.

[10]For example, see John Jefferson Davis, *Worship and the Reality of God* (Downers Grove, Ill.: IVP Academic, 2010), pp. 18, 194.

[11]"U.S. Religious Landscape Survey," March 7, 2009, http://religions.pewforum.org/reports#.

[12]Ed Stetzer, Richie Stanley and Jason Hayes, *Lost and Found: The Younger Unchurched and the Churches That Reach Them* (Nashville: Broadman & Holman, 2009), p. 51.

[13]"U.S. Religious Landscape Survey," March 7, 2009, as cited in Davis, *Worship and the Reality of God*, p. 20.

embraced a tenet of faith so inimical to the clear teaching of Scripture lends support to the concern of some that there is a serious disciple-making deficit currently at work in evangelical churches.[14] Second, how likely is it that evangelical church members who have embraced the notion of religious relativism will be willing and able to participate in the fulfilling of the Great Commission Christ gave his church (i.e., to keep making disciples until the end of the age)?[15]

An observation made by retired missionary Lesslie Newbigin—that Europe and North America had become mission fields themselves—precipitated what has come to be known as the missional church movement.[16] There is a sense that this movement can be viewed as an attempt by evangelical churches in the West to mount a theologically informed ministry response to the post-Christian condition they find themselves in. Of special note is the fact that at the heart of the missional ministry impulse is a pneumatological question: *What is the Holy Spirit up to in this or that ministry location, and how might/should we cooperate with him?*[17]

The importance of the Holy Spirit to the missional conversation is evident in a number of ways. For one thing, in his subsequent writings

---

[14]For example, see Bill Hull, *The Disciple-Making Pastor* (Grand Rapids: Revell, 1988), p. 12; Dallas Willard, *The Divine Conspiracy: Rediscovering Our Hidden Life in God* (San Francisco: HarperSanFrancisco, 1998), p. 301; and George Barna, *Growing True Disciples: New Strategies for Producing Genuine Followers of Christ* (Colorado Springs: WaterBrook, 2001), pp. 7-8.

[15]While it is my contention that religious relativism, especially among evangelicals, is a problem that should be proactively addressed, there is an upside to the reality that we live in a religiously pluralistic society. John Stackhouse reminds the evangelical community that "extensive religious plurality can offer an opportunity for Christians to shed the baggage of cultural dominance that has often impeded or distorted the spread of the gospel. It may be, indeed, that the decline of Christian hegemony can offer the Church the occasion to adopt a new and more effective stance of humble service toward societies it no longer controls" (John G. Stackhouse, *Humble Apologetics: Defending the Faith Today* [New York: Oxford University Press, 2002], p. 36). I will have more to say about a humble versus dogmatic, arrogant approach to communicating the faith to post-Christians in chap. 5. However, citing this quote here provides me with an opportunity to make the point that my concern to address religious relativism is not motivated by a desire to squelch religious freedom or to preserve the illusion of Christian hegemony in the West.

[16]Roxburgh and Boren, *Introducing the Missional Church*, p. 9. See also Tim Stafford, "God's Missionary to Us, Part 1," December 9, 1996, www.christianitytoday.com/ct/1996/december9/6te24a.html; and "God's Missionary to Us, Part 2," December 9, 1996, www.christianitytoday.com/ct/1996/december9/6te24b.html.

[17]Roxburgh and Boren, *Introducing the Missional Church*, pp. 20, 52, 70, 86.

Newbigin encouraged his readers to always keep in mind that the mission of the church must ever be Christ's mission *as discerned through the inspirational activity of the Holy Spirit*. According to Newbigin, listening to and being empowered by the Holy Spirit is absolutely crucial to the missional endeavor. It was in support of this thesis that he wrote:

> *His* mission. It is of the greatest importance to recognize that it remains his mission. . . . Even Jesus himself speaks of his words and works as not his own but of those of the Father. His teaching is the teaching of the Father, and his mighty works are the work of the Father. So also in the Synoptic Gospels, the mighty works of Jesus are the work of God's kingly power, of the Spirit. So also with the disciples. It is the Spirit who will give them power and the Spirit who will bear witness. It is not that they must speak and act, asking the help of the Spirit to do so. It is rather that in their faithfulness to Jesus they become the place where the Spirit speaks and acts.[18]

In a similar vein, the multiple authors of the widely read *Missional Church* provide a description of the earmarks of "missional communities" that is pregnant with references to the crucial role played by the Holy Spirit. This critical passage reads thusly:

> The distinctive characteristic of such communities is that the Holy Spirit creates and sustains them. Their identity (who they are), their character (how they are), their motivation (why they are), and their vocation (what they do) are theological, and thus missional. That is, they are not formed solely by human intentions and efforts, individual or collective, but instead by God's empowering presence: "The Spirit of God is the dynamic, life-giving power of the Church, the unseen Lord, Master, Guide, and Inspirer of the Christian community." Through the power of the Holy Spirit a "people sent" are cultivated through the practices by which they are formed, trained, equipped, and motivated as missional communities.[19]

This same influential group of authors goes on to declare, "The church owes its origin, its destiny, its structure, its ongoing life, its

---

[18]Newbigin, *Gospel in a Pluralist Society*, pp. 118-19.
[19]Guder, *Missional Church*, p. 142, cited in R. P. C. Hanson, "The Divinity of the Holy Spirit," *Church Quarterly* 1, no. 4 (1969): 302.

ministry—in short—its mission—to the divine Spirit of life, truth, holiness."[20]

Finally, a recent work devoted to the task of encouraging evangelical churches to do a better job of effecting ministry in a post-Christian context is the aforementioned *Introducing the Missional Church* written by Alan J. Roxburgh and M. Scott Boren. This book is one of the latest in a stream of works that sound the call for evangelical churches to adopt a more missional approach to ministry in their respective communities. Such a move, insist these authors, requires that evangelical churches become more *incarnational* and less *attractional* in their approach to ministry. Leaders of evangelical churches should be less preoccupied with getting the unchurched into their church buildings and more concerned about presenting the gospel in loving, compassionate ways to the people living in the neighborhoods where their communities of faith are located. But how does this mobilization happen? In the process of encouraging this incarnational approach to ministry, Roxburgh and Boren comment on the importance of church leaders learning how to allow the Holy Spirit to effect missionally faithful ministry through the ordinary members of evangelical churches:

> Our rock-bottom conviction is that the Spirit of God is among the people of God. By this we mean that the Spirit is not the province of ordained leaders or superspiritual people; instead the Spirit is in what we call the ordinary people of a local church. Furthermore, we don't mean that this requires people to become like the superspiritual. Instead we mean that the Spirit is actually at work in our ordinary, common lives. This means that God's future—putting into action God's dream for the whole world—is among God's people. At one level this may sound obvious. It's not! When choosing among politicians or entertainers or when selecting a new pastor, we look for someone out of the ordinary—someone who is bigger than life. This is not how God is creating a new world. God works among ordinary, everyday men and women.
>
> Very practically, a missional church is formed by the Spirit of God at work in the ordinary people of God in a local context. A practical implication is that this imagination changes the focus of leadership.

---

[20]Guder, *Missional Church*, p. 145.

Rather than having plans, programs, strategies, and goals, they ask how they can call forth what the Spirit is doing among the people. When this happens, the potential for discovering the wind of the Spirit is exciting.[21]

While I am led to wonder who and what Roxburgh and Boren have in mind when referring to the "superspiritual," and certainly hope that their intent in this excerpt is not to suggest that the Holy Spirit never does his missional work in phenomenal ways, I, an evangelical with a Pentecostal-charismatic heritage, deeply appreciate their focus on the ministry empowerment provided by the Holy Spirit and his desire to use ordinary people of God to accomplish God's extraordinary purposes.

MORE ON THE PURPOSE OF THIS BOOK

The upshot of this observation that the Holy Spirit plays a crucial role in the missional approach to ministry is this: If it is true that some of the most influential missiologists of our day see a crucial connection between ecclesiology and pneumatology—the doctrine of the church and the doctrine of the Spirit—does this not imply the need for a *missional pneumatology*—a theology of the Spirit that can enable evangelical churches in the West to respond to its increasingly post-Christian environment in a missionally faithful manner? Assuming that it does, this is the reason why this book was written.[22]

---

[21]Roxburgh and Boren, *Introducing the Missional Church*, p. 122.

[22]Over the years a number of books have been authored by missiologists and theologians which address the Holy Spirit's role in world missions. For example, see Allan Anderson, *An Introduction to Pentecostalism* (New York: Cambridge University Press, 2004); Harry R. Boer, *Pentecost and Missions* (Grand Rapids: Eerdmans, 1961); Frederick Dale Bruner, *A Theology of the Holy Spirit: The Pentecostal Experience and the New Testament Witness* (Grand Rapids: Eerdmans, 1970); Arthur F. Glasser, *Announcing the Kingdom: The Story of God's Mission in the Bible* (Grand Rapids: Baker Academic, 2003); A. J. Gordon, *The Holy Spirit in Missions* (Harrisburg, Penn.: Christian Publications, 1968); Melvin L. Hodges, *A Theology of the Church and its Mission: A Pentecostal Perspective* (Springfield, Mo.: Gospel Publishing House, 1977); Marguerite G. Kraft, *Understanding Spiritual Power: A Forgotten Dimension of Cross-Cultural Mission and Ministry* (Maryknoll, N.Y.: Orbis, 1995); L. Grant McClung Jr., ed., *Azusa Street and Beyond: Pentecostal Missions and Church Growth in the Twentieth Century* (South Plainfield, N.J.: Bridge Publishing, 1986); Paul A. Pomerville, *The Third Force in Missions* (Peabody, Mass.: Hendrickson, 1985); David Shibley, *A Force in the Earth: The Charismatic Renewal and World Evangelism* (Altamonte Springs, Fla.: Creation House, 1989); John V. Taylor, *The Go-Between God:*

Once again, the purpose of this book is to provide the evangelical church in the West with a practical biblical theology of the Spirit that will encourage and enable an engagement in missional ministry that is both faithful and hopeful (i.e., because it is faithful to the person and work of the Spirit of mission, it is also hopeful regarding that mission's ultimate success).[23] To be even more specific, this volume aims at being a practical theology of the Spirit to guide pastors and church leaders in forming biblically informed, Spirit-empowered, missionally faithful churches. As a result, the work is not intended to function as a fully comprehensive pneumatology. The goal is, rather, a *missional* pneumatology that surveys what the Bible as a whole has to say about the Holy Spirit's apparent penchant for involving God's people in the fulfilling of God's purposes in their churches and neighborhoods by inspiring them to engage in prophetic speech and action (i.e., by inspiring them to speak and act toward others on behalf of the risen Christ in a manner

---

The Holy Spirit and the Christian Mission (New York: Oxford University Press, 1979); Charles Van Engen, *God's Missionary People* (Grand Rapids: Baker Academic, 1991); Wright, *Mission of God*; John White, *When the Spirit Comes with Power: Signs and Wonders Among God's People* (Downers Grove, Ill.: InterVarsity Press, 1988). As helpful as all these books are, what is missing is a book that provides a practical biblical theology of the Spirit that aims at helping evangelicals form missionally faithful churches. This present volume is an attempt to fill this void.

[23]I offer this work in full knowledge that respected missiologist Arthur Glasser warned that nothing short of a thoroughgoing study of what all Scripture has to say about mission can actually motivate a faithful response on the part of Christians to that mission: "Only if the church understands the full biblical revelation of God concerning the mission of God's people, stimulated by confronting Scripture with today's questions, will they be responsibly challenged to offer to God the devotion of heart, strength, time, and resources essential to its completion. . . . It has become increasingly difficult to defend the modern missionary movement by supplementing this concern with appeals to the Great Commission (Matt. 28:18-20), in the tradition of William Carey and Hudson Taylor. Nor can greater credibility be gained by broadening the base through appealing to proof-texts carefully selected to support such related themes as the sending character of God, the compassionate compulsion of the Spirit, the example of the apostolic church, and the relation between missionary obedience and the second coming of Christ. . . . An overall approach to Scripture must be taken that will allow each part to make its contribution so that the total concern of God for the nations might be understood" (Arthur F. Glasser, "Kingdom and Mission: A Biblical Study of the Kingdom of God and the World Mission of His People," unpublished syllabus, Fuller Theological Seminary, Pasadena, Calif., 1992). Still it is my hope that *in combination with other more comprehensive treatments of the Spirit in mission* the survey of pertinent texts related to the theme of prophetic speech and action presented in this work will inform and inspire toward a greater missional faithfulness and hopefulness on the part of evangelicals living in an increasingly post-Christian ministry context.

that somehow represents the kingdom of God to them in evangelizing, edifying or equipping ways).[24]

SOME FOUNDATIONAL MISSIOLOGICAL AND PNEUMATOLOGICAL PRESUPPOSITIONS

The ambitious aim of this book is grounded in several foundational missiological and pneumatological presuppositions. Given the importance of these a priori assumptions, it is imperative that they be identified and explained.

The meaning of missional. I have referred to this project as an attempt at a *missional* pneumatology. Given the current confusion regarding what the word *missional* means, I want to make clear from the outset what I have in mind when I use this term.[25]

There appears to be consensus among contemporary mission scholars that the term *missional* refers to the idea that the goal of the church should not be to simply pursue its own purposes but to pursue God's purposes. The authors of *Missional Church* contrast "missional" with a traditional

---

[24]In secular usage the original sense of the Greek noun *prophētēs* was "one who proclaims"; the idea of a prophet as "one who predicts" came later. Likewise, the primary meaning of the Greek verb *prophēteuō* in antiquity was "to proclaim" (see H. Kramer, in *Theological Dictionary of the New Testament: Abridged in One Volume*, ed. Gerhard Kittel and Gerhard Friedrich [Grand Rapids: Eerdmans, 1985], p. 952). In terms of the way these words are used in the New Testament not much changes. The Greek noun *prophētēs* "is normally a biblical proclaimer of a divinely inspired message," and "to prophesy" (*prophēteuō*) means "to proclaim a divinely imparted message" (G. Friedrich, in *Theological Dictionary of the New Testament: Abridged in One Volume*, ed. Gerhard Kittel and Gerhard Friedrich [Grand Rapids: Eerdmans, 1985], p. 960). This is all to say that in this book I will not be using the word *prophetic* in the sense of predicting the future but simply as a "speaking forth on behalf of God." Furthermore when I refer to the phenomenon of "prophetic speech and action," what I have in mind is someone saying or doing something on behalf of God due to a prompting by the Holy Spirit. I will argue in chap. 2 of this book that in the book of Acts this prophetic speech and action usually takes the form of someone being prompted by the Holy Spirit to say or do something in the life of another that has the effect of evangelizing them (bringing them to faith in Christ), edifying them (encouraging, building them up in their walk with Christ) or equipping them (providing that which is necessary for their survival or the accomplishment of their own mission in Christ).

[25]The fact that *Introducing the Missional Church* includes a chapter titled "Just Give Me a Definition: Why *Missional Church* Is So Hard to Define" serves to verify the haze I speak of (Roxburgh and Boren, *Introducing the Missional Church*, pp. 27-45). The current confusion regarding the term *missional* has also been alluded to in several *Christianity Today* articles. For example, see J. Todd Billings, "What Makes a Church Missional?" March 5, 2008, www.christianitytoday.com/ct/2008/march/16.56.html; and Alan Hirsch, "Defining Missional" (December 12, 2008), www.christianitytoday.com/le/2008/fall/17.20.html.

church's preoccupation with "institutional maintenance."[26] In *Breaking the Missional Code*, Ed Stetzer and David Putnam contrast being missional with a church's preoccupation with its own preferences:

> Simply put, being missional does not mean doing things the way we like them. It means to take the gospel into the context where we have been called . . . and to some degree, to let the church take the best shape that it can in order to reach a specific culture. However, the problem is our preferences. You can't be missional and pick what *you* like at the same time.[27]

We have already seen that at the heart of the missional movement is a pneumatological question: *What is the Holy Spirit up to in this or that ministry location, and how might/should we cooperate with him?* This question not only bespeaks of the importance of the Holy Spirit to the missional endeavor, it also indicates the importance of the practice of contextualization. The multiple authors of *Missional Church* explain:

> A missional ecclesiology is contextual. Every ecclesiology is developed within a particular cultural context. There is but one way to be the church, and that is incarnationally, within a specific concrete setting. The gospel is always translated into a culture, and God's people are formed in that culture in response to the translated and Spirit-empowered Word. All ecclesiologies function relative to their context. Their truth and faithfulness are related both to the gospel they proclaim and to the witness they foster in every culture.[28]

In chapter four of this book I will treat the concept of contextualization in more depth, providing some biblical and theological support for its practice in the process. For now, it is sufficient to indicate that, according to the previous quote, at its heart the missional impulse is to faithfully translate the truth of the gospel into diverse, unique cultures, so that those living in those cultures might be formed by the gospel within their cultures, "in response to the translated and Spirit-empowered Word."[29]

---

[26]Guder, *Missional Church*, p. 7.

[27]Stetzer and Putnam, *Breaking the Missional Code*, p. 50.

[28]Guder, *Missional Church*, p. 11.

[29]According to Stetzer and Putnam: "Here is the message—'repentance and forgiveness of sins

Now, with regard to the means by which this missional ministry is achieved, it should also be noted from the outset that in the pages that follow I will be referring to a biblically informed, Spirit-empowered missional ministry that encourages a faithful fulfilling of the Great Commission (Mt 28:18-20), while at the same time being careful to obey the Great Commandment (Mt 22:36-40), and engaging in creation care.[30] In other words, it is my conviction that a faithful engagement in missional ministry will involve *both* gospel proclamation toward the end of disciple making *and* a loving engagement in social action toward the goal of a more peaceful, just, humane society, and a clean, healthy environment.[31] While I am willing to concede that God's great concern to reconcile lost human beings to himself (2 Cor 5:17-20) does not comprise the entirety of what it means to be missional, I am convinced that the Bible clearly demonstrates the importance of disciple making to it.

This caveat is made necessary by the history of the use of the term *missio Dei*. In his book *The Mission of God*, Christopher Wright explains that the term *missio Dei* (the mission or sending of God) was coined by German missiologist Karl Hartenstein as a way of summarizing the teaching of Karl Barth. According to Wright, "Barth and Hartenstein wanted to make clear that mission is grounded in an intratrinitarian movement of God himself and that it expresses the power of God over history, to which the only appropriate response is obedience."[32]

According to missiologist Van Sanders, the original reason for the

---

to be preached in his name to all nations.' When it becomes something other than repentance and forgiveness, then the gospel itself is lost in the process" (Stetzer and Putnam, *Breaking the Missional Code*, p. 39; see also pp. 93, 185).

[30]It should be pointed out that not all advocates for the missional church emphasize the dynamic of creation care. Personally, I absolutely believe that Christ's followers should pursue this agenda. However, since this is a work of biblical theology, and the biblical support for an engagement in creation care is less prominent than that which exists for gospel proclamation and social action, the bulk of this book's discussion of missional ministry will center mainly in the latter two missional dynamics (as do all of the missional works cited by me in this work).

[31]Two excellent works that promote a holistic embrace of both disciple making and social action are Ronald J. Sider, *Good News and Good Works: A Theology for the Whole Gospel* (Grand Rapids: Baker, 1993); and Ronald J. Sider, Philip N. Olson and Heidi Rolland Unruh, *Churches That Make a Difference: Reaching Your Community with Good News and Good Works* (Grand Rapids: Baker, 2002).

[32]Wright, *Mission of God*, pp. 62-63.

coining of the term *missio Dei* by Hartenstein in 1934 was to address the European church's "anemic mission practice of that time."[33] Sanders goes on to assert, however, that eventually the Latin phrase *missio Dei* began to be used in a manner that went beyond the scriptural call to reach all the nations with the gospel of Christ:

> In the 1950's and 1960's . . . *[m]issio Dei* came to mean more than just the task of making disciples of all *ta ethnē* by the Church. Dutch missiologist Johannes Hoekendijk said the "mission of God was to establish Shalom—'peace, integrity, community, harmony and justice'—or humanization in this world." The World Council of Churches (WCC) adopted this understanding of *missio Dei*. This interpretation fostered a sociopolitical view of *missio Dei* and "meant that the church should act in partnership with the sending God, not by world evangelization and church planting, but by directly promoting political and economic human good."[34]

For his part Wright essentially confirms Sanders's analysis of the historical distortion of the original meaning of the term *missio Dei*, and in the process echoes the concern that in some quarters the concept has come to represent the idea that the mission of God excludes any evangelistic activity on the part of the church.[35] Missiologist Lesslie Newbigin registered a similar concern when he wrote,

> The concept of *missio Dei* has sometimes been interpreted so as to suggest that action for justice and peace as the possibilities are discerned within a given historical situation *is* the fulfillment of God's mission, and that the questions of baptism and church membership are marginal or irrelevant. That way leads very quickly to disillusion and often to cynical despair.[36]

---

[33]Van Sanders, "The Mission of God and the Local Church," in *Pursuing the Mission of God in Church Planting*, ed. John M. Bailey (Alpharetta, Ga.: North American Mission Board, 2006), p. 24.

[34]John A. McIntosh, "Missio Dei," in *Evangelical Dictionary of World Missions*, ed. A. Scott Moreau (Grand Rapids: Baker, 2000), p. 632, cited in Sanders, "Mission of God and the Local Church," p. 25.

[35]Wright, *Mission of God*, p. 63.

[36]Newbigin, *Gospel in a Pluralist Society*, p. 138, emphasis in the original. Stetzer and Putnam speak to this issue also, commenting on the inappropriate, unnecessary manner in which some missional advocates feel the need to speak in a completely disparaging manner of the church

The history of the term *missio Dei* notwithstanding, I believe that a careful read of Scripture does support the idea that God's redemptive concern extends beyond individual human beings to creation as a whole. Genesis 1:26-30 can be interpreted in such a way as to indicate that God expects human beings to develop the creation, to carry on his work of creating a world that reflects his original plans and intentions for the planet. Furthermore, Romans 8:21 indicates that a future liberation awaits not only human beings but creation itself. Likewise, Colossians 1:15-20 specifies that God's plan is for "all things" (all creation) to be eventually reconciled in Christ. And, finally, Revelation 21:5 boldly declares that God will someday make "everything" new. Taken together, these passages can be interpreted in such a way as to at least infer that God's redemptive concern ultimately extends beyond the salvation of individual souls, to human cultures, to the welfare of the planet itself.

Thus, on the whole, I find myself resonating with Christopher Wright when he suggests that *"fundamentally, our mission (if it is biblically informed and validated) means our committed participation as God's people, at God's invitation and command, in God's own mission within the history of God's world for the redemption of God's creation."*[37] In my mind, the value of this conception of the church's mission is in the way it emphasizes (1) the reality that our God is a missionary God who has a plan for the world he created,[38] (2) the fact that God desires to use his people toward the accomplishment of his mission, and (3) the need for our sense of mission to be informed by an understanding of God's purposes for this world (rather than our own).

That said, I will go on to indicate that I resonate even more with the missional trajectory set by Scot McKnight who defines the gospel as *"the work of God to restore humans to union with God and communion with others, in the context of a community, for the good of others and the world."*[39]

---

growth and church health movements (see Stetzer and Putnam, *Breaking the Missional Code*, pp. 49-50).

[37]Wright, *Mission of God*, pp. 22-23.

[38]See Guder, *Missional Church*, p. 4, emphasis in original.

[39]Scot McKnight, *Embracing Grace: A Gospel for All of Us* (Brewster, Mass.: Paraclete Press, 2005), p. xiii.

The value of this summary of the essence of the Christian gospel rests in its suggestion that disciple making will necessarily be at the heart of missional activity. I also appreciate the way it succeeds at the important task of holding disciple making, social action and creation care in a healthy tension, all the while reminding the church that it exists to serve God and others rather than itself.[40]

The Spirit and God's mission. A second foundational presupposition—a set of presuppositions really—has to do with the crucial role the Holy Spirit plays in the achievement of God's missional purposes. Simply looking over a list of the many titles attributed to the Holy Spirit in Scripture indicates his significance. In addition to the epithet "Holy Spirit," he is also referred to numerous times in the New International Version of the Bible as the "Spirit of the Lord," the "Spirit of God" and simply the "Spirit." He is also known in Scripture as the "Spirit of judgment" and "Spirit of fire" (Is 4:4); "Spirit of wisdom and of understanding" (Is 11:2); "Spirit of counsel and of power" and "Spirit of knowledge and of the fear of the LORD" (Is 11:2); "Spirit of the Sovereign LORD" (Is 61:1); "Spirit of your Father" (Mt 10:20); "Spirit of truth" (Jn 14:17; 15:26; 16:13: 1 Jn 4:6); "Spirit of holiness" (Rom 1:4); "Spirit of Christ" (Rom 8:9; 1 Pet 1:11); "Spirit of Jesus" (Acts 16:7); "Spirit of Jesus Christ" (Phil 1:19); "Spirit of life" (Rom 8:2); "Spirit of him who raised Jesus from the dead" (Rom 8:11); "Spirit of sonship" (Rom 8:15); "Spirit who is from God" (1 Cor 2:12); "God's Spirit" (1 Cor 3:16); "Spirit of our God" (1 Cor 6:11); "Spirit of the living God" (2 Cor 3:3); "Spirit of his Son" (Gal 4:6); "Spirit of wisdom and revelation" (Eph 1:17); "Holy Spirit of God" (Eph 4:30); "Spirit of grace"

---

[40]If Newbigin, Roxburgh and Boren, Stetzer and Putnam, and the authors of *Missional Church* are any indication, I suspect that this proposed understanding of what it means to be missional will resonate with a good number of my evangelical readers. For even the main progenitors of the missional conversation seem to have room in their understanding of being missional for gospel proclamation and disciple making (see Newbigin, *Gospel in a Pluralist Society*, pp. 119, 123, 128-40; Roxburgh and Boren, *Introducing the Missional Church*, pp. 54, 87; Stetzer and Putnam, *Breaking the Missional Code*, pp. 30-42, 79-81, 83-84; and Guder, *Missional Church*, pp. 12, 238, 247; see also Frost and Hirsch, *Shaping of Things to Come*, p. 11; Dan Devadatta, "Strangers but Not Strange: A New Mission Situation for the Church (1 Peter 1:1-2 and 17-25)," in *Confident Witness—Changing World: Rediscovering the Gospel in North America*, ed. Craig Van Gelder [Grand Rapids: Eerdmans, 1999], pp. 111-12, 121-24; Hunter, *To Change the World*, p. 226).

(Heb 10:29); "Spirit of glory and of God" (1 Pet 4:14); and "Counselor" (Jn 14:16, 26; 15:26; 16:7).

In addition to the Holy Spirit's general work of creation implied by the Genesis 1 creation narrative (see Gen 1:2),[41] the Bible also speaks of his role in giving natural life to all of God's creatures in passages such as Genesis 2:7, Job 33:4 and Psalm 104:24-30.

But the Scriptures go on to indicate that the Holy Spirit also figures prominently with regard to the dynamic of spiritual life. In this regard, the New International Version contains thirty-one verses that speak of the Holy Spirit "coming upon" various people, another seventeen verses that refer to people being "filled" with the Holy Spirit, and one verse that speaks of the Spirit coming to "rest" upon an individual (Is 11:2).

To what end does the Spirit fill or indwell human beings? A short list of some of the effects the Holy Spirit produces within the lives of human beings as indicated by the New Testament includes such things as:

- convicting them of sin and their need for a savior (Jn 16:7-11)

- enabling them to experience the "new birth" (Jn 3:3-8)

- assuring them that they have become God's children (Rom 8:15-16)

- leading them into a deeper understanding of Christ (Jn 16:12-15)

- serving as a guarantee of their heavenly inheritance (Eph 1:13-14)

- inspiring among them a vital, joyful, prophetic worship experience (Eph 5:18-20)

- manifesting his presence and power in their lives in various edifying, community-building ways (1 Cor 12:4-8)

- empowering them to actually obey God's moral commands (Rom 8:1-4)

- producing within them the very personality and character traits of Christ himself (Gal 5:22-25)

- enabling them to pray according to the will of the Father (Rom 8:26-27)

---

[41]See John V. Taylor, *The Go-Between God: The Holy Spirit and the Christian Mission* (New York: Oxford University Press, 1972), p. 26.

- empowering them to boldly and effectively bear witness to their risen Lord (Acts 1:8)

- providing them with an amazingly precise degree of ministry guidance (Acts 16:6-10)[42]

- enabling them to stand firm in the faith and to intercede for others in this regard (Eph 6:10-18)

- enabling them to experience a dynamic, despair-defeating sense of hope (Rom 15:13)

All of the effects listed here, when considered together, suggest that being filled with or led by the Holy Spirit is a very important part of the Christian life.

The importance of the Spirit to the Christian life stands to reason since, from the Council of Constantinople in A.D. 381 onward the full divinity of the Holy Spirit has been recognized as the orthodox view among Christians,[43] and this critical creedal article is due in no small part to the fact that the Bible contains many passages that refer to the Holy Spirit in such a way as to suggest that he, along with God the Father and Christ the Son, form an eternal triune Godhead (e.g., Lk 3:22; Jn 14:26; 15:26; Acts 7:55; Eph 2:18, 22; Heb 9:14).[44]

As for the relationship between the Holy Spirit and the other two members of the Trinity, nearly all Bible readers are aware of Jesus' assertion that "God is spirit" (see Jn 4:23-24). Going further, the New Testament also contains passages which suggest that a special connection exists between the Holy Spirit and Jesus (e.g., Mt 1:18, 20; Lk 1:35; Jn 1:32-33; 7:39; 14:26; 15:26; 16:15; 20:22; Acts 2:33; 16:7; Rom 8:9; Phil 1:19; 1 Pet 1:11). Some theologians have suggested that

---

[42]Though I have provided one passage from the book of Acts that is illustrative of this pneumatic effect in our lives, in chap. 2 I make a case for the idea that the book of Acts is replete with passages that could just have easily been pressed into service here.

[43]Donald McKim, *Theological Turning Points: Major Issues in Christian Thought* (Louisville: Westminster John Knox Press, 1989), p. 19.

[44]John Thompson alludes to the eternality of the Spirit in the theology of Karl Barth when he writes: " [Because] the Spirit comes from the Father *and* the Son in the economy of salvation it does so eternally in the life of God" (John Thompson, *The Holy Spirit in the Theology of Karl Barth* [Allison Park, Penn.: Pickwick, 1991], p. 30, cited in Donald G. Bloesch, *The Holy Spirit: Works and Gifts* [Downers Grove, Ill.: InterVarsity Press, 2000], pp. 272-73).

the Holy Spirit can be thought of as the eternal personification of the love that flows between the eternal Father and co-eternal Son (see Rom 5:5).[45]

Proceeding further still, we are specifically told that both the Father and the Son played a role in the sending of the Spirit into the world (Jn 14:26; 15:26).[46] Commenting on the doctrine of the *filioque* (the Spirit proceeding from the Father and the Son), theologian Donald Bloesch asserts not only that the *filioque* "lends support to the idea of the intratrinitarian communion between Father and Son" but also that the received doctrine "is supportive of the gospel witness, namely, that the Spirit unites his own mission with that of Christ and thereby chooses to serve the mission of Christ."[47] Thus, the fact that both the Father and the Son seem to have been responsible for sending the Spirit into the world does more than connote the idea of mission, it veritably demands it!

Indeed, I want to make the observation, based on everything stipulated so far, that being *missional is the heartbeat of the Holy Spirit*. According to the divine self-revelation we find in sacred Scripture, God desires humans to experience the life-giving community (divine dance) that is at the heart of the Trinity.[48] The biblical narrative reflects how this community was lost and is now being restored through the agency

---

[45]For example, Augustine thought of the Spirit as the "mutual bond of love between the Father and the Son" (McKim, *Theological Turning Points*, p. 20). Versions of this basic idea have appeared in the writings of an eclectic group of theologians over years. See, e.g., C. S. Lewis, *Mere Christianity* (New York: HarperSanFrancisco, 1952), pp. 175-76; Stanley Grenz, *Theology for the Community of God* (Grand Rapids, Eerdmans, 1994), p. 101; Ray Anderson, *An Emergent Theology for Emerging Churches* (Downers Grove, Ill.: InterVarsity Press, 2006), p. 48; Jürgen Moltmann, *The Trinity and the Kingdom* (Minneapolis: Fortress Press, 1993), pp. 57, 142; and Karl Barth, *Church Dogmatics*, vol. 1: *The Doctrine of the Word of God*, pt. 1 (Peabody, Mass.: Hendrickson, 1936), p. 480.

[46]For more on this see Christopher J. H. Wright, *The Mission of God's People: A Biblical Theology of the Church's Mission* (Grand Rapids: Zondervan, 2010), pp. 210-11.

[47]Bloesch, *Holy Spirit*, p. 272.

[48]See Clark Pinnock, *Flame of Love: A Theology of the Holy Spirit* (Downers Grove, Ill.: InterVarsity Press, 1996), p. 31. Again, in a provocative move, Bloesch demurs somewhat on the idea of the divine dance when he writes: "The God of the Bible is neither the self-contemplating God of classical philosophy nor the dancing God of the new spirituality but the seeking and redeeming God who enters into the travail and pain of the world" (Bloesch, *Holy Spirit*, p. 273). It is interesting that while Bloesch seems to be somewhat critical of the idea of the divine dance, he expresses this in such a way as to underscore the missionary heart of the Trinity!

of all three members of the Trinity, working together to effect not only the *regeneration* and *sanctification* of lost human beings, but their *participation* in the ministry of reconciliation as well (2 Cor 5:17-20).[49] The Bible goes on to indicate very clearly the crucial role the Holy Spirit plays in a person's justification (e.g., 1 Cor 6:11), regeneration (e.g., Jn 3:5), sanctification (e.g., Rom 8:1-14) and participation in ministry (e.g., Acts 1:8). With regard to their ministry formation in particular, we have already noted that the Scriptures teach us that the Holy Spirit is Christ's Spirit (Acts 16:7; Rom 8:9; Phil 1:19; 1 Pet 1:11) and that his ultimate goal is to empower Jesus' apprentices to participate in the intimate, interactive relationship with God that Jesus himself possessed and that had such a positive missional impact on those around him (see Jn 16:7-15; 2 Cor 3:18). All of this points toward the fact that the Spirit's empowerment in our lives will not simply be about boundary marking—who is in and who is out—but about mission. *The Holy Spirit is all about the enablement of Christ's followers to glorify the Father, in the name of the Son, in such as way as to encourage lost and hurting human beings to accept the invitation to join the divine dance, experiencing justification, sanctification and empowerment for ministry themselves in the process.* The esteemed missiologist Arthur Glasser put it this way:

> So then, we do not want to limit the Holy Spirit only to the work of awakening faith (justification) and to the work of perfecting faith (sanctification). The Spirit must primarily be seen as the driving force behind any and all movements of the people of God outward, beyond the frontiers of faith, to share the gospel with those who have not yet heard it. Mission means movement from Christ by his Spirit to the world he reconciled. As such it stands in sharpest contrast to the individualistic or ecclesiastical introversion so common in large segments of the contemporary Christian scene.[50]

In other words, the Holy Spirit is the "Spirit of mission."[51] In *The Min-*

---

[49]I am deliberately conflating such soteriological dynamics as adoption, election, justification, etc., into the concept of regeneration in order to keep the discussion as broad and nonsectarian as possible.

[50]Glasser, *Announcing the Kingdom*, p. 263

[51]Though he does not to my knowledge refer to the Holy Spirit as the "Spirit of Mission," evangelical theologian Clark Pinnock provides tacit support for this view in his book *Flame of Love.*

istry of the Spirit, Roland Allen surveys the work of the Holy Spirit in the book of Acts and comes to the following conclusion regarding the Spirit's identity:

> These considerations are surely sufficient to convince us that the book of Acts is strictly a missionary book. But we have seen that it is the record of the acts of men moved by a Spirit given to them. The conclusion is irresistible, that the Spirit given was, in St Luke's view, a Spirit which impelled to missionary work, in fact a missionary Spirit.[52]

It is this recognition of the Holy Spirit as a missionary Spirit that makes a biblical theology of the Holy Spirit in mission not only possible but necessary as well.

The prospect of a missional faithfulness. Though I will assert in this work that the faithfulness of the Spirit makes it possible for us to offer him a missional engagement that is faithful and hopeful in response, such an interaction is not guaranteed. For while the Scriptures speak of the controlling (Rom 8:6), compelling (Lk 2:27; 20:22), and inspiring (Mt 22:43; 1 Cor 12:3) effects the Holy Spirit can have on people, they also seem to indicate that the Holy Spirit is not an impersonal force (as in Star Wars)[53] but a divine person capable of possessing and producing such personal attributes as love, joy, peace, patience, kindness, goodness, faithfulness, gentleness, self-control, righteousness and hope (Lk 10:21; Rom 14:17; 15:13, 30; Gal 5:22-23; 1 Thess 1:6).

Furthermore, according to the Scriptures, the Holy Spirit can and must be related to in an interpersonal manner. Various biblical texts indicate that the Spirit should be *followed* (Mt 4:1; Lk 4:1; Rom 8:14; Gal 5:18), *fellowshiped with* (2 Cor 13:14; Phil 2:1), *lived by* (Gal 5:16, 25), *lived according to* (Rom 8:4, 5, 13), *kept in step with* (Gal 5:25) and *learned*

Grounding his treatment of the Spirit in the "Christian understanding of God as pure relationality," Pinnock goes on to suggest that the work of the Spirit in creation, redemption and restoration is all about "moving humanity toward personal communion and participation in the divine nature," which he insists "was God's everlasting purpose" (Pinnock, *Flame of Love*, pp. 22, 23). This, I suggest, is another way of saying that being missional is the heartbeat of the Spirit.

[52]Roland Allen, *The Ministry of the Spirit* (Grand Rapids: Eerdmans, 1960), p. 17.

[53]See Gordon Fee, *God's Empowering Presence: The Holy Spirit in the Letters of Paul* (Peabody, Mass.: Hendrickson, 1994), p. 569. Interestingly, systematic theologian Donald Bloesch rather provocatively refers to the Spirit as both a force and a person (Bloesch, *Holy Spirit*, p. 274).

from (1 Cor 2:13). Unfortunately, they also specify that it is possible for the Spirit of God to be *lied to* (Acts 5:3), *tested* (Acts 5:9), *resisted* (Acts 7:51), *grieved* (Eph 4:30), *rejected* (1 Thess 4:8), *quenched* (1 Thess 5:19) and even *insulted* (Heb 10:29). Even more biblical passages convey the idea that the Holy Spirit bids our obedience or, to put it bluntly, can and should be cooperated with (Gal 3:3; 5:16-25; 6:8; Eph 4:3).

The fact that the Holy Spirit is personal and seeks to interact with us in an interpersonal manner might imply that his invitation to include us in his ministry of accomplishing the mission of God is likewise personal in the sense that it is *contingent* on a personal response. Thus, a delicate tension between the sovereignty of God and the responsibility of human beings is evident here.[54] However, while recognizing the need to reckon with the possibility that it is possible for Christ's followers to do otherwise, I will repeatedly contend in this work that an embrace of a theological realism (more about this in chap. 3) accompanied by a bedrock conviction that the Holy Spirit is faithful to God's mission and God's people is a compelling combination that, at the very least, greatly encourages and enables a missional engagement that is both faithful and hopeful in response (see 2 Cor 5:14-15).[55] Once again, it is the aim of this book to increase the numbers of evangelical believers in the West who, having embraced a biblically informed missional pneumatology, are indeed *willing* and *eager* to become empowered partners with the Holy Spirit in the execution of the purposes of God in their everyday worlds through prophetic speech and action.

AN OVERVIEW OF WHAT LIES AHEAD

A few more clarifying comments are in order at this point regarding the nature and structure of this book.

---

[54]Commenting on the apostle Paul's view of the relationship between the Christ follower and the Holy Spirit, Gordon Fee indicates that "the Spirit has not come to 'take over,' as it were, so that our human responsibility is diminished." Fee also states that "the coming of the Spirit does not overtake or overwhelm. . . . The Christian life is *by the Spirit;* but *we* cry, or walk, or conform our behavior, or follow, as the case may be" (Fee, *God's Empowering Presence*, p. 569).

[55]James Davison Hunter emphasizes that "at root, a theology of faithful presence begins with an acknowledgement of God's faithful presence to us and that his call upon us is that we be faithfully present to him in return. This is the foundation, the logic, the paradigm" (Hunter, *To Change the World*, p. 243).

I have already indicated that the work is a *biblical* theology of the Spirit in mission. Among other things, this means that what I am presenting here is a synthetic argument that does not depend on one key text or even a few texts, but rather requires an overview—a survey of pertinent biblical passages from the whole of Scripture that culminates in the New Testament. Furthermore, since my goal is to produce a *practical* biblical theology, my approach in this volume will not be to address every possible issue related to the Holy Spirit in mission but to focus on the formation of a *missional* pneumatology that can enhance the ability of evangelical church leaders and members to form missionally faithful churches. Finally, due to its practical theological application, the pastor-teacher in me has strived to make the content of this work accessible and useful to professional and lay church leaders, as well as to those who function in the academy. I can only hope that I have achieved a modicum of success at this ambitious endeavor.

Now for a few words about how the book is structured.

Chapter one presents an overview of what the Bible as a whole seems to say about the connection between the coming of the Holy Spirit into people's lives and the phenomenon of prophetic activity. According to the Bible, something remarkable really can be expected to occur when a person experiences a dramatic, empowering encounter with the Holy Spirit: he or she will receive a special *capacity* to engage in prophetic speech and action.

The focus of chapter two is on the connection between prophetic activity (Spirit-inspired speech and action) and missional faithfulness. A close examination of the ministry practices of the earliest Christians will reveal how important it is that at least some of our attempts at evangelism (*kerygma*), edification (*koinōnia*) and equipping (*diakonia*) be conducted in a prophetic manner, unmistakably empowered by the Holy Spirit. Included in this chapter will be several accounts of prophetic activity occurring in our day that serve as contemporary examples of the kind of prophetic evangelism, edification, and equipping the book of Acts describes.

Chapter three makes a case for the idea that the remarkable spread of

Pentecostal and charismatic Christianity around the world in recent years can be attributed, at least in part, to the dynamic of prophetic activity taking place in the lives of rank-and-file church members. This realization offers hope that a similar missional faithfulness can be experienced in Western, industrialized nations should the dynamic of prophetic activity be rediscovered by the evangelicals living within them.

Picking up where the previous chapter left off, chapter four will explore some reasons why and ways how evangelicals living in the post-Christian West can engage in the same kind of missional faithfulness described in the previous chapters, and do so with it a sense of hopefulness in our hearts. Toward the accomplishment of this huge objective, this chapter will provide a careful, biblically informed and well-illustrated analysis of how the dynamic of prophetic activity can play an important role in the missional ministry strategies promoted by some of the contemporary era's best missiological minds. This chapter argues that a recovery of prophetic speech and action on the part of rank-and-file evangelicals living in the West can take our attempts to be missional to a whole new level.

The no-nonsense focus of chapter five is on some vital leadership issues: what local church leaders, denominational officials and members of the academy can do in order to encourage rank-and-file evangelicals to embrace the missional pneumatology discussed and proffered in the first four chapters of this work.

The book ends with a brief conclusion that not only recaps the basic contours of my pneumatological proposal but also strives to inspire Christians, one last time, to unite with all evangelicals around the goal of missional living in the power of the Spirit.

Missiologist Arthur Glasser began his book *Announcing the Kingdom* with these words: "The whole Bible, both Old and New Testaments, is a missionary book, the revelation of God's purpose and action in mission in human history."[56] Likewise, in his massive work *The Mission of God* Christopher Wright boldly contends that "mission is not just one of a list of things that the Bible happens to talk about, only a bit more

---

[56]Arthur F. Glasser, *Announcing the Kingdom*, p. 17.

urgently than some. Mission is, in that much abused phrase, 'what it's all about.' "[57]

After lamenting the inability of most North American churches to reduce "the level of lostness in their community," evangelical missiologist Van Sanders offers what I think is best described as a "prescriptive word of hope":

> Multitudes of North American churches need to return to God's ways of doing His mission. The gap that exists in many churches today between God's way of mission and their actual practices can be overcome. When churches strive to embrace God's mission practices and patterns in the power of the Holy Spirit, individual Christians are renewed to be faithful witnesses of Christ and churches corporately demonstrate the missionary nature of Christianity.[58]

It is sentiments such as these that inspired me to write this book. If there were ever a time since the days of the earliest Christians when the world needed the local church to function in a way that makes it hard for people to relativize Jesus as just another path to God, it is now. This is happening in the Majority World. The question is: Can it happen here in the West?

While I am convinced it can and intend to do my best to explain why and how, this book is a challenging read that will call for some serious rethinking of previously held convictions on the part of Pentecostal and charismatic evangelicals and non-Pentecostal and noncharismatic evangelicals alike. Furthermore, embracing the proposal put forward here will likely change our lives in dramatic ways, not the least of which will be our having to embrace a little spiritual ambiguity while letting go of the idea that our days are ours to do with as we wish.

Then again, I am also convinced that the Christian life becomes a truly exciting adventure only when God is free to break into our days at any moment, just as he did in the case of an ordinary, rank-and-file believer like Ananias (of Damascus) in Acts 9:10-20, providing us with a special ministry assignment, calling for us to speak and act propheti-

---

[57]Wright, *Mission of God*, p. 22.
[58]Sanders, "Mission of God and the Local Church," p. 13.

cally toward others in his name.[59] My experience has been that this does not happen every day, and not always in dramatic ways. But when this biblically supported phenomenon does occur, it is very exciting and often results in fruitful ministry activity.

In *The Drama of Doctrine*, Kevin Vanhoozer describes the local church as a theater in which Spirit-empowered speech and actions are on public display.[60] This is the great need in our day, is it not—to allow the risen Christ to reveal himself through *our* Spirit-inspired speech and actions to people who desperately need him? I am absolutely convinced that contemporary Christians living in the West can live more missionally faithful lives in the power of the Spirit, and that a remarkably persuasive alternative to a rampant religious relativism can be offered by this era's evangelical community to the post-Christian culture in which it exists. Let us begin now the process of learning how.

---

[59]F. D. Bruner is careful to observe that Ananias was neither an apostle nor a bishop, just an ordinary disciple (Bruner, *Theology of the Holy Spirit*, p. 190).

[60]Kevin J. Vanhoozer, *The Drama of Doctrine: A Canonical Linguistic Approach to Christian Theology* (Louisville: Westminster John Knox Press, 2005), pp. 406-7.

1

"WOULD GOD THAT ALL THE LORD'S PEOPLE WERE PROPHETS"

The Biblical Connection Between the Coming of the Spirit and Prophetic Activity

I AM AN EVANGELICAL HOPING to inspire fellow evangelicals to embrace a theology of the Spirit that will produce a greater missional faithfulness in an increasingly post-Christian ministry environment. I fully realize that if I am to succeed in this endeavor, I must be able to demonstrate that the pneumatology I am proposing possesses a biblical warrant. A commitment that lies at the center of what it means to be evangelical is an allegiance to the authority of Scripture.[1] We evangelicals want our beliefs and behaviors to be biblically informed. In this chapter I will attempt to demonstrate that the Bible as a whole does indeed evidence a connection between empowering encounters with God's Holy Spirit (the Spirit of mission) and the phenomenon of prophetic activity—speaking and acting on God's behalf.

The challenge will be for me to make the case for this connection in such a way as to convince my readers without exhausting them in the process. In order to accomplish this I will do my best to move as swiftly as possible through surveys of what the Old and New Testaments have

---

[1]See Mark Noll, *American Evangelical Christianity: An Introduction* (Malden, Mass.: Blackwell, 2001), p. 13; and Alister McGrath, *Evangelicalism and the Future of Christianity* (Downers Grove, Ill.: InterVarsity Press, 1995), pp. 53-87.

to say about what typically occurs when the Holy Spirit comes upon God's people. In some places I will slow down and provide some clarifying commentary. In other places I will simply allude to relevant episodes or present applicable biblical passages with especially pertinent sections highlighted for easier identification.

OLD TESTAMENT SUPPORT FOR THE CONNECTION

A common criticism of the approach taken by many traditional Pentecostal scholars as they attempt to make their case for an empowering, phenomenon-producing anointing with the Holy Spirit is that they focus their attention almost exclusively on the New Testament book of Acts.[2] However, since the goal of this book is to work out a biblical theology of the Spirit that focuses on particular aspects of the Spirit's missional work, what is called for is a consideration of the whole of biblical teaching that culminates with the New Testament. Hence my decision to commence this study with a careful examination of some pertinent passages found in the Old Testament.

Empowerment in general. Many Old Testament passages speak in a very general way of the relationship between the coming of the Holy Spirit upon individuals and the experience of divine empowerment. For example, several passages in the book of Judges refer to the Spirit of the Lord coming upon Samson "in power" (Judg 14:6, 19; 15:14). Similar language is also used of empowering encounters experienced by Saul (1 Sam 10:6, 10; 11:6) and David (1 Sam 16:13). Isaiah's prophecy includes a prediction that the Spirit of the Lord will rest upon the Messiah, endowing him with the "Spirit of counsel and of power" (Is 11:2). Finally, Micah 3:8 seems to associate an in-filling of the Spirit of the Lord with an empowerment for prophetic ministry.

---

[2]See, e.g., James D. G. Dunn, *Baptism in the Holy Spirit* (Philadelphia: Westminster Press, 1970), pp. 3, 5, 103; and Frederick Dale Bruner, *A Theology of the Holy Spirit* (Grand Rapids: Eerdmans, 1970), pp. 63-69. This tendency to focus exegetical attention on passages from the book of Acts is acknowledged by other Pentecostalism scholars: see, e.g., Allan Anderson, *An Introduction to Pentecostalism* (New York: Cambridge University Press, 2004), p. 191; Roger Stronstad, *The Charismatic Theology of St. Luke* (Peabody, Mass.: Hendrickson, 1984), p. 5; Robert Menzies, *Empowered for Witness* (Sheffield, U.K.: Sheffield Academic Press, 1994), pp. 237, 245-46; and Amos Yong, *The Spirit Poured Out on All Flesh* (Grand Rapids: Baker Academic, 2005), pp. 83-85.

It is interesting that the passages just cited are located in various sections of the Old Testament—the historical books and the prophets. At the very least it seems clear that the Old Testament as a whole can be understood as containing a number of passages that associate the coming of the Spirit of the Lord upon people as having the effect of empowering them to say and do things they would not otherwise be able to say and do.

Now that a connection between the coming of the Spirit and divine empowerment in general has been made, let's go on to ponder a possible connection between the coming of the Spirit and prophetic activity (in the form of speech and action) in particular. Biblical scholar Wilf Hildebrandt insists that the Old Testament does indeed present us with numerous passages that refer to the Spirit (*rûaḥ*) in relation to the gift of prophecy.[3] If this assertion is correct, a connection between the coming of Spirit and prophetic activity should not be difficult to discern.

Prophetic speech. As indicated in this book's introduction, I am using the phrase "prophetic speech" to refer not to foretelling, but forth-telling. To speak prophetically is, most basically, to say something to God or on behalf of God to others, as a result of the prompting of the Spirit.

In *Knowing the Holy Spirit Through the Old Testament*, Christopher Wright includes a chapter titled "The Prophetic Spirit" and a subsection titled "God's Prophets and God's Spirit."[4] Throughout these pages Wright asserts the Old Testament understanding of the connection between the phenomenon of prophetic activity and the Holy Spirit.[5] However, he begins his treatment of the prophetic Spirit not with one of the prophetic books but further back in time and canonical placement to, of all places, the book of Numbers.

Near the beginning of the Old Testament we read that Moses, himself a prophet, had been leading the people of Israel single-handedly for some time. To say that he was suffering from burnout would be an

---

[3]Wilf Hildebrandt, *An Old Testament Theology of the Spirit of God* (Peabody, Mass.: Hendrickson, 1995), p. 151.

[4]Christopher J. H. Wright, *Knowing the Holy Spirit Through the Old Testament* (Downers Grove, Ill.: IVP Academic, 2006), pp. 63-86.

[5]For example, see ibid., p. 75.

understatement. The truth was that Moses was completely fried—ready to throw in the leadership towel![6]

Having expressed his radical frustration in a prayerful lament, God responded by instructing Moses to select seventy elders who would begin to share the leadership load with him. The plan was for these seventy elders to gather with Moses at the Tent of Meeting at which time God would allow them to share in the spiritual anointing that had thus far rested on Moses alone. Please notice the effect the coming of the Spirit had upon these seventy elders:

> Then the LORD came down in the cloud and spoke with him, and he took of the Spirit that was on him and put the Spirit on the seventy elders. *When the Spirit rested on them, they prophesied*, but they did not do so again. However, two men, whose names were Eldad and Medad, had remained in the camp. They were listed among the elders, but did not go out to the Tent. *Yet the Spirit also rested on them, and they prophesied* in the camp. A young man ran and told Moses, "Eldad and Medad are prophesying in the camp." (Num 11:25-27, emphasis added)

The story goes on to indicate that Joshua, Moses' aide-de-camp, became alarmed at the fact that two of the seventy elders were prophesying in the camp. Notice now what happened when Joshua pleaded with Moses to make these two men cease their prophetic activity:

> Joshua son of Nun, who had been Moses' aide since youth, spoke up and said, "Moses, my lord, stop them!" But Moses replied, "Are you jealous for my sake? *I wish that all the LORD's people were prophets and that the LORD would put his Spirit on them!*" Then Moses and the elders of Israel returned to the camp. (Num 11:28-30, emphasis added)

Thus, in Numbers 11:29 we hear Moses express the wish "that all the LORD's people were prophets and that the LORD would put his Spirit on them!" In the process of expressing this wistful longing, it certainly seems as if Moses equates the coming of the Spirit with some sort of prophetic capacity. We should also take note of the fact that Moses seems to articulate here a yearning for a day when this empow-

---

[6]Ibid., p. 47.

ering experience might be available to all of God's people rather than only a select few.

As the narrative presented in the Old Testament continues, we find a plethora of passages that report some sort of prophetic activity occurring as a result of God's Spirit coming on people who belong to him. For example, in 1 Samuel 10:1-11 we find the interesting story of Samuel's recruitment of Saul to become the first king of Israel. According to the biblical account, Samuel not only functioned prophetically in Saul's life—making some predictions that, once fulfilled, would provide Saul with a confirmation of his call to the throne (1 Sam 10:1-4)—Samuel also predicted that Saul himself would soon experience the phenomenon of prophetic utterance as a result of his own empowering encounter with the Holy Spirit. Thus, 1 Samuel 10:5-7 reads:

> After that you will go to Gibeah of God, where there is a Philistine outpost. As you approach the town, you will meet a procession of prophets coming down from the high place with lyres, tambourines, flutes and harps being played before them, and they will be prophesying. *The Spirit of the LORD will come upon you in power, and you will prophesy with them;* and you will be changed into a different person. Once these signs are fulfilled, do whatever your hand finds to do, for God is with you. (1 Sam 10:5-7, emphasis added)

Not surprisingly, the narrative goes on to report that Samuel's predictions came true, just as he said. In fact, 1 Samuel 10:9-11 seem to underscore the connection between the coming of the Spirit and the phenomenon of prophetic utterance. These verses read:

> As Saul turned to leave Samuel, God changed Saul's heart, and all these signs were fulfilled that day. When they arrived at Gibeah, a procession of prophets met him; *the Spirit of God came upon him in power, and he joined in their prophesying.* When all those who had formerly known him saw him prophesying with the prophets, they asked each other, "What is this that has happened to the son of Kish? Is Saul also among the prophets?" (1 Sam 10:9-11, emphasis added)

While our reading of Samuel's recruitment of Saul makes it clear that Saul's experience of prophetic speech was spasmodic rather than

perpetual, the book of 1 Samuel as a whole makes evident that this was
not the only time it occurred. Later on in 1 Samuel 19 we read of Saul
and his henchmen engaging in prophetic utterance as a result of the
Holy Spirit coming upon them. Saul and David had experienced a fall-
ing out. Saul was on the hunt for David—his goal being to eliminate
this young rival for the throne. As we look over the passage that describes an episode that took place during this desperate search, we
should pay special attention to verses 20, 21 and 23. The passage as a
whole reads:

> When David had fled and made his escape, he went to Samuel at Ramah
> and told him all that Saul had done to him. Then he and Samuel went to
> Naioth and stayed there. Word came to Saul: "David is in Naioth at
> Ramah"; so he sent men to capture him. But when they saw a group of
> prophets prophesying, with Samuel standing there as their leader, *the Spirit
> of God came upon Saul's men and they also prophesied.* Saul was told about it,
> and he sent more men, and *they prophesied too.* Saul sent men a third time,
> and *they also prophesied.* Finally, he himself left for Ramah and went to the
> great cistern at Secu. And he asked, "Where are Samuel and David?"
>
> "Over in Naioth at Ramah," they said.
>
> So Saul went to Naioth at Ramah. But *the Spirit of God came even
> upon him, and he walked along prophesying until he came to Naioth.* He
> stripped off his robes and also prophesied in Samuel's presence. He lay
> that way all that day and night. This is why people say, "Is Saul also
> among the prophets?" (1 Sam 19:18-24, emphasis added)

As an aside, I will briefly articulate here the view that the collective
"prophesying" referred to in these passages probably took the form of
ecstatic, extemporaneously delivered orations and songs of praise and
theological reflection very similar to what can be found in the Old
Testament book of Psalms. While prophesying can involve making
predictions regarding the future, it need not. This view is supported by
the fact that (1) David, the author of many of the psalms, is identified
in Scripture as a prophet (Acts 2:25-30) and a Spirit-anointed singer of
songs (2 Sam 23:1); (2) at least one of the psalms in the book of Psalms
is explicitly referred to by David as an "oracle" (Ps 36:1); (3) 2 Samuel
23:1-7 serves as an another example of a psalm-like oracle attributed to

David; (4) the Old Testament contains references to such prophesying being accompanied by musical instruments (e.g., 1 Chron 25:1, 3); (5) the Scriptures present us with other psalm-like orations that are explicitly portrayed as prophetic utterances (e.g., Lk 1:67-79); and (6) the apostle Paul seems to suggest that one of the consequences of being filled with the Spirit is that church members will "speak to one another with psalms, hymns and spiritual songs," and will sing and make music in their hearts to the Lord (Eph 5:19).

Returning to our survey, Numbers 24:1-3 also connects the coming of the Holy Spirit upon a person with the phenomenon of prophetic activity; here we read of the Holy Spirit coming upon Balaam, empowering him to prophesy in a positive manner over the nation of Israel (much to the chagrin of Balak, son of Zippor, king of Moab!). This passage reads:

> Now when Balaam saw that it pleased the LORD to bless Israel, he did not resort to sorcery as at other times, but turned his face toward the desert. When Balaam looked out and saw Israel encamped tribe by tribe, *the Spirit of God came upon him and he uttered his oracle.* (Num 24:1-3, emphasis added)

The following are some other Old Testament examples indicating a connection between the coming of the Holy Spirit and the phenomenon of prophetic speech:

> *Then the Spirit came upon Amasai, chief of the Thirty, and he said . . .* (1 Chron 12:18, emphasis added)

> *The Spirit of God came upon Azariah son of Oded. He went out to meet Asa and said to him . . .* (2 Chron 15:1-2, emphasis added)

> *Then the Spirit of the LORD came upon Jahaziel son of Zechariah, the son of Benaiah, the son of Jeiel, the son of Mattaniah, a Levite and descendant of Asaph, as he stood in the assembly. He said . . .* (2 Chron 20:14-15, emphasis added)

> *Then the Spirit of God came upon Zechariah son of Jehoiada the priest. He stood before the people and said,* "This is what God says . . . (2 Chron 24:20, emphasis added)

"Therefore prophesy against them; prophesy, son of man."

Then the Spirit of the LORD came upon me, and he told me to say: "This is what the LORD says . . . " (Ezek 11:4-5, emphasis added)

I have presented these numerous Old Testament passages in order to make the point that we do not have to jump straight away into the book of Acts in order to find biblical support for the idea that a connection exists between the coming of the Holy Spirit and the phenomenon of prophetic utterance. A careful and honest reading of the Old Testament will readily demonstrate that it is possible to discern in its pages a thematic pattern that really should not go unnoticed by any evangelical interested in forging a theology of the Spirit that is biblically informed. To be more specific, this survey of pertinent Old Testament passages has indicated that when the Holy Spirit rested or came upon an individual, the phenomenon of prophecy in the sense of speaking either to God or to others on behalf of God often occurred.

Prophetic action. So far, we have looked at passages that speak of the Spirit of God coming upon people in an empowering manner in general and in a way that produced prophetic utterances in particular. There is also a collection of Old Testament passages that seems to connect the coming of the Holy Spirit with prophetic action. As we are about to see, to act in a prophetic manner as I am envisioning it means doing something toward others on behalf of God at the Spirit's prompting.

On the one hand, some of these passages speak of Spirit-inspired acts of *warfare* engaged in by Israelite judges and kings such as Othniel, Gideon, Jephthah, Samson and Saul:

The Spirit of the LORD came upon him, so that he became Israel's judge and went to war. The LORD gave Cushan-Rishathaim king of Aram into the hands of Othniel, who overpowered him. (Judg 3:10, emphasis added)

Then the Spirit of the LORD came upon Gideon, and he blew a trumpet, summoning the Abiezrites to follow him. He sent messengers throughout Manasseh, calling them to arms, and also into Asher, Zebulun and Naphtali, so that they too went up to meet them. (Judg 6:34-35, emphasis added)

Then the Spirit of the LORD came upon Jephthah. He crossed Gilead and Manasseh, passed through Mizpah of Gilead, and from there he advanced against the Ammonites. (Judg 11:29, emphasis added)

Then the Spirit of the LORD came upon him in power. He went down to Ashkelon, struck down thirty of their men, stripped them of their belongings and gave their clothes to those who had explained the riddle. Burning with anger, he went up to his father's house. (Judg 14:19, emphasis added)

As he approached Lehi, the Philistines came toward him shouting. *The Spirit of the LORD came upon him in power. The ropes on his arms became like charred flax, and the bindings dropped from his hands. Finding a fresh jawbone of a donkey, he grabbed it and struck down a thousand men.* (Judg 15:14-15, emphasis added)

When Saul heard their words, *the Spirit of God came upon him in power, and he burned with anger. He took a pair of oxen, cut them into pieces, and sent the pieces by messengers throughout Israel, proclaiming, "This is what will be done to the oxen of anyone who does not follow Saul and Samuel." Then the terror of the LORD fell on the people, and they turned out as one man.* (1 Sam 11:6-7, emphasis added)

On the other hand, there are other Old Testament passages that seem to speak in a predictive manner of the effects that will be produced as a result of the Spirit of God coming upon Israel's future Messiah. These Spirit-prompted behaviors are less militaristic and more peace-producing. Of course these messianic passages achieved a literal fulfillment in the person of Christ. However, while not denying this literal fulfillment, is there not also room for a more figurative one as well? Might the Holy Spirit, in principle, produce in Christ's followers the same kind of behaviors he produced in Christ (see Gal 5:22-25; 2 Cor 3:17-18)? Understood in this figurative, general manner these passages might then be interpreted to suggest that the coming of the Holy Spirit might prompt in someone's life the *pursuit of justice* and an engagement in a *missional ministry to the poor and hurting:*

Here is my servant, whom I uphold,
   my chosen one in whom I delight;

I will put my Spirit on him
  and he will bring justice to the nations.
He will not shout or cry out,
    or raise his voice in the streets.
A bruised reed he will not break,
    and a smoldering wick he will not snuff out.
In faithfulness he will bring forth justice;
    he will not falter or be discouraged
till he establishes justice on earth.
    In his law the islands will put their hope. (Is 42:1-4, emphasis added)

The Spirit of the Sovereign LORD is on me,
    because the LORD has anointed me
    to preach good news to the poor.
He has sent me to bind up the brokenhearted,
    to proclaim freedom for the captives
    and release from darkness for the prisoners,
to proclaim the year of the LORD's favor
    and the day of vengeance of our God,
to comfort all who mourn,
    and provide for those who grieve in Zion—
to bestow on them a crown of beauty
    instead of ashes,
the oil of gladness
    instead of mourning,
and a garment of praise
    instead of a spirit of despair.
They will be called oaks of righteousness,
    a planting of the LORD
for the display of his splendor. (Is 61:1-3, emphasis added)

But as for me, *I am filled with power,*
    with the Spirit of the LORD,
    and with justice and might,
to declare to Jacob his transgression,
    to Israel his sin. (Mic 3:8, emphasis added)

"Are these not the words the LORD proclaimed through the earlier
prophets when Jerusalem and its surrounding towns were at rest and

prosperous, and the Negev and the western foothills were settled?"

And the word of the LORD came again to Zechariah: "This is what the LORD Almighty says: *'Administer true justice; show mercy and compassion to one another. Do not oppress the widow or the fatherless, the alien or the poor. In your hearts do not think evil of each other.'*

"But they refused to pay attention; stubbornly they turned their backs and stopped up their ears. *They made their hearts as hard as flint and would not listen to the law or to the words that the LORD Almighty had sent by his Spirit through the earlier prophets.* So the Lord Almighty was very angry." (Zech 7:7-12, emphasis added)

The bottom line is that the Old Testament sometimes speaks of the Spirit of God inspiring people to take action on God's behalf. Though in some places these Old Testament texts seem to associate the coming of the Holy Spirit with acts of warfare designed to free God's people from their oppressors, there are other passages where the coming of the Spirit produces benevolent rather than violent behaviors. Furthermore, we should also keep in mind that in the New Testament the anointing of the Spirit is never associated with warfare but with behaviors such as gospel proclamation, peacemaking and benevolent social action![7]

A particularly important passage. As we conclude this survey of what the Old Testament has to say about what we can expect from an encounter with God's Holy Spirit, we must not overlook a passage located in the prophecy of Joel that has tremendous implications for a biblically informed theology of the Spirit. Near the end of the Old Testament era the prophet Joel felt compelled by God to announce that the plaintive wish expressed by Moses back at the beginning of the Old Testament era—that all of God's people might be filled with God's Spirit and become involved in prophetic activity—would someday come true. This prophetic promise reads this way:

And afterward,
    I will pour out my Spirit on all people.
    Your sons and daughters will prophesy,

---

[7]See Edward Henry Bickersteth, *The Holy Spirit: His Person and Work* (Grand Rapids: Kregel, 1959), p. 23, for a brief discussion of the progressive manner in which the activity of the Holy Spirit is revealed in the Old Testament.

> your old men will dream dreams,
> your young men will see visions.
> Even on my servants, both men and women,
> I will pour out my Spirit in those days. (Joel 2:28-29)

Many scholars have observed that this remarkable prophecy seems to promise a future era in salvation history when all kinds of sociological barriers will be contravened within the covenant community as a result of God's Spirit coming upon *all* of his servants. According to Joel, age, gender and socioeconomic status will become irrelevant as all kinds of people are empowered by the Spirit to engage in the kind of prophetic activity that was once enjoyed by prominent, male elders only.

As important as this sociological observation is, some scholars believe that something even more profound is being promised in Joel 2:28-29. For example, having made the connection between Moses' wish as reported in Numbers 11:29 and Joel's promise presented in this passage, Wilf Hildebrandt suggests that biblical prophecy "has a forward anticipatory outlook to a period where God would have immediate and intimate connection with all his people."[8] In other words, a time is coming, says the prophet Joel, when all of God's people will be enabled by the Spirit of mission to do things that prophets do: hear God's voice, receive ministry assignments, speak and act in his name.

NEW TESTAMENT SUPPORT FOR THE CONNECTION

We have seen that the Old Testament provides support for the idea of a connection between the coming of the Spirit and the phenomenon of prophetic activity. But does the New Testament as well? I believe it does, not simply in the book of Acts, but because of their strong emphasis upon pneumatology, the Gospel of Luke and the Pauline letters as well.[9] That said, it is also true that more than one scholar has sug-

---

[8]Hildebrandt, *Old Testament Theology of the Spirit of God,* p. 205.
[9]Most introductions to the New Testament comment on the fact that the Gospel of Luke contains a special emphasis on the Holy Spirit (as compared with the other Synoptic Gospels Matthew and Mark). For example, see Donald Guthrie, *New Testament Introduction* (Downers Grove, Ill.: InterVarsity Press, 1970), p. 93; John Drane, *Introducing the New Testament* (San Francisco: Harper & Row, 1986), pp. 187-88; Merrill C. Tenney, *New Testament Survey* (Grand

gested that the biblical book we know as the Acts of the Apostles is poorly named given the importance of the Holy Spirit to the story it tells.[10] Thus, while our survey of the New Testament will extend beyond the book of Acts, it should not surprise us to find within this particular book a plethora of pertinent texts.[11]

I am not alone in holding the view that the New Testament as a whole and book of Acts in particular demonstrate a connection between the coming of the Spirit and the phenomenon of prophetic speech and action. For example, speaking of the New Testament witness, John Michael Penney states that

> the main strand of Holy Spirit activity, whether in relation to Jesus or to his disciples, is conceived broadly in terms of a prophetic power evidenced in word and deed. In particular the terms filled with/full of the Holy Spirit are accompanied by "prophetic" speech, while the anointing of the Spirit or the Spirit coming upon someone is conceived as an empowering of words which effect salvation or deliverance."[12]

Similarly, in his treatise on the Spirit in Luke-Acts, Robert P. Menzies insists that "Luke consistently portrays the Spirit as a source of prophetic inspiration, which (by granting special insight and inspiring speech) empowers God's people for effective service."[13]

Rapids: Eerdmans, 1985), pp. 184-85; Everett Harrison, *Introduction to the New Testament* (Grand Rapids: Eerdmans, 1971), p. 204; Ralph P. Martin, *New Testament Foundations: A Guide for Students* (Grand Rapids: Eerdmans, 1975), 1:252-55; Walter A. Elwell and Robert W. Yarbrough, *Encountering the New Testament: A Historical and Theological Survey* (Grand Rapids: Baker, 1998), p. 104; Robert H. Gundry, *A Survey of the New Testament* (Grand Rapids: Zondervan, 1994), p. 209. See also Stronstad, *Charismatic Theology of St. Luke*, p. 35. It should be noted that many of the Lukan passages from which we derive New Testament support for the connection between the coming of the Spirit and prophetic activity possess parallels in Matthew and Mark.

[10]For a balanced, thoughtful discussion of this issue see John R. W. Stott, *The Message of Acts* (Downers Grove, Ill.: InterVarsity Press, 1990), pp. 32-34.

[11]Interestingly, Amos Yong makes the observation that if a theology is designed to respond to a "yearning to experience afresh the power of the Holy Spirit manifest in the first-century church" it would seem logical to focus on Luke-Acts since Luke is the New Testament author "most concerned with, and interested in, the operations of the Spirit" (Yong, *Spirit Poured Out*, p. 27).

[12]John Michael Penney, *The Missionary Emphasis of Lukan Pneumatology* (Sheffield, U.K.: Sheffield Academic Press, 1997), p. 47. See also Hildebrandt, *Old Testament Theology of the Spirit of God*, pp. 205-7.

[13]Menzies, *Empowered for Witness*, p. 44. See also pp. 174, 186, 188, 202, 226, 230, 238, 239-40, 249, 250, 258-59.

Harry R. Boer says something similar without using the word *prophetic*. He writes:

> The being filled [*sic*] with the Spirit at Pentecost manifested itself in *irrepressible speaking* about the great works of God that came forth from the human spirit wholly seized by the divine Spirit. Pentecost momentarily placed in sharp and dramatic relief that the Church that had come into being in her New Testament form is a speaking, proclaiming Church and that she addresses all men and all nations with her message.[14]

Similarly, over against a tendency among some Christians to become preoccupied with their inner spiritual life, Arthur Glasser makes the following cogent observation:

> In Acts, whenever mention is made of believers being filled with the Holy Spirit, the account always goes on to mention speech (Acts 2:2; 4:8, 31; 7:55-56; 9:17-20; 10:44-46; 13:9-10; 13:52–14:1; 19:6; etc.). Whereas it is true that the fruit of the Spirit described in Galatians 5:22-23 is largely his provision of inward graces, Acts would have us understand that a primary work of the Spirit is to open people's mouths and get them to bear witness to Jesus Christ. Indeed, "the higher gifts" of the Spirit are those that make possible the oral ministry of God's Word (1 Cor 12:31; 14:1-3).[15]

James D. G. Dunn has contended that "for the first Christians, the Spirit was most characteristically a divine power manifesting itself in inspired utterance" (see Acts 1:16; 3:18; 4:25; 28:25).[16]

Finally, Roger Stronstad, referring to Luke-Acts, writes: "The Gospel is the story of Jesus, the unique Charismatic Prophet; the Acts is the story of His disciples, a community of Charismatic prophets. As Luke describes it, their respective ministries of salvation are possible only through the anointing, empowering, and leading of the Holy Spirit."[17]

As we press ahead to survey the pertinent New Testament passages, following the lead of missiologist Arthur Glasser, I do not provide a

---

[14]Harry R. Boer, *Pentecost and Missions* (Grand Rapids: Eerdmans, 1961), p. 102.

[15]Arthur F. Glasser, *Announcing the Kingdom* (Grand Rapids: Baker Academic, 2003), p. 263.

[16]James D. G. Dunn, *The Christ and the Spirit: Pneumatology* (Grand Rapids: Eerdmans, 1997), p. 11.

[17]Stronstad, *Charismatic Theology of St. Luke*, pp. 34-35.

thorough recapitulation of the arguments on either side of the scholarly debate concerning the supposed incompatibility of the pneumatologies put forward by Paul and Luke.[18] Rather, presuming the unity of the Bible and that all the biblical materials point to the one and the same divine reality of the Spirit, while at same time not discounting the diversity that does exist in the biblical witness, I am going to press ahead with the assumption in place that Luke intended to present his readers with a pneumatology that, while not incompatible with the apostle Paul's, differed somewhat from it—a *complementary* pneumatology that includes the notion of multiple in-fillings with the Spirit occurring subsequently to the experience of conversion that result in charismatic empowerment for mission.[19] For reasons already stated in the previous quotes, and on which I will elaborate in chapter three, I am inclined to refer to this complementary pneumatology or theology of the Spirit as "missional."[20] I am convinced that a careful study of the New Testament as a whole will provide support for the thesis that there is a connection between ongoing in-fillings with the Holy Spirit and the phenomenon of prophetic activity.

---

[18]See Glasser, *Announcing the Kingdom*, p. 270.

[19]Menzies, *Empowered for Witness*, pp. 240-41. See also Stronstad, *Charismatic Theology of St. Luke*, pp. 11-12. For his part, Frank Macchia speaks of the possibility of integrating the Lukan, Pauline and Johannine pneumatologies "along the lines of a pneumatological soteriology that views the Spirit as the very substance of the Christ life" (Frank D. Macchia, *Baptized in the Spirit* [Grand Rapids: Zondervan, 2006], pp. 16, 28-29). Likewise, Simon Chan speaks of the need for Pentecostals to link Lukan pneumatology with Pauline pneumatology (Simon Chan, *Pentecostal Theology and the Christian Spiritual Tradition* [New York: Sheffield Academic Press, 2000], p. 12). In a similar move Amos Yong seems to link the Pauline and Lukan pneumatologies when he suggests that "the one baptism in the Holy Spirit, taken as a New Testament metaphor for the full salvific work of God . . . demands a variety of experiences, each of which could be significant of conversion in different areas or at deeper levels, including that of being redirected toward bearing more focused and intensive witness to the gospel. . . . Put succinctly, the baptism in the Holy Spirit refers both to Christian initiation (but understands salvation in a dynamic Wesleyan rather than forensic Lutheran/Reformed sense) *and* empowerment for service (but understands this as holding out the possibility of multiple deepening and intensifying experiences of the Spirit rather than only as 'second'or 'third' works of grace" (Yong, *Spirit Poured Out*, p. 119).

[20]Frank Macchia attempts to construct a Pentecostal doctrine of Spirit baptism that succeeds at integrating Paul's soteriological view of the Spirit with Luke's vocational perspective (Macchia, *Baptized in the Spirit*, pp. 57-59). Since his approach is to ground both pneumatologies in an overarching theology of the kingdom of God (see ibid., pp. 60, 63, 79, 91, 256, 282), I would offer that if we can connect the "kingdom of God" with God's mission toward the world, then Macchia's theology of the Spirit ends up being "missional" as well.

Prophetic activity in the infancy narratives of Luke 1–2. The early chapters of the Gospel of Luke present us with several instances of common folk delivering psalm-like orations in an extemporaneous manner. Many scholars are convinced that Luke expected his readers to understand these ecstatic utterances as occasions of Spirit-enabled prophetic speech similar to those which occurred during the Old Testament era. This would have constituted a startling and therefore effective introduction to Luke's Gospel narrative.

The roughly four hundred years that stand between the completion of the Old Testament epoch and the commencement of the New is referred to by biblical scholars as the "intertestamental era." Robert Menzies sees the characters described in Luke 1–2 as inhabiting a "world of pietistic Judaism"[21] heavily influenced by the literature composed during this intertestamental age.[22] According to Menzies, on the one hand, the intertestamental literature exhibits a tendency to "identify the Spirit of God with prophetic inspiration."[23] On the other hand, the same literature also attests to a perceived dearth of Spirit-inspired prophetic activity during this long period of time.[24] This would have made the story narrated in the early chapters of Luke's Gospel all the more compelling for its first-century audience. Says Menzies, "the silence of spirit-inspired prophetic activity to which the intertestamental literature attests is shattered at the very outset of the narrative, and pneumatic inspiration constitutes a recurring motif."[25] Roger Stronstad puts it this way:

This dramatic outburst of Charismatic or prophetic activity is best in-

---

[21]Menzies, *Empowered for Witness*, p. 107. See also Stronstad, *Charismatic Theology of St. Luke*, p. 36.
[22]Menzies, *Empowered for Witness*, pp. 106-7. See also Stronstad, *Charismatic Theology of St. Luke,* p. 38.
[23]See Menzies, *Empowered for Witness*, pp. 49-102, for a fascinating, if disputed, analysis of various diaspora Palestinian and Essene texts composed during the intertestamental period, as well as texts that are a part of the Rabbinic tradition. On the other hand, see Penney, *Missionary Emphasis*, pp. 29-35, for a critique of Menzies' thesis.
[24]Menzies, *Empowered for Witness*, p. 107. See also Stronstad, *Charismatic Theology of St. Luke*, p. 36; and Roger Stronstad, *The Prophethood of All Believers* (Cleveland, Tenn.: CPT Press, 2010), p. 39.
[25]Menzies, *Empowered for Witness*, p. 107. See also Stronstad, *Charismatic Theology of St. Luke*, p. 36.

terpreted against the background of intertestamental Judaism. . . . [T]he extra-canonical literature of this period, though it is characterized by diversity, witnesses to a threefold perspective on the Spirit: 1) in Judaism the Spirit is almost always the Spirit of prophecy, 2) this prophetic gift of the Spirit has ceased with the last of the writing prophets, and 3) the revival of the activity of the Spirit is expected only in the messianic age—however it might be variously conceived.[26]

In other words, from the very outset of the story it is narrating, Luke's Gospel endeavors to help its readers understand that a new era in salvation history has dawned. The Holy Spirit is active again, enabling men and women to engage in dramatic, prophetic activity just as in the days of old. This revival of prophetic activity can mean only one thing: the messianic age has finally arrived!

Thus, it should not surprise us to find that the first reference to the Holy Spirit actually coming upon someone in Luke's Gospel occurs in Luke 1:11-17 where we read of the angel Gabriel announcing to Zechariah that a son would be born to him in his old age. The promise to this aged priest was that this son, to be named John, would engage in an important prophetic ministry as the forerunner to the Messiah. Furthermore, in keeping with his special prophetic calling, the baby "will be filled with the Holy Spirit even from birth" (Lk 1:15). There it is: the first New Testament passage demonstrating a connection between the coming of the Spirit upon someone and the phenomenon of prophetic activity.[27]

Later in Luke 1 we read of Mary, already with child as a result of her own empowering encounter with the Holy Spirit (Lk 1:35), arriving at Elizabeth's home. The narrative tells us that when Elizabeth heard Mary's greeting she was filled with the Holy Spirit. Luke 1:41 reads: "When Elizabeth heard Mary's greeting, the baby leaped in her womb, and Elizabeth was filled with the Holy Spirit" (Lk 1:41).

Here we have yet another New Testament reference to the Holy Spirit coming upon someone. A careful reading of the story would seem

---

[26]Stronstad, *Charismatic Theology of St. Luke*, p. 38. See also Stronstad, *Prophethood of All Believers*, p. 39.

[27]See Stronstad, *Charismatic Theology of St. Luke*, p. 37.

to indicate that Elizabeth went on to experience the phenomenon of prophetic speech. As we look at Luke 1:42-45, pay close attention to the *manner* and *content* of Elizabeth's verbal response to the experience of being filled with the Spirit. The passage in question reads:

> In a loud voice she exclaimed: "Blessed are you among women, and blessed is the child you will bear! But why am I so favored, that the mother of my Lord should come to me? As soon as the sound of your greeting reached my ears, the baby in my womb leaped for joy. Blessed is she who has believed that what the Lord has said to her will be accomplished!"

In this particular case, the prophetic speech in question took the form of a fervent, spontaneous, ejaculatory pronouncement of blessing directed at Mary and her unborn child. Not a few scholars recognize this as a prophetic utterance.[28] Evidently, Luke intended his readers to assume that Elizabeth's knowledge of what was happening to Mary was divinely conferred and that the entire utterance was spontaneous, ecstatic, fervent and prompted by the Spirit having suddenly come upon her.

Going forward, we have already taken notice of the fact that Luke 1:35 refers to the Holy Spirit coming upon Mary in order to effect her pregnancy. Since Elizabeth's prophetic utterance refers to Mary as having already conceived, it seems safe to assume that Mary's empowering encounter with the Holy Spirit had already occurred. Indeed, it appears that it is simply the sound of Mary's voice that prompts Elizabeth's encounter with the Spirit: as if Mary, or the holy child she is carrying, is not only a bearer of the Spirit but a prophetic purveyor of him (see Acts 8:15; 9:17; 10:44; 19:6).

Furthermore, Luke 1:46-55 goes on to provide an account of an apparent prophetic utterance offered by Mary herself in response to the one just proffered by Elizabeth. Robert Menzies argues not only for a connection between Mary's encounter with the Spirit referred to in Luke 1:35 with her speech in Luke 1:46-55, but also for her speech's inspired, prophetic qualities.[29]

---

[28]Penney, *Missionary Emphasis,* p. 33; Menzies, *Empowered for Witness,* p. 108. See also Stronstad, *Charismatic Theology of St. Luke,* p. 37; and Stronstad, *Prophethood of All Believers,* p. 40.
[29]Menzies, *Empowered for Witness,* p. 115. See also Stronstad, *Prophethood of All Believers,* p. 40;

The next reference to someone being filled with the Spirit in Luke's infancy narratives concerns Zechariah, the father of John the Baptist. Once Elizabeth had given birth to her son, and Zechariah had obeyed the angelic instruction to name the child John, he had his own empowering encounter with the Holy Spirit. It is difficult, if not impossible, to recognize Zechariah's oration (Lk 1:67-79) as anything other than a Spirit-enabled prophetic utterance since the preamble to this oration reads: "His father Zechariah was filled with the Holy Spirit and prophesied" (Lk 1:67).[30]

The next reference in Luke's Gospel to someone being filled with the Holy Spirit occurs in Luke 2:25-35 and presents us with yet another account of prophetic activity. Mary and Joseph had taken Jesus to the temple in order to "present him to the Lord" (Lk 2:22-24). Luke describes for his readers a righteous, devout, already Spirit-filled man named Simeon. The fact that Simeon's encounter with the Holy Spirit had produced within him a prophetic capacity is indicated by the fact that, as Luke tells it, "It had been revealed to him by the Holy Spirit that he would not die before he had seen the Lord's Christ" (Lk 2:26). In other words, the Spirit-filled Simeon was apparently receiving prophetic revelations from the Lord. Going further, Luke tells his readers that, prompted to do so by the Holy Spirit, Simeon rushed to the Temple courts where he seems to have expected this prophetic revelation to be fulfilled (Lk 2:27). Sure enough, in some revelatory manner Simeon was able to recognize the baby Jesus as Israel's future Messiah. Then, taking this infant into his arms, Simeon gave expression to what appears to be yet another example of prophetic speech (Lk 2:27-32).[31]

But Simeon's experience of the prophetic didn't conclude with his expression of Spirit-inspired praise. He went on to engage in prophetic ministry to Joseph and Mary, who, according to Luke, were understandably stunned by Simeon's having referred to their child in various ways as Israel's long awaited Messiah (Lk 2:33). In 1 Corinthians 14:1-3

Penney, *Missionary Emphasis*, p. 33.

[30]See Stronstad, *Charismatic Theology of St. Luke*, p. 37. See also Stronstad, *Prophethood of All Believers*, p. 40; Penney, *Missionary Emphasis*, p. 33.

[31]See Stronstad, *Charismatic Theology of St. Luke*, p. 37; see also Menzies, *Empowered for Witness*, p. 115.

the apostle Paul indicates that when the Holy Spirit prompts Christ's
followers to prophesy to one another, his intention is that the recipients
of this ministry might be strengthened, encouraged and comforted.
Though Simeon's prophetic message to Jesus' parents (especially Mary)
was not, strictly speaking, a comforting one, surely it was intended to
strengthen, prepare and, in a sense, encourage them.

Immediately following his account of Simeon's Spirit-enabled prophetic ministry, Luke introduces his readers to a woman named Anna,
whom he describes as a prophetess. Though Luke does not refer explicitly to the role the Holy Spirit played in Anna's prophetic ministry, he
does make it clear that she, having experienced some form of supernatural revelation as to the baby Jesus' messianic identity, was prompted
to (1) offer prophetic words of praise on his behalf, and (2) begin bearing witness to the Messiah's arrival to everyone in her world (Lk 2:38).
I want to suggest that, for a variety of possible reasons, Luke simply did
not consider it necessary to explicitly refer to the presence of the Holy
Spirit in Anna's life. For one thing, as we have already seen, many Old
Testament passages, as well as various texts composed during intertestamental era, seem to connect prophetic activity with the empowerment provided by the Spirit of the Lord. For another, Luke seems to
take pains to indicate that the episode concerning Anna was nearly
contemporaneous with the one concerning Simeon, whose relationship
with the Holy Spirit was explicitly indicated. Surely the fact that Luke's
account of Anna's episode begins with the words "Coming up to them
at that very moment" (Lk 2:38) is not without significance. For all these
reasons, scholarly support for the prophetic nature of Anna's speech
and actions is not lacking.[32]

Prophetic activity in the inauguration narrative of Luke 3:1–4:44.
The inauguration narrative is Luke's way of describing the commencement of Jesus' public, prophetic ministry.[33] Even though Luke has pre-

---

[32]See, e.g., Stronstad, *Prophethood of All Believers*, p. 40. See also Penney, *Missionary Emphasis*, p. 33.

[33]Stronstad writes: "A close reading of Luke's history of the origin of Christianity compels the reader to conclude that Jesus ministers, from first to last, as the eschatological, anointed prophet" (*Prophethood of All Believers*, p. 37). Furthermore, Stronstad makes the observation that "Jesus identifies himself as prophet in his inaugural sermon at Nazareth (Lk. 4.16-30).

viously referred to Jesus as the Son of God whose very birth was caused by the Holy Spirit having "come upon" his mother, the third Gospel indicates that Jesus experienced his own empowering encounter with the Spirit on the occasion of his water baptism. Luke 3:21-22 reads:

> When all the people were being baptized, Jesus was baptized too. And as he was praying, heaven was opened and the Holy Spirit descended on him in bodily form like a dove. And a voice came from heaven: "You are my Son, whom I love; with you I am well pleased."

While this passage provides support for the idea that the Bible as a whole seems to teach that a connection exists between the coming of the Holy Spirit and some sort of prophetic activity, it does so in an ironic manner. In all of the cases of Spirit-endowment we have looked at thus far, it had been the recipient of the Holy Spirit that either speaks or acts prophetically. In this case, it is the dispenser of the Spirit that "prophesies"—God himself!

Given the immediate context of the story of Jesus' baptism—the temptation episode in Luke 4:1-13, the story of his rejection at Nazareth in Luke 4:14-30 and the accounts of his ministries of exorcism and healing in Luke 4:31-44—many New Testament scholars understand the voice from heaven as bringing to Jesus a prophetic message at the outset of his public ministry. This message was intended to encourage and strengthen him "in the face of the satanic and human opposition he must face."[34]

And yet we should also keep in mind that some biblical scholars have alluded to the possibility that the inauguration stories of Jesus' baptism, temptation, rejection at Nazareth and subsequent engagement in charismatic ministries form an integrated narrative designed to portray the "launching of the public ministry of Jesus—the charismatic Christ."[35] If such a literary connection is justified, then there is a sense in which Luke may have intended his readers to associate the prophetic

---

Because this is programmatic for Jesus' entire ministry, Luke placed this episode immediately after Jesus' baptism and temptation, and thereby at the beginning of Jesus' ministry" (ibid., pp. 37, 53).

[34]Stronstad, *Charismatic Theology of St. Luke*, pp. 40-41.

[35]Ibid., p. 39.

speech uttered by Jesus in the synagogue at Nazareth (Lk 4:14-21) with the account of his water baptism and reception of the Spirit. This would mean that, as Luke tells the story, Jesus himself did eventually prophesy in response to his own reception of the Spirit.[36]

At the very least, given the fact that Jesus' subsequent ministry was so very rich with prophetic speech and action, we can safely assume that his experience with the Spirit on the occasion of his water baptism served to endow him with the phenomenon of *prophetic capacity*.[37]

Prophetic activity alluded to in Jesus' preparation of his disciples (Lk 12:11-12). This is somewhat of a special case, but one that should

---

[36]Something similar may have occurred in the case of Saul of Tarsus. Though no prophetic speech per se is indicated in Acts 9:17, the subsequent verses in Acts 9 imply an engagement in prophetic ministry, and 1 Cor 14:18 makes it clear that at some point the apostle Paul did begin to engage in the practice of glossolalia (speaking in tongues), a form of prophetic speech.

[37]This line of thinking assumes that in his *kenosis* or self-emptying Jesus became just as dependent on the Spirit for his ministry anointing as any other human minister would be. With that thought in mind, I would like to brave the frigid waters and ask: Could it be that this notion of *prophetic capacity* might function as a new starting point in the ongoing dialogue between Pentecostals and charismatics and non-Pentecostals or charismatics with regard to the question of phenomena and Spirit-infillings? I suggest that given the increasingly post-Christian ministry environment in which we Western Christians are presently situated, the focus of evangelical theologians and church leaders—Pentecostal-charismatic and non-Pentecostal-charismatic—needs to move past the old pneumatologies championed thus far toward a theology of the Spirit that can produce within the rank and file of all our churches an increased ability to live missionally faithful, hopeful lives. Might it be possible for all sides to come together around the idea that when the Holy Spirit comes upon a follower of Christ, at the very least we can agree that this experience results in the impartation of prophetic capacity? While I cannot speak for those on the non-Pentecostal-charismatic side of this debate, nor for the leaders of classical Pentecostal denominations, I can attest that there are a number of Pentecostal-charismatic academics and church leaders who recognize the need and potential for such a meeting of the minds. For example, Pentecostal theologian Frank Macchia lends support for this notion when, after providing an affirming comment on a current trend among many Pentecostals to "accent the gift of the Spirit given in regeneration and to view the Pentecostal experience of Spirit baptism as empowerment for witness as a 'release' of an already-indwelling Spirit in life," he writes, "Implied is that all Christians are charismatic. Christians at whatever level of spiritual maturity find their ministries enhanced with greater power and effectiveness through an experience of Spirit baptism" (Macchia, *Baptized in the Spirit*, p. 77). Later in this same work Macchia refers to Spirit baptism as "an empowering calling and gifting for a living witness to Jesus that is the birthright of every Christian as a bearer of the Spirit" (ibid., p. 79). Furthermore, I recently heard Pentecostal statesman Jack Hayford deliver an address in which he made a distinction between being Pentecostal with an "uppercase 'P' " and being one with a "lowercase 'p.' " That is, being a Pentecostal whose major concern is the doctrine of initial, physical evidence, and being a Pentecostal who actually practices prophetic speech (*glossolalia*) on a regular basis with a missional effect (Jack Hayford, "The Pentecostal Pilgrimage and the Emerging Church," Second Annual Pentecostal Leaders Series, The Lewis Wilson Institute for Pentecostal Studies, Costa Mesa, Calif., February 17, 2011).

be included in our survey since it links the Holy Spirit with prophetic activity. In addition to the several Lukan passages that portray prophetic speech occurring as a result of the Holy Spirit having come upon someone, in Luke 12:11-12 we find Jesus speaking a strange word of comfort to his disciples that refers to their future experience of Spirit-inspired speech in a missional context: "When you are brought before synagogues, rulers and authorities, do not worry about how you will defend yourselves or what you will say, *for the Holy Spirit will teach you at that time what you should say*" (Lk 12:11-12, emphasis added)

That it is a type of prophetic speech Jesus has in mind here is connoted more clearly in Matthew's version of this same ministry promise:

> On my account you will be brought before governors and kings as witnesses to them and to the Gentiles. But when they arrest you, do not worry about what to say or how to say it. At that time you will be given what to say, *for it will not be you speaking, but the Spirit of your Father speaking through you.* (Mt 10:18-20, emphasis added)

This is a strange promise Jesus makes to his disciples. On the one hand, he is assuring them they will be persecuted, sometimes in formal, legal, even regal settings. Clearly this would be an intimidating bit of news. But on the other hand Jesus goes on to assure his disciples that at such times they will not be alone. They can count on the Holy Spirit to be faithful during these types of "trials," even to the point of prophetically inspiring their apologetic responses.

Prophetic activity in the book of Acts. So far in our study of what the Bible as a whole has to say about what can be expected when the Holy Spirit comes upon people, we have discerned the presence of a "prophetic story" within the "biblical story" as a whole. This prophetic story is made up of three "chapters" and begins, first of all, with Moses making the wish that someday all of God's people would be filled with the Spirit and thereby endowed with the capacity to function prophetically (Num 11:29). The next chapter in the prophetic story occurs when we read of the prophet Joel making the bold announcement that what Moses wished for will someday occur: all of

God's people, regardless of age, gender and socioeconomic status, will be filled with the Holy Spirit and thereby enabled to prophesy (Joel 2:28-29). The final chapter unfolds when we find an inspired apostle Peter boldly announcing that with the coming of the Holy Spirit on the day of Pentecost, both Moses' wish and Joel's promise have been fulfilled (Acts 2:14-18)![38] This concluding chapter to the prophetic story is so critical to our understanding of what the Bible as a whole has to say about the connection between the coming of the Spirit and the phenomenon of prophetic activity that it warrants an especially close inspection.

In Acts 1:8 Luke has Jesus making a promise of his own: his disciples will receive a supernatural empowerment to bear witness for him as a result of the Holy Spirit coming upon them. The utterance of this promise, followed by Jesus' bodily ascension into heaven, precipitated an extended prayer meeting attended by eleven of Jesus' disciples, a few family members and a number of other followers (Acts 1:13-14). Acts 2 tells us that Jesus' promise was fulfilled on the day of Pentecost.

> When the day of Pentecost came, they were all together in one place. Suddenly a sound like the blowing of a violent wind came from heaven and filled the whole house where they were sitting. They saw what seemed to be tongues of fire that separated and came to rest on each of them. All of them were filled with the Holy Spirit and began to speak in other tongues as the Spirit enabled them. (Acts 2:1-4)

This passage reveals yet another occasion in Luke-Acts where the reader finds someone being filled with the Holy Spirit. Luke makes it crystal clear in Acts 2:4 that the phenomenon of glossolalia, speaking in tongues, was Spirit-enabled. The question is: Is glossolalia to be considered a form of prophetic speech? Luke answers this question for us in the two pericopes (sections of Scripture) that follow.

Acts 2:5-13 conveys the image of Jesus' followers spontaneously, ecstatically, publicly "declaring the wonders of God" in tongues that were

---

[38]Support for this connection is provided in Veli-Matti Kärkkäinen, *Pneumatology* (Grand Rapids: Baker Academic, 2002), p. 31. See also Wright, *Knowing the Holy Spirit*, p. 53; and Yong, *Spirit Poured Out*, p. 83.

foreign to them but well known to the members of a crowd of onlookers that had quickly gathered around them. Granted, Luke tells us that the missional effect this prophetic speech had on the crowd of onlookers was mixed. Witnessing the prophetic activity of the Spirit-filled disciples caused some in the crowd to mock and to accuse the disciples of being drunk in public. Observing the same prophetic activity caused others in the crowd to experience great amazement and to pose the question, "What does this mean?"

Acts 2:14-18 serves as the preface to Peter's "Pentecostal Sermon," which itself should be viewed as prophetic speech.[39] This preface to Peter's sermon makes it clear that the glossolalia referred to in Acts 2:4, 11, constitutes a form of prophecy. Notice in the following passage the way the apostle Peter makes the connection between the disciples' glossolalia and the fulfillment of the promise made by the prophet Joel that someday all of God's people would be enabled by the Spirit to prophesy.

> Then Peter stood up with the Eleven, raised his voice and addressed the crowd: "Fellow Jews and all of you who live in Jerusalem, let me explain this to you; listen carefully to what I say. These men are not drunk, as you suppose. It's only nine in the morning! No, this is what was spoken by the prophet Joel:
>
> "In the last days, God says,
> I will pour out my Spirit on all people.
> Your sons and daughters will prophesy,
> your young men will see visions,
> your old men will dream dreams.
> Even on my servants, both men and women,
> I will pour out my Spirit in those days,
> and they will prophesy." (Acts 2:14-18)

Actually, a close comparison of Acts 2:18 and Joel 2:29 indicates that Luke has Peter going out of his way to equate glossolalia with the phenomenon of prophecy. Peter's concluding phrase "and they will proph-

---

[39]William W. Menzies and Robert P. Menzies, *Spirit and Power: Foundations of Pentecostal Experience* (Grand Rapids: Zondervan, 2000), pp. 194-95.

esy" is not a part of Joel 2:29. Peter has added that phrase as if to under-score an important theological point: Moses' wish and Joel's promise have been fulfilled in the events of Pentecost![40]

Indeed, it has been suggested that Luke intended for the outpouring of the Spirit on the day of Pentecost to be interpreted as an event that harks back to the transference of the Spirit and accompanying ministry anointing from Moses to the seventy elders described in Numbers 11. Just as Numbers 11 depicts how the Spirit and accompanying ministry anointing that had rested on Moses was transferred to the seventy elders, Acts 2 depicts a transferring of the Spirit and accompanying ministry anointing that had been resident in Jesus to his apostolic community.[41] Thus the connection is not simply between Pentecost and Joel's promise, but between Pentecost and Moses' wish that someday all of God's people would be endowed with a prophetic capacity. Roger Stronstad puts it this way: "the pouring out of the Spirit on the day of Pentecost inaugurates nothing less than God's people as the prophethood of all believers."[42]

The idea that Luke was being careful to make this theological point finds support in the fact that the remainder of the book of Acts is filled with stories of Christ's followers being empowered by the Holy Spirit to engage in prophetic speech and action. Robert Menzies observes that "Out of 59 references to the Spirit of God in Acts, 36 are unequivocally linked to prophetic activity."[43] My own observation

---

[40]See Stronstad, *Prophethood of All Believers*, p. 69; Clark Pinnock, *Flame of Love* (Downers Grove, Ill.: InterVarsity Press, 1996), p. 134; Glasser, *Announcing the Kingdom*, p. 264.

[41]Stronstad, *Prophethood of All Believers*, pp. 69-70. Likewise, Clark Pinnock writes, "At Pentecost the church received the Spirit and became the historical continuation of Jesus' anointing as the Christ. The One baptized in water and Spirit now baptizes the disciples. He transferred Spirit to them so that his actions could continue through their agency. The bearer of the Spirit now baptizes others with the Spirit, that there might be a continuation of his testimony in word and deed and a continuation of his prophetic and charismatic ministry" (Pinnock, *Flame of Love*, p. 118). See also Christopher J. H. Wright, *The Mission of God's People* (Grand Rapids: Zondervan, 2010), p. 43.

[42]Stronstad, *Prophethood of All Believers*, pp. 69-70. Likewise, Gordon Fee writes, "With the outpouring of the Spirit at the end of the age, the early Christians understood the prophecy of Joel 2:28-30 to have been fulfilled, so that 'prophecy' not only became a renewed phenomenon, but was also potentially available to all, since all now possessed the Spirit in fullness (cf. Acts 2:17-18)" (Gordon Fee, *God's Empowering Presence* [Peabody, Mass.: Hendrickson, 1994], p. 170).

[43]Menzies, *Empowered for Witness*, p. 258.

is that no less than twenty-one of the twenty-eight chapters of the book of Acts portray some sort of prophetic activity taking place: (1) disciples speaking prophetically to God, (2) disciples prophetically hearing from God, (3) disciples prophetically speaking and acting on behalf of God with the result that even more disciples are made and the church is built up!

For example:

- A previously timid Peter was now willing and able to stand and deliver a powerful Spirit-inspired sermon that resulted in thousands of converts to the Christian faith (Acts 2).[44]

- Somehow Peter seemed to know that he was supposed to lift a lame man to his feet, thereby effect his healing, and then boldly preached to an astonished crowd about the resurrected Jesus (Acts 3).

- Peter was enabled by the Holy Spirit to offer a bold response to the religious leaders of Israel who wanted to know by what power he and John had been able to heal that lame man in the temple (Acts 4).

- After a fresh in-filling with the Holy Spirit, the entire Christian community began to proclaim the gospel in an extraordinarily bold manner (Acts 4)!

- Peter seemed to know that God was about to exercise divine discipline in the lives of two church members—Ananias of Jerusalem and his wife Sapphira—who were guilty of lying to Holy Spirit (Acts 5).

- Stephen was empowered by the Holy Spirit to bear witness to the resurrected Jesus even as he was becoming the church's first martyr (Acts 7).

- An angel of the Lord told Philip to go to a certain location (out in the desert) and wait there for a certain ministry opportunity. Once there, the Spirit enabled Philip to effectively evangelize and baptize a high-standing member of the court of the queen of Ethiopia! After

---

[44]Stronstad provides substantial exegetical support for the notion that Peter's Pentecostal sermon was a "pneuma discourse—speech inspired by the Holy Spirit" (Stronstad, *Prophethood of All Believers*, pp. 68-70).

this ministry had concluded, the Spirit continued to provide specific direction to Philip in his missional endeavors (Acts 8).

- The Lord spoke to Ananias of Damascus in a vision, sending him to pray for the man who would become the apostle Paul (Acts 9).

- The Holy Spirit told Peter to go with some Gentiles to Caesarea in order to do ministry there (Acts 10).

- As Peter preached the gospel in an extemporaneous manner to the Gentiles in Cornelius's house, the Spirit came upon them, enabling them to engage in prophetic speech of their own (both glossolalia and ecstatic praise in the vernacular) (Acts 10).

- The Holy Spirit, speaking through a prophet named Agabus, informed the church in Antioch that a famine would soon adversely affect the disciples living in the region of Judea (Acts 11).

- An angel spoke to Peter, giving him specific instructions, helping him escape the prison into which he had been thrown (Acts 12).

- The Holy Spirit spoke to the church leaders in Antioch, instructing them to send Paul and Barnabas off on their first missionary assignment to Cyprus and Asia Minor (Acts 13).

- Paul was inspired by the Holy Spirit to boldly and prophetically confront a perverse Jewish sorcerer who was impeding the ministry of the gospel (Acts 13).

- The Holy Spirit inspired the leaders of the church in Jerusalem not to require that Gentiles be circumcised in order to become Christ followers and church members (This was a huge development in the history of the church!) (Acts 15).

- Paul received some fairly specific and important ministry instructions delivered in various ways by the Holy Spirit. (As a result, the gospel crossed the Aegean Sea and invaded Europe. This too was a huge event in the history of the church!) (Acts 16).

- The Lord spoke to Paul in a vision, encouraging him to continue ministering in Corinth despite the adversity he was experiencing (Acts 18).

- Apollos (in some Greek manuscripts), having been "instructed in the way of the Lord" was able to speak with "fervor in the Spirit" (Acts 18).

- After the apostle Paul prayed for some newly baptized folks in Ephesus, the Holy Spirit came upon them, enabling them to engage in prophetic speech (glossolalia and prophecy uttered in the vernacular) (Acts 19).

- Paul kept hearing the Holy Spirit warn him that his future involved prison and hardships (Acts 20).

- The Spirit used various church members in Tyre and Caesarea to deliver prophetic messages to Paul, further preparing him for the adversity he would soon experience (Acts 21).

- Paul rehearsed the prophetic manner in which the Lord had warned him to flee Jerusalem years earlier just after his conversion (Acts 22).

- The Lord spoke to Paul in a very personal way, assuring him that he would not die in Jerusalem but would have the opportunity to preach the gospel in Rome (Acts 23).

- Paul rehearsed the prophetic manner in which he had been called to a prophetic ministry (Acts 26).

- The apostle Paul was able to minister comfort and assurance to his fellow shipmates because he had had an encouraging conversation with an angel the night before (Acts 27).

What should we make of the many incidents of prophetic activity presented in the book of Acts? At the very least, we must acknowledge that the Holy Spirit played a huge role in the birth and expansion of the Christian movement. I want to go on to suggest, however, that our survey of Luke-Acts has yielded a remarkable degree of support for the idea that a connection exists between the coming of the Spirit and the phenomenon of prophetic activity.

Going even further, I want to underscore the opinion put forward by not a few scholars that while Luke's work as a historian should not be undervalued, he was doing more than writing a history. Luke was also a theologian, composing with the help of the Spirit a document

that was intended to function prescriptively as well as descriptively.[45]
To be more precise, I am convinced that the Holy Spirit was using
Luke to create a document that would perpetually remind the church
of the need to engage in prophetic activity in order to remain missionally faithful.

Though the evidence does not support the idea that the story of the
disciple Ananias (of Damascus) being sent by the Holy Spirit to minister to a dazed and confused Saul of Tarsus (Acts 9:10-20) was, strictly
speaking, paradigmatic for Luke of what Christ wants all of his Spirit-
filled followers to be able to do, *it must be acknowledged that Luke's message overall seems to be that that all Spirit-filled believers possess the capacity,
like Ananias, to hear God's voice, receive ministry assignments, speak and act
on Christ's behalf, make new disciples, and build up the church, offering a
powerful refutation of religious relativism in the process!*[46]

References to prophetic activity in the writings of the apostle Paul.
Earlier in this chapter I alluded to the idea that Paul and Luke seem to
present their readers with different though compatible theologies of
the Spirit. Scholars refer to Paul's pneumatology as "soteriological,"
and to Luke's as "charismatic" or "vocational." I then indicated my
preference for the term *missional.* Though this distinction is valid, it

---

[45]For example, Pentecostal scholar Roger Stronstad makes the assertion that Luke's historical
accounts provide a solid foundation for a theology of the Spirit that should be taken seriously
by contemporary followers of Christ. Stronstad writes, "In principle, Luke's narratives are an
important and legitimate data base for constructing a Lukan doctrine of the Spirit. Thus,
rather than providing a flimsy foundation upon which to erect a doctrine of the Holy Spirit, as
is commonly alleged, the historical accounts of the activity of the Spirit in Acts provide a firm
foundation for erecting a doctrine of the Spirit which has normative implications for the mission and religious experience of the contemporary church" (Stronstad, *Charismatic Theology of
St. Luke*, p. 9). Furthermore, the view that Luke was a theologian as well as a historian is also
supported by evangelical scholars William Klein, Craig Blomberg and Robert Hubbard Jr.,
who write, "many interpreters of Acts succumb to false dichotomies between theology and
history. . . . But, as in his Gospel, Luke did not compile history for history's sake; rather he
compiled it to teach his readers what he believed God was accomplishing in the world and
what God was commanding believers to do in and through the events he narrated" (William
W. Klein, Craig L. Blomberg and Robert L. Hubbard Jr., *Introduction to Biblical Interpretation*
[Dallas: Word, 1993], pp. 344-45, cited in Penney, *Missionary Emphasis*, p. 13).
[46]While it is true that Acts 9:10-20 does not refer to the Holy Spirit specifically, its context in
the two-volume work Luke-Acts (see Acts 1:1) suggests that Luke assumed his readers would
understand that it was through the agency of the Holy Spirit that God communicated with
Ananias, prompting his subsequent engagement in missional ministry to a blinded and bewil-
dered Saul of Tarsus on behalf of the risen Christ.

should not be viewed as absolute. I believe that it is possible to identify passages in Paul's writings that seem to connect the phenomenon of prophetic activity with the coming of the Spirit and which suggest that the activity of the Spirit in the lives of believers can and should exercise a missional effect.[47]

First, I want to bring attention to a couple of passages that seem to suggest that *it is through prophetic means that the Spirit assures believers of their soteriological status before God*. In Romans 8:15-16 we are told that through the Spirit believers are enabled to "cry, Abba, Father" and thereby to have their hearts assured that they belong to God. This passage says, "For you did not receive a spirit that makes you a slave again to fear, but you received the Spirit of sonship. And by him we cry, 'Abba, Father.' The Spirit himself testifies with our spirit that we are God's children" (Rom 8:15-16).

Paul says essentially the same thing in Galatians 4:6.[48] "Because you are sons, God sent the Spirit of his Son into our hearts, the Spirit who calls out, 'Abba, Father.'"

Certainly, these references to the Holy Spirit prompting disciples to employ a certain form of speech, and to the inner testimony of assurance he provides in the process, can be understood metaphorically. But is it not also possible that Paul had in mind that as a result of receiving the Spirit, a person might literally give expression to a form of Spirit-inspired speech whereby he or she is enabled to communicate with God in a direct, intimate, spontaneous and impassioned manner?[49]

Even more support for the idea that Paul was open to the idea that the Holy Spirit might prompt a believer to give expression to some form of prophetic speech is provided by the apostle's reference in Romans

---

[47]Support for this idea is provided in Kärkkäinen, *Pneumatology*, p. 32. Certainly this was the case with Paul himself as Acts 13:9-12 makes clear.

[48]Gordon Fee's treatment of these two passages overlaps greatly. See Fee, *God's Empowering Presence*, pp. 561-62.

[49]C. K. Barrett acknowledges the possibility that due to his use of the violent word *krazomen* in Rom 8:15 (translated as "we cry"), Paul may have had a Spirit-inspired utterance in mind here (cf. 1 Cor. 14:15) (C. K. Barrett, *The Epistle to the Romans*, Harper's New Testament Commentaries [New York: Harper & Row, 1957], p. 164). A form of the same Greek verb is used in Galatians 4:6 and is translated as "calls out." Gordon Fee makes the point that it is the believer who speaks, but at the Spirit's prompting (Fee, *God's Empowering Presence*, pp. 568-69).

8:26-27 to the aid the Holy Spirit provides believers when it comes to prayer. This passage reads:

> In the same way, the Spirit helps us in our weakness. We do not know what we ought to pray for, but the Spirit himself intercedes for us with groans that words cannot express. And he who searches our hearts knows the mind of the Spirit, because the Spirit intercedes for the saints in accordance with God's will.

Most scholars agree that the plain sense of this passage is that in one way or another the Holy Spirit assists spiritually confused believers by inspiring them to pray in a manner that is in accordance with God's will. Yes, it is true that scholarly debate surrounds the issue of whether Paul had glossolalia in mind here or a literal groaning inspired by the Spirit.[50] Either way, it appears that Paul meant to suggest that at times the Spirit will actually speak or pray *through* the believer, offering effective intercession on his or her behalf in the process.[51]

Further exegetical support for the idea that Paul recognized the connection between the coming of the Spirit and prophetic speech is to be found in his first letter to the Corinthians. In 1 Corinthians 12:3 the apostle refers to the dynamic of "speaking by the Spirit." Paul goes on to list various ways the Holy Spirit can and will manifest himself through members of Christ's body.[52] Though all of the manifestations

---

[50]Eminent New Testament scholars F. F. Bruce and C. K. Barrett both acknowledge the possibility that Paul may have had glossolalia in mind in Romans 8:26 (F. F. Bruce, *Romans*, Tyndale New Testament Commentaries [Downers Grove, Ill.: InterVarsity Press, 2008], p. 165; C. K. Barrett, *Epistle to the Romans*, p. 168). For his part, Pentecostal biblical scholar Gordon Fee is a bit less ambivalent. He writes: "Several matters, therefore, join to suggest that Origen probably had it right, in understanding these sentences as a whole and this phrase in particular to refer to a kind of private ('to oneself') praying in tongues that Paul speaks about as part of his resolution of the practice of uninterpreted tongues in the worshiping community in Corinth" (Fee, *God's Empowering Presence*, p. 580). According to Fee, Ernst Käsemann also sees a reference to prayer in tongues at work in this passage. See Ernst Käsemann, "The Cry for Liberty in the Worship of the Church," in *Perspectives on Paul* (London: SCM Press, 1971), p. 135.

[51]Fee feels the need to make it clear that the Spirit is not enabling us to intercede for others. "To the contrary, the appeal is before God on *our* behalf, the Spirit's appealing to God for us because in our weakness we do not know how to pray in our own behalf" (Fee, *God's Empowering Presence*, p. 579).

[52]Fee asserts that the gifts listed in this passage are "above all *manifestations* of the Spirit's presence in their midst, chosen because they are, like tongues itself, extraordinary phenomena" (ibid., p. 165).

of the Spirit listed by Paul in 1 Corinthians 12 can be seen in one way or another to be prophetic and missional in nature, in verse 8 he refers to "messages" of wisdom and revelation that are provided by the Spirit,[53] and in verse 10 he alludes to the gift of "prophecy" proper,[54] which, according to Gordon Fee, "consisted of spontaneous, Spirit-inspired, intelligible messages, orally delivered in the gathered assembly, intended for the edification or encouragement of the people."[55]

Evidently, Paul viewed the ability to prophesy an especially important, valuable spiritual gift.[56] As is well known, there is a sense in which 1 Corinthians 14 is all about this particular form of prophetic speech. Paul begins this chapter by commending this particular "spiritual gift" to the Corinthians (1 Cor 14:1).[57] Paul goes on in the chapter to explain why he holds the gift of prophecy in such high esteem. First, there is its ability to bring messages to fellow church members that result in their

---

[53]Fee refers to those who "have suggested that Paul here has in mind a supernatural endowment of knowledge, factual information that could not otherwise have been known without the Spirit's aid, such as frequently occurs in the prophetic tradition" (ibid., p. 167). In a note related to this discussion, Fee indicates that "Peter's 'knowledge' of Ananias and Sapphira's misdeed in Acts 5:1-11 is often looked upon as this gift in action" (ibid., p. 167 n. 310). Fee goes on to indicate that since the gift known as the "message of knowledge" "is so closely tied to the 'message of wisdom,' the two should probably be understood as parallel in some way. Most likely, therefore, it is a 'Spirit utterance' of some revelatory kind" (ibid., p. 167).

[54]Ibid. p. 165. Fee refers here to William Baird's grouping of "prophecy, discerning prophecies, tongues, interpretation of tongues" as "gifts of inspired utterance" (William Baird, *The Corinthian Church: A Biblical Approach to Urban Culture* [New York: Abingdon, 1964], p. 139). Fee also explains that for Paul "the prophet was one who under inspiration of the Spirit spoke to God's people (e.g., Mic 3:8)" (Fee, *God's Empowering Presence*, p. 169). See also F. D. Bruner's treatment of the operation of this spiritual gift in Pentecostal churches in Bruner, *Theology of the Holy Spirit*, pp. 142-43.

[55]Fee, *God's Empowering Presence*, p. 170. I should point out that Fee essentially dismisses the notion of "personal prophecy, whereby someone prophesies over another as to very personal matters in their lives." On the one hand, I ultimately resonate with the spirit in which this critique is offered and the goal of its execution. The type of missional prophetic activity I am seeking to promote in these pages should not be confused with the kind of "personal prophecy" that goes on in many charismatic prayer meetings. On the other hand, even though Fee allows that some form of personal prophecy might have been going on in those situations reflected in 1 Tim 1:18; 4:14, I still wonder if his critique could be more nuanced in the light of what he, himself, has to say about the prophetic aspects of the messages of wisdom and knowledge, as well as such passages as Acts 9:10-20; 13:9-11. That said, I also wonder if perhaps for Fee the community versus private setting is what is at issue as well as the interpersonal nature of the prophetic activity (see ibid., pp. 170-71).

[56]See Pinnock, *Flame of Love*, p. 134; and Fee, *God's Empowering Presence*, pp. 215, 217-21.

[57]Fee, *God's Empowering Presence*, p. 215.

"strengthening, encouragement and comfort" (1 Cor 14:3).[58] Second, *when conducted properly*, a charismatic worship service earmarked by valid prophetic utterances will have a positive missional effect on any unbelievers who happen to be in attendance (1 Cor 14:24-25). Commenting on this passage, Fee writes:

> Once more prophecy is set forth as the alternative to the unintelligibility of uninterpreted tongues. In this case it is viewed as leading directly to the conversion of the visiting unbeliever. This passage in particular implies that prophesying is *potentially available* to all believers, since all are Spirit people. That is, Paul does not say, "If the prophets all prophesy," but "If *all* prophesy . . . the unbeliever will be convicted by *all* [not all prophets] . . . and he or she will be judged by *all*." The nature of this argumentation excludes the option that this gift was limited to a group of authoritative people who were known in the community as "the prophets."[59]

Paul concludes the chapter by admonishing the Corinthians to be eager to prophesy and not to forbid speaking in tongues (1 Cor 14:39). It should be pointed out that Paul evidently believed that there is a way for missionally faithful churches to engage in these kinds of prophetic behaviors in a manner that is fitting and orderly—that is, not weird, chaotic, disruptive, off-putting or counterproductive (1 Cor 14:40).[60]

Finally, Paul's letter to the Ephesians contains a fascinating passage which, all by itself, serves to indicate that there is within the apostle's essentially soteriological pneumatology an understanding of how being filled with the Spirit will produce a capacity for Christ's followers to minister to one another through prophetic speech. Ephesians 5:18-20 says:

> Do not get drunk on wine, which leads to debauchery. Instead, be filled with the Spirit. Speak to one another with psalms, hymns and spiritual songs. Sing and make music in your heart to the Lord, always giving thanks to God the Father for everything, in the name of our Lord Jesus Christ.

---

[58]Ibid., pp. 217-19.
[59]Ibid., p. 244, emphasis in original.
[60]Ibid., p. 261.

At the very least this passage suggests that being filled with the Spirit (something which the Greek verb form indicates should happen over and over again)[61] will result in the capacity to engage in prophetic speech (ecstatic praise and thanksgiving) and prophetic action (submitting to one another *in the fear of Christ*). Gordon Fee takes pains to indicate that "what is often missed in our English translations is that all of vv. 19-21 take the form of a series of participles that modify the primary imperative in v. 18."[62] This means that the circumstances by which Paul's readers are to obey the primary imperative "be filled with the Spirit" are indicated in such qualifying phrases as:

- "speaking *to each other* with psalms, hymns, and Spirit songs"

- "singing and making music *to the Lord*, with your hearts"

- "giving thanks *to God* for all things in the name of the Lord Jesus Christ"

- "submitting yourselves *to one another* in the fear of Christ."[63]

Presumably, Paul meant for his readers to understand that this interpersonal ministry by means of prophetic speech and action would have the effect of producing ongoing spiritual maturation among church members. The possibility exists, however, that he also intended his readers to understand that such interpersonal prophetic ministry was

---

[61]Referring to the command in Eph 5:19 to be filled with the Spirit, biblical commentator Frances Foulkes writes: "the tense of the verb, present imperative in the Greek, should be noted, implying as it does that the experience of receiving the Holy Spirit so that every part of life is permeated and controlled by Him is not a 'once for all' experience. In the early chapters of the Acts of the Apostles it is repeated a number of times that the apostles were 'filled with the Holy Spirit.' The practical implication is that the Christian is to leave his life open to be filled constantly and repeatedly by the divine Spirit" (Frances Foulkes, *Ephesians*, Tyndale New Testament Commentaries [Downers Grove, Ill.: InterVarsity Press, 2008], p. 159). This observation would also have application as a corrective against any pneumatological view of a Spirit baptism that does not allow for ongoing experiences of in-filling. Ironically, though James Dunn and the classical Pentecostal denominations differ on the use of the term *Spirit baptism*, and whether an initial Spirit infilling resulting in empowered witness should be viewed as a second or even third work of grace, my sense is that most classical Pentecostals would agree with Dunn that "one does not enter the new age or the Christian life more than once, but one may be empowered or filled with the Spirit many times (Acts 2.4; 4.8, 31; 9.17; 13.9; Eph 5.18)" (Dunn, *Baptism in the Holy Spirit*, p. 54). See also Bruner, *Theology of the Holy Spirit*, pp. 171-72, 214, 241; and Glasser, *Announcing the Kingdom*, p. 311.

[62]Fee, *God's Empowering Presence*, p. 719.

[63]Ibid.

key to the accomplishment of the important moral and missional imperatives to which he had been referring throughout the whole section of which this passage is a part (Eph 4:17–5:21).[64]

These are just a few passages culled from the writings of the apostle Paul which, along with those we identified in Luke-Acts and those included in our survey of the Old Testament, offer strong support for the idea that the Bible as a whole evidences a dynamic connection between empowering encounters with God's Holy Spirit and the phenomenon of prophetic activity. Why is seeing and embracing this dynamic connection so important? Though I have already hinted at the answer to this question, I provide a formal, much more thorough response to it in chapter two. And in the process, I will put forward a rather provocative ministry theory.

---

[64]Fee asserts that this passage functions as a "transition as Paul moves toward brining closure to the long section of paranesis that began in 4:17" (ibid., pp. 718-19).

2

"YOU SHALL RECEIVE POWER"

The Connection Between Prophetic Activity
and Missional Faithfulness

SPEAKING OF THE RESULT OF THE outpouring of the Holy Spirit on the day of Pentecost, the authors of the hugely influential book *Missional Church: A Vision for the Sending of the Church in North America* write:

> While the Spirit is "the unseen Lord," the movement of the Holy Spirit has real and visible effects. The experience of the Spirit brings "the touch of God's presence, the power of God's healing, the liberating experience of forgiveness, the reality of fraternal community, the joy of celebration, the boldness in witness, the blossoming of hope, and the fruitfulness in mission."[1]

We have seen that the coming of the Spirit upon the first followers of Christ did indeed produce some real and visible effects, which I am describing in an overarching manner as prophetic activity. The purpose of this chapter is to explore a possible connection between this prophetic activity and a "boldness in witness," a "blossoming of hope" and a "fruitfulness in mission." The thesis of this chapter is that because of the faithfulness of the Spirit of mission, there is indeed a biblically discernible connection between prophetic activity and a missional faithfulness and hopefulness (that this faithful missional engagement

---

[1]Darrell Guder, ed., *Missional Church* (Grand Rapids: Eerdmans, 1998), p. 146. Quote cited is from Mortimer Arias, *Announcing the Reign of God* (Philadelphia: Fortress, 1984), p. 61.

will also prove fruitful). While we must ever be on guard against the sacrifice of faithfulness for the sake of efficiency, and a tendency among North American churches to allow our prominent cultural ethos of pragmatism to feed a desire to capture the Spirit in formulas and principles, perhaps even to manage or control the Spirit for *our* church growth ends (i.e., to help us feel successful), the fact remains that the God of the Bible is interested in our being fruitful in our walk with Christ with the result that more people are brought into the faith (e.g., see Mt 5:13-14; Jn 15:8, 16; Acts 2:41, 47; 5:14; 9:31; 11:26; 16:5; 28:23; Col 1:6, 10).

With this goal in mind, I want to remind us of the fact that a chief earmark of the post-Christian ministry context in which we currently find ourselves is a rampant embrace of the notion of religious relativism. It just so happens that this is not the first time that a group of sincere Christ followers has had to wrestle with this thorny ministry obstacle. The fact is that a rampant religious relativism was rife in the world the earliest Christians inhabited as well.

Historian John Ferguson asserts that "the attitudes of many in the ancient Roman Empire in the first century concerning alien religious beliefs and practices were marked by tolerance, accommodation, and openness to syncretism."[2] Harold Netland, professor of philosophy and intercultural studies, reminds us that in the Roman Empire in the first century "the idea that there are multiple ways in which to relate to the divine, with each culture having its own distinctive traditions for doing so, was widespread."[3] Thus the historical evidence strongly suggests that a commitment to religious relativism was commonplace in the first-century Roman world.

Biblical support for the idea that the early church's first-century ministry context was awash with religious relativism is not lacking either. For instance, more than likely it was a vestigial tendency toward

[2]John Ferguson, *The Religions of the Roman Empire* (Ithaca, N.Y.: Cornell University Press, 1970), chap. 12, cited in Harold Netland, *Dissonant Voices: Religious Pluralism and the Question of Truth* (Vancouver: Regent College Publishing, 1991), p. 12. See also Harold Netland, *Encountering Religious Pluralism: The Challenge to Christian Faith & Mission* (Downers Grove, Ill.: InterVarsity Press, 2001), p. 25.
[3]Netland, *Encountering Religious Pluralism*, pp. 25-26.

syncretism (and the religious relativism that promotes this practice) at work in the lives of the Corinthian church members that caused the apostle Paul to issue more than one stern warning against participating in the pagan religious rituals so common in Corinth (1 Cor 10:21; 2 Cor 6:14-18). And, of course, we are well aware of the religiously relativistic environment that Paul encountered in Athens that so influenced the tack he took when preaching to them.

> Paul then stood up in the meeting of the Areopagus and said: "Men of Athens! I see that in every way you are very religious. For as I walked around and looked carefully at your objects of worship, I even found an altar with this inscription: TO AN UNKNOWN GOD. Now what you worship as something unknown I am going to proclaim to you." (Acts 17:22-23)

Thus, it certainly appears that the first-century world in which the earliest Christians lived had much in common with our own. Our post-Christian ministry context is eerily similar to the pre-Christian one inhabited by the earliest followers of Christ!

Herein lies the problem: because the Christian faith purports to put people in touch with the truth about the way things are (e.g., 1 Tim 2:4; 2 Tim 2:25; Tit 1:1; Heb 10:26; 1 Jn 2:20-21; 2 Jn 1:1-4), the way human beings should behave (e.g., Eph 5:1-17), and the true path to God and eternal blessedness (e.g., Jn 14:6; Acts 4:12; 1 Tim 2:5-6), a rampant religious relativism represents a ministry challenge that, as Paul's experience in Athens shows, can be quite formidable. What is a contemporary evangelical Christian living in the post-Christian West, who sincerely believes that the way of Jesus is true in a manner that other religious paths are not, supposed to do?

In brief, it is my contention that in our post-Christian day and place we contemporary evangelicals must *assume responsibility to imitate the missional ministry practices of the early church as reflected in Luke-Acts*. For despite the fact that the church was birthed into such a religiously relativistic environment, the testimony is that for all its imperfections the faithful Spirit of mission was able to use the early church to turn the world upside down (see Acts 17:6 KJV), and launch a movement that would impact the entire world.[4]

To be more specific, I am committed to the idea that the kind of missional ministry practices that are required if we evangelicals are to succeed at mitigating the embrace of religious relativism by our co-workers, friends, neighbors and loved ones must be prophetic—Spirit-enabled—in nature. In chapter one, I did my best to demonstrate that nearly every page of Luke's Acts of the Apostles contains a reference to some sort of prophetic, Spirit-enabled activity. As some scholars are fond of saying, Luke viewed the church as a "community of Charismatic prophets" on a mission to re-present the risen Christ to the world through prophetic words and works.[5] Going further, I want to suggest in this chapter that *the kind of missional ministry that does the best job of mitigating religious relativism is prophetic in nature—that is, it involves Spirit-inspired words and works, prophetic speech and actions.*[6]

Commenting on the method by which the Jerusalem church gave witness to Christ, Roger Stronstad writes:

> As Luke reports it there are two complementary and interdependent aspects to this witness by the community of Spirit-baptized and empowered prophets. On the one hand, the disciples will witness by works of power. These works of power are the many "signs and wonders [which] were taking place through the apostles" (Acts 2:43). On the other hand, the disciples will witness by words of power. These words of power are words inspired by the Spirit, such as, but not restricted to, the two pneuma discourses of Peter who witnessed when he was "filled with the Holy Spirit" (Acts 2:4; 4:8). This witness of the disciples as a

---

[4]Roland Allen emphasizes the fact that the earliest witnesses for Christ were motivated by a Spirit-instilled conviction that "the need of men [and women] could be satisfied only in Jesus Christ" (Allen, *The Compulsion of the Spirit: A Roland Allen Reader*, ed. David Paton and Charles H. Long [Grand Rapids: Eerdmans, 1983], p. 65). He goes on to insist that the experience that cemented this conviction in place was the earliest Christians' experience of the Holy Spirit: "When the Holy Spirit reveals Christ to the soul, whatever the previous religion or morality of the man may have been, he is conscious that he could not do without Christ" (ibid., p. 67).

[5]Roger Stronstad, *The Charismatic Theology of St. Luke* (Peabody, Mass.: Hendrickson, 1984), p. 34. See also Stronstad, *The Prophethood of All Believers* (Cleveland, Tenn.: CPT Press, 2010), pp. 15, 25, 65-66, 70, 71-84, 114, 115-121; Frank D. Macchia, *Baptized in the Spirit* (Grand Rapids: Zondervan, 2006), p. 76; and Amos Yong, *The Spirit Poured Out on All Flesh* (Grand Rapids: Baker Academic, 2005), p. 140.

[6]In chap. 4 I will elaborate on how prophetic activity can impact ministry in our current post-Christian context.

community of Spirit-Baptized prophets echoes the pattern of the ministry of Jesus. In other words, just as it had been reported that Jesus was a "prophet mighty/powerful in deed/work and word" (Lk. 24.19), so Luke reports that the disciples were a prophetic community powerful in works—signs and wonders—and powerful words—prophetic speech.[7]

Now an approach taken by some Pentecostal-charismatic scholars as they treat the ministry practices of the earliest Christians is to direct their readers' attention to passages in Acts that fall into two broad categories: Spirit-enabled miraculous signs (works) and Spirit-inspired sermons (words).[8]

This is certainly one way to go. However, I feel "led" to take a slightly different tack. There is a difference to be made, I believe, between a ministry *means* and a ministry *end*. Fully embracing the notion that Jesus desires his church to follow his lead and impact the world through an engagement in Spirit-inspired words and works (ministry means), I suggest that the ministry accounts presented in the book of Acts actually indicate that the prophetic ministry engaged in by the earliest Christians pursued three basic ministry ends: *evangelism* (bringing people to faith in Christ), *edification* (building people up in their walk with Christ) and *equipping* (providing the various kinds of support necessary for people to accomplish the unique mission they have received from Christ).

I will elaborate on each of these ministry aims. However, for now, I will summarize as plainly as possible my ministry proposal. My contention is that (1) the kind of ministry we evangelicals desperately need to recover from the book of Acts and engage in today involves a Spirit-empowered (prophetic) approach to *evangelism, edification* and *equipping,* (2) these ministry ends need to be pursued via the means of both prophetic *words* and *works,* and (3) these ministry ends pursued via these ministry means possess a special ability to re-present the presence and power of the risen Christ to everyone involved.

My personal ministry experience and academic research indicate that it is extremely difficult, if not impossible, for ministry recipients

---

[7]Stronstad, *Prophethood of All Believers,* p. 81.
[8]See, e.g., ibid., pp. 80-84.

(or even those looking on) to continue to embrace the notion of religious relativism when, through some disciple's prophetic activity (speech and action), the reality of the risen Christ has become unmistakably obvious to them. The historical record is unassailable: the earliest Christians behaved in such a way as to defeat the notion held by many of their contemporaries that all religions are more or less effective. I am proposing that a similar engagement in prophetic evangelism, edification and equipping will produce the same kind of ministry effects in our day.

PROPHETIC EVANGELISM

Christians used to debate the relative merits of words versus works, gospel proclamation versus social action. It is hard to imagine such a debate gathering much steam these days. At least not among evangelical believers who, while remaining opposed to a purely social gospel, have nevertheless come to realize that many hungry, sick and oppressed people in our world will need to experience Christ's love before they will be willing or able to confess his lordship.[9]

That said, I use the term *prophetic evangelism* to refer to sermons (verbal presentations of the gospel) and acts of compassion that tend to be delivered in an extemporaneous and spontaneous manner as a result of an explicit sense that the disciple is being prompted by the Holy Spirit to do so in a particular way at a particular time. Furthermore, I want to stipulate that missional, prophetic *acts of compassion* can be *spectacularly miraculous* (such as exorcisms and physical healings) or *subtly miraculous* (such as a sacrificial sharing of one's resources with those in need or a willingness to be reconciled with previously estranged entities).[10]

---

[9]Once again, two books that do a great job of helping readers maintain a healthy, biblically informed perspective on the tension between gospel proclamation and social action are Ronald J. Sider, *Good News and Good Works: A Theology for the Whole Gospel* (Grand Rapids: Baker, 1993); and Ronald J. Sider, Philip N. Olson and Heidi Rolland Unruh, *Churches That Make a Difference: Reaching Your Community with Good News and Good Works* (Grand Rapids: Baker, 2002).

[10]Frank Macchia registers a concern that Luke's emphasis on pneumatological empowerment for witness be defined more broadly and deeply than "mere prophetic speech (Menzies) or charismatic gifting (Stronstad)" to include "a certain quality of communal life that is rich in praise

It needs to be further stipulated that this emphasis on prophetic evangelism is not to say that evangelistic sermons and acts of compassion that are institutionalized, in the sense that they are preplanned and structured, cannot be empowered by the Spirit. In no way do I mean to suggest that evangelicals should refrain from engaging in institutionalized, preplanned and structured evangelistic activities.

What I do want to suggest however is that (1) in the book of Acts (and to a lesser degree in the third Gospel) Luke seems to present to us several stories that portray Spirit-filled disciples engaging extemporaneously in evangelistic preaching and acts of compassion (both spectacular and subtle) that are obviously the direct result of a special, in the moment, prophetic prompting to do so;[11] and (2) we contemporary evangelicals must recover this capacity to engage in prophetic evangelism if we are to do an adequate job of re-presenting the reality of the risen Christ in our religiously pluralistic and relativistic ministry context.

Roland Allen was convinced that the *spontaneous* missionary activity of huge numbers of ordinary Christians accounts for the "rapid and wide expansion of the Church in the early centuries."[12] He then goes on to assert:

> This spontaneous activity of the individual, rooted as it is in a universal instinct, and in a Grace of the Holy Spirit given to all Christians, is not peculiar to any one age or race. We are familiar with it today. It constantly shows itself, and would repeat the history of the early Church, if it were not that our fears have set up barriers in the way of its proper fruition.[13]

---

and acts of self-giving" (Macchia, *Baptized in the Spirit*, p. 16). Furthermore, says Macchia, a charismatic community made up of people who have been (are being) baptized into divine love should be one in which barriers between previously estranged people are continually being broken down (ibid., pp. 14, 79, 157-68).

[11]While this is true, given what we have learned about Luke's desire to portray the church in Jerusalem as a "prophetic" or "charismatic" community, I believe it is theoretically possible to view each one of his references in Acts 1–7 to a sermon or act of compassion that resulted in disciple making as an example of prophetic evangelism, whether an empowerment by the Spirit is explicitly referred to or not!

[12]See Allen, *Compulsion of the Spirit*, p. 34.

[13]Ibid., p. 35.

It is my contention that much of the "spontaneous" missional activity Allen refers to was Spirit prompted in the prophetic sense I am describing in this book. In the next few paragraphs I want to provide some examples from the book of Acts of the kind of prophetic evangelism I am advocating. After that, I will share a story from my own ministry history that illustrates what this form of evangelism might look like in our time.

Peter's Pentecostal sermon. Acts 2:1-13 tells us that the outpouring of the Holy Spirit on the day of Pentecost resulted in a collective experience of prophetic praise and proclamation that soon drew a crowd. In Acts 2:14 we read that a Spirit-filled apostle Peter "stood up with the Eleven, raised his voice and addressed the crowd." So effective was the Spirit-inspired sermon uttered by Peter that day that it resulted in three thousand new believers undergoing water baptism (Acts 2:41).[14]

The healing of the lame man and resulting impromptu sermons. In Acts 3:1-11 we read of Peter somehow feeling led to minister healing to the lame man stationed at the entrance to the temple. Then, Acts 3:12-26 indicates that Peter, taking advantage of the fact that an amazed crowd had quickly gathered, began to boldly and articulately proclaim the gospel in an extemporaneous manner.

In Acts 4:1-7 we discover that Peter's impromptu sermon in the temple precinct attracted the notice of the Sanhedrin, along with the high priest and certain members of his family. After a season of questioning, verse 8 indicates that Peter, *empowered by a fresh in-filling of the Spirit*, proceeded to boldly and extemporaneously proclaim to Jerusalem's unbelieving Jewish leaders the fact of the resurrection and the doctrine of soteriological exclusivity (i.e., that Jesus is the only means of salvation). While Luke does not report any conversions among the Jewish leaders, neither does he abjectly discount the possibility that converts were made that day among rank-and-file worshipers who had observed a miraculous ministry of mercy extended to a lame man, and had heard Peter's bold, fervent, extemporaneous, Spirit-empowered sermon.

Stephen's speech and martyrdom. Acts 7:2-53 is a record of the testi-

---

[14]Roger Stronstad refers to this as one of Peter's "pneuma discourses" (Stronstad, *Prophethood of All Believers*, pp. 81, 83).

mony that Stephen, a Spirit-filled deacon in the Jerusalem church (see Acts 6:5), gave while on trial before the Sanhedrin. Acts 6:5, 6:10 and 7:55 seem to suggest that either Stephen's initial in-filling with the Spirit had endowed him with a prophetic capacity that was ongoing or that he was continually experiencing fresh in-fillings with the Holy Spirit (see Acts 4:8, 31). While the exegetical evidence will not allow for interpretive certainty, Luke 12:12, Acts 6:10 and Acts 7:51 point toward the likelihood that Luke intended his readers to perceive the speech presented in Acts 7 as prophetic—a Spirit-enabled sermon delivered in a manner that was both extemporaneous and bold at the same time.[15]

Certainly, Luke intended his readers to understand the prophetic nature of the subsequent statements made by Stephen: his claim to be able to see Jesus standing at the right hand of God in heaven (Acts 7:56), his plea that Jesus might receive his spirit (Acts 7:59) and the prayer in which he forgave his executioners (Acts 7:60). People simply do not say and do these kinds of things without being empowered by the Holy Spirit to do so!

The missional impact of Stephen's prophetic activities is not really in question since Luke's reference to the "great wonders and miraculous signs" Stephen was enabled to perform (Acts 6:8) strongly suggests that he, like Peter and Paul, had a preaching ministry that was aided by these compassionate demonstrations of the risen Christ's reality. But what of the prophetic speech before the Sanhedrin—the longest speech presented in the book of Acts? In what sense was this prophetic utterance missional? Luke includes an important detail in Acts 7:58: one of the witnesses to Stephen's majestic martyrdom was a young man named Saul. A possible connection between Saul's observation of the way Stephen died and his own eventual conversion is not out of the question (see Acts 26:14). Neither is it beyond the realm of possibility that observing Stephen's dignified demise played a role in a number of priests and Pharisees eventually becoming followers of Christ (see Acts 6:7; 15:5).

---

[15]Ibid., p. 90.

Philip's preaching and witnessing endeavors. Acts 8 presents the ministry exploits of another Spirit-filled deacon of the Jerusalem church named Philip (Acts 6:5). Like Stephen, Philip's prophetic capacity issued forth in a ministry of prophetic evangelism. Luke tells us that, apparently led by the Spirit to do so, Philip went down to a city in Samaria and began proclaiming the gospel there, pairing his preaching with a compassionate engagement in exorcisms and physical healings (Acts 8:5-13). Eventually joined by the apostles Peter and John, who had been sent to make sure that the Samaritan believers received the Holy Spirit (Acts 8:14-17),[16] the mission seems to have been hugely successful both in terms of disciples made and races reconciled.

However, Luke has yet to conclude his report of this charismatic deacon's engagement in prophetic, crosscultural evangelism. Acts 8:26-39 provides a fascinating account of Philip's evangelistic encounter with "an Ethiopian eunuch, an important official in charge of all the treasury of Candace, queen of the Ethiopians," who was headed home after having gone to Jerusalem to worship (v. 27). That this is an obvious instance of "prophetic evangelism" is indicated by the fact that (1) Philip received supernatural instruction to leave the successful ministry still taking place in Samaria and to travel to a deserted location where the encounter with the Ethiopian court official was to take place (v. 26); (2) Philip received even more specific instruction from the Holy Spirit to go to and stay near the chariot in which the Ethiopian court official was riding (v. 29); (3) the fact that the Ethiopian court official happened to be reading a passage from the book of Isaiah that is pregnant with messianic significance seems to have been something other than merely coincidental (vv. 28, 32); (4) Luke seems to be suggesting as well that the Ethiopian court official's invitation for Philip to join him in his chariot and to serve as his tutor was likewise providential; (5) obviously, Philip's presentation of the gospel to the Ethiopian court official was not only extemporaneous but Spirit-empowered as well, as indicated by the court

---

[16]Classical Pentecostals and charismatics frequently use this passage to argue against the notion of a sacrament-centered pneumatology, which insists that the reception of the Holy Spirit is formalized in water baptism. For a broad and balanced discussion of this issue, see Macchia, *Baptized in the Spirit*, pp. 72-75.

official's request to be baptized immediately (vv. 35-38); and finally, (6) some scholars believe that Luke's reference to the Spirit whisking Philip away so that he might continue preaching in other locations (vv. 39-40) was intended to indicate that the entire evangelistic experience had occurred under the auspices of the Holy Spirit.[17]

Peter's sermon in the home of Cornelius. A final biblical example of prophetic, race-reconciling evangelism can be found in Acts 10, where we find the well-known story of Peter reluctantly preaching the gospel to the household of a Roman centurion named Cornelius. The story is so familiar that I will limit my commentary to just four observations: first, that Cornelius and his household had been supernaturally prepared for this momentous evangelistic encounter is indicated by Acts 10:1-8; second, according to Acts 10:9-22 Peter received specific instructions from the Holy Spirit to participate in this evangelistic endeavor; third, it is interesting that Peter makes reference in his sermon to Jesus' own engagement in prophetic evangelism (Acts 10:38); fourth, the fact that Luke intended his readers to understand Peter's extemporaneously delivered sermon as having been inspired by the Spirit is evidenced by the fact that before Peter could conclude his prophetic sermon, his Gentile listeners experienced their own in-filling with the Spirit, accompanied by their own engagement in prophetic speech (Acts 10:44-46)!

Other passages that reflect prophetic evangelism in the book of Acts. The accounts already alluded to are only a sampling of the many presented in the book of Acts that serve as examples of the phenomenon I am referring to as prophetic evangelism through both words and works. Other pertinent passages include Acts 9:32-35, 11:19-21, 13:6-12, 14:1-3, 14:8-18, 16:13-14, 19:11-20 and 28:23-31. These passages should be pondered in a prayerful, judicious manner.

---

[17]For example, Roger Stronstad writes, "Philip's witness to the Ethiopian is both introduced and concluded by references to the Holy Spirit, on the narrative strategy of inclusio (Acts 8:29, 39). Thus, Luke's report about Philip's twofold ministry, first in Samaria, and secondly, to the Ethiopian court official, shows that on the one hand, he witnessed by works which were empowered by the Spirit, and on the other hand, he witnessed by words of wisdom which were inspired by the Spirit. In other words, Philip is another example of the many disciples who were prophets powerful in works and word" (Stronstad, *Prophethood of All Believers*, p. 93).

A contemporary example of prophetic evangelism. Having examined some biblical support for the concept, the question now is: Does this kind of evangelism occur in our time and place? I am absolutely convinced that it does. I do not consider myself a prophet or even someone who has been given the spiritual gift of prophecy. The truth is that I have yet to have a good experience with anyone who has introduced himself or herself to me as a prophet! This does not mean, however, that over the course of my ministry career (thirty-five years and counting) I have not found myself involved in, be it ever so reluctantly at times, ministry endeavors that I would ultimately have to describe as prophetic.

For example, back in the day when I functioned as a youth pastor, I had been reading a book titled *The Cross and the Switchblade*.[18] This book tells the story of David Wilkerson's remarkable Spirit-directed outreach to the drug addicts and gang members of New York City—an outreach that began in the 1950s and that resulted in the founding of the very successful worldwide ministry known as Teen Challenge.

At the same time that I was reading this inspirational book, my everyday commute to and from the church I served took me past a small neighborhood park that was often filled with quite a few rambunctious kids whose ages ranged from about twelve to eighteen. Judging by the rowdy behaviors I was able to observe each day as I drove past this small park, I got the impression that these kids—more a gaggle than an actual gang—were probably unchurched.

With the story of David Wilkerson's ministry foray into the heart of Harlem still haunting me, it did not take long for me to begin to sense a prompting in my heart that I was supposed to approach this group of park rats and share with them the good news concerning Jesus Christ and the difference his loving lordship would make in their lives both now and forever.

I have to honestly say that I resisted this prompting as long as I could. First, as a twenty-two-year-old, I was only a few years older than the most senior member of the group I was being instructed by

---

[18]David Wilkerson, *The Cross and the Switchblade* (New York: Berkley Publishing, 1977).

the Holy Spirit to "confront." (We thought of personal evangelism in terms of a confrontation back in the 1970s!) Second, I had only become a Christ follower myself a few years earlier at the age of nineteen and had yet to complete my ministry education. Finally, though I was doing reasonably well at leading the youth ministry of the church I had been converted in, the truth is that I am an introvert by nature, and the idea of boldly approaching this gaggle of park rats in an unannounced manner and sharing the gospel with them was *way* out of my comfort zone!

Still, the prompting persisted. In point of fact, over the course of the week or so that I wrestled with it, it became more and more intense. Finally, I could no longer withstand the pressure the Holy Spirit was applying to my conscience. One day as I drove by the park I spied a good number of the kids up to no good. *For heaven's sake,* I remember thinking to myself, *if David Wilkerson could take the gospel to Harlem, I can take it into this little neighborhood park!* So, on an impulse, I quickly swerved my 1971 Mach 1 Mustang to the side of the road, literally skidding to a stop on the sandy shoulder. In a flash, I flung open the car door and jumped out, heading across the street toward where the park rats were standing, wide-eyed and open-mouthed (them, not me).

Back in those days, some churches required their youth pastors to wear a coat and tie to work every day. At least mine did. So, the sight of a guy in a suit, bringing his car to an abrupt stop, emerging from it quickly and then striding toward them in a determined, forthright manner, caused the gaggle to assume that I was some version of "the man." As a result, they began to scatter in all directions!

As they attempted to scurry away, I called out to them, assuring them that I was not there to hurt or roust them in any way. Remarkably, all of them returned and stood in front of me, about a dozen-and-a-half rowdy teens. (Are you sensing the Spirit's participation in all this yet?)

After taking a moment to collect myself, I opened my mouth and began my impromptu ministry presentation, saying simply, "Hey, I could be wrong, but I have this strong feeling that God wants me to tell you guys a story." I then proceeded to share the gospel with them in the form of a parable—a pretty lame parable as I recall. And yet the Holy

Spirit was obviously involved in all this: prompting the meeting and then empowering the message.

How do I know the Spirit was involved? First, there is the fact that I was there. Second, I was able somehow to call all these understandably skittish teens back together again. Third, in the moment, I was able to articulate the gospel of Christ using a parable that was, though quite unsophisticated, ultimately successful. At the conclusion of my impromptu gospel presentation, at my invitation, every single one of those park rats knelt in the grass, raised their hands toward heaven as a sign of surrender to God and followed along as I helped them pray aloud a version of the "sinner's prayer"!

It really did happened just like that. My youth group grew by about 30 percent as a result of my visit to the park that day. It all started with a prompting from the Spirit to speak and act in Christ's name.

Every so often I get a phone call from either Joe or George. George is the older brother, Joe the younger. I have known these guys for over thirty-two years now (as of this writing). A couple of years ago, around 4 p.m. on a Father's Day, the phone rang and I answered it. It was Joe. He asked how my Father's Day was going. He spoke of having spent the day with his own family around him, helping him celebrate "his" day. He told me that I had been on his mind all day long, hence the phone call. Then, choking up as he spoke, he said "Gary, I just wanted to tell you again how grateful I am that you pulled your car over, came into the park, and shared the message of Jesus with us that day so long ago." Joe was one of those park rats. He is still serving Christ three decades later.

Prophetic, ad hoc, Spirit-prompted and empowered evangelism really can occur in our place and time. Speaking to myself as well as anyone else: what would happen if more evangelical church members became open to the idea that on any given day the Spirit of God might send them, like Philip, on a special ministry assignment? How hard is it to say to someone, when appropriate, "Hey, I could be wrong, but I just have this strong feeling that God wants me to tell you a story"? We might be surprised at how many hearts the Holy Spirit has already prepared for such an encounter.

PROPHETIC EDIFICATION

Disciple-making pastors tend to think of edification as the spiritual growth phase that follows evangelism. After someone embraces the Christian faith, he or she needs to be *edified*—established, instructed, built up—in it. Paul seemed to be referring to the edification process in his letter to the Colossians when he wrote: "So then, just as you received Christ Jesus as Lord, continue to live in him, rooted and built up in him, strengthened in the faith as you were taught, and overflowing with thankfulness" (Col 2:6-7).

Perhaps an even more important Pauline passage to consider as we attempt to wrap our minds around the concept of "prophetic" edification is 1 Corinthians 14:1-4, where Paul clearly refers to the edificational value inherent in the spiritual gift of prophecy:

> Follow the way of love and eagerly desire spiritual gifts, especially the gift of prophecy. For anyone who speaks in a tongue does not speak to men but to God. Indeed, no one understands him; he utters mysteries with his spirit. But everyone who prophesies speaks to men for their strengthening, encouragement and comfort. He who speaks in a tongue edifies himself, but he who prophesies edifies the church.

In this passage we witness Paul encouraging his readers to exercise their prophetic capacity in a way that serves to edify—strengthen, encourage and comfort—fellow church members.

Putting all this together, when I refer to "prophetic edification" I have in mind occasions in which a disciple, obeying an explicit prompting from the Holy Spirit to do so, offers in an extemporaneous manner words or works that have the effect of encouraging, comforting and strengthening a fellow disciple or group of disciples.

As with prophetic evangelism, I am not suggesting that edificational ministries that are institutionalized (preplanned and structured) cannot be empowered by the Spirit. For instance, I have long held that really good biblical preaching and teaching, well prepared and much prayed over, can function prophetically in the lives of congregation members, making it possible for them to sense God speaking to them personally and existentially in an especially profound manner.

While all of this is true, I have also experienced an engagement in edificational ministry that is prophetic in the sense that it is more *immediately* prompted and empowered by the Holy Spirit. What follows are some biblical and contemporary examples of this phenomenon.

Simeon's ministry to Mary and Joseph. In chapter one we took note of the Spirit-prompted edification provided by Simeon to the parents of the child Jesus (Lk 2:21-35). Though his prophetic words may have been of small comfort, they were undoubtedly intended to strengthen their hearts in the face of the challenges that lay ahead.

The Ananias incident. Perhaps the classic example of this phenomenon is the story I referred to in this book's introduction—the case of Ananias (of Damascus) being sent by God to find the recently blinded Saul of Tarsus, pray for his healing and Spirit in-filling and then to effect his water baptism and, by implication, his first bit of Christian instruction (Acts 9:10-20). While I will have more to say about this story in a subsequent section, I wish to emphasize here that the prophetic nature of Ananias's edificational ministry to the future apostle Paul should not go unnoticed.[19]

Some negative examples: Ananias and Sapphira, and Simon the sorcerer. What I am about to suggest may prove controversial. I believe that Luke may have had an edificational goal in mind when he included the terrible story of Ananias (of Jerusalem) and Sapphira lying to the Holy Spirit and experiencing divine discipline as a result (Acts 5:1-10). Serving as a negative example for the rest of the prophetic community, this story's message of admonition and warning came through loud and clear as Acts 5:11 indicates: "Great fear seized the whole church and all who heard about these events."

In other words, the end result of *Peter's Spirit-directed responses* to Ananias and Sapphira was that other church members were instructed and edified in their faith.[20] Acts 9:31 supports the idea that "living in

---

[19]Once again, it should be noted that the context of Acts 9:10-20 infers that God communicated with Ananias through the agency of the Holy Spirit, providing Ananias with his ministry assignment.

[20]Gordon Fee indicates that some biblical scholars see the spiritual gift known as the "message of knowledge" at work in this story (Gordon Fee, *God's Empowering Presence: The Holy Spirit in the Letters of Paul* [Peabody, Mass.: Hendrickson, 1994], p. 167).

the fear of the Lord" was viewed by Luke as a good thing. So, negative example though it may be, this tragic and frightening story really does qualify as a biblical example of prophetic edification.[21]

Another example of prophetic edification performed in a negative confrontational manner is the story of Simon the Sorcerer. In Acts 8:13-19 we are told that even though Simon had expressed faith in the lordship of Christ and had experienced water baptism, he committed a huge faux pas when he attempted to purchase from Peter and John the authority to confer the Holy Spirit through the laying on of his hands.

Luke tells us that Peter labeled Simon's request not only foolish but sinful. In his rebuke of Simon (Acts 8:20-23), Peter dared to diagnose the condition of the man's heart—that he was "full of bitterness and captive to sin." I suppose it is possible that Peter was simply intuiting Simon's inner motives based on his outer actions, but I hope this was not the case. Far too many Christians make the mistake of presuming to know the heart motives of others, both inside and outside the church. Nothing hurts like being misunderstood, much less demonized, by a fellow follower of Christ! So, while I cannot prove it to be the case, I prefer to think that Peter's negative edificational speech to Simon was a result of divine prompting and empowerment. I am hopeful also that Luke intended his readers to interpret Acts 8:24 as an indication that this case of negative prophetic edification, in the end, proved successful.

Barnabas and the church at Antioch. Another example of prophetic edification, more positive in tone, process and result, can be found in Acts 11:19-26, which tells the story of how the church in Jerusalem, having heard of the revival that had broken out among both Jews and

---

[21]It can be maintained that this tragic story was also intended by Luke to underscore the importance to the Spirit of mission of the church's engagement in prophetic action toward the poor. Some scholars have pointed out that the instructive tale of Ananias and Sapphira follows on the heels of a passage (Acts 4:31-37) which suggests that one of the fruits of the Spirit is an eager willingness to care for the poor in a generous manner. For Luke to proceed immediately to the story of Ananias and Sapphira would seem to indicate a contrasting connection between the sincerity and humility of Barnabas displayed in Acts 4:36-37, and the lack thereof in Ananias and Sapphira portrayed in Acts 5:1-11 (see James D. G. Dunn, *Baptism in the Holy Spirit* [Philadelphia: Westminster Press, 1970], p. 51). Since the issue at hand is ministry relief for the poor, the importance of this missional ministry dynamic is brought to the fore and its importance to the Holy Spirit is suggested.

Greeks in Syrian Antioch, was careful to send Barnabas to investigate. Luke makes a point of telling his readers in Acts 11:24 that Barnabas was "a good man, full of the Holy Spirit and faith." After commenting on Barnabas's success at bringing people in Antioch to faith in Christ, Luke goes on to explain in Acts 11:26 that Barnabas was also careful to engage in the ministry of edification.

What supports the notion that Barnabas's edificational activity should be considered prophetic is not that we are told that he was led of the Lord to edify this or that disciple, but that he was led to go to Tarsus, find Saul in particular, and then bring him to Antioch so that he could serve as a partner in a teaching ministry to the disciples there. That Luke intended this to be viewed as a prophetic, Spirit-directed ministry move is supported by the fact that in Acts 13:1-3 Barnabas seems to be referred to as a prophet as well as a teacher.[22]

Priscilla, Aquila and Apollos. Finally, while the text does not explicitly say so, the context of Acts 18:24-26 might suggest that the edificational ministry that Priscilla and Aquila provided Apollos possessed a prophetic component. Luke provides at least one reference in the larger pericope to a revelatory experience (see Acts 18:9-10), and the varied comings and goings of Paul, Priscilla, Aquila and Apollos subsequently described (see Acts 18:11-28) give the impression that they were moving about as a consequence of some divine direction. All of this might argue for the idea that Luke intended his readers to understand that the involvement of Priscilla and Aquila in the completion of Apollos's Christian education was at the behest of the Holy Spirit.

A few contemporary examples of prophetic edification. Using these various biblical accounts of prophetic edification as a spring board, I will relate a few simple stories from my own ministry experience.

There was the time when I was meeting with a fairly new disciple who was complaining of having hit a wall in his spiritual journey: the joy had dissipated; all enthusiasm for the things of the Lord had disappeared. After talking with him for a while, explaining to him that periods of both consolation and desolation were to be expected as part of

---

[22]Indeed, Roger Stronstad refers to Barnabas as one of five charismatic prophets highlighted by Luke in the book of Acts (Stronstad, *Prophethood of All Believers*, pp. 93-94).

the spiritual journey, I felt a very strong impression that I should put to him a particularly pungent question: "Do you by any chance happen to have a problem with pornography?" The stunned look on his face was priceless. The Lord had used my prophetic question to pierce the young man's façade and provide him with an opportunity to surrender to Jesus a moral struggle that had been "eating his lunch."

How did I know to ask the probing question about pornography? Please keep in mind that this event occurred in the 1980s, long before the Internet served to popularize pornography and cause the numbers of males addicted to it to skyrocket. Furthermore, it is important to know that this kind of confrontational counseling is not something I engage in every day. In other words, it is my contention that this really was a simple matter of the Spirit of God prompting me to engage in edificational ministry in an impromptu, ad hoc, prophetic manner.

On a different occasion I was counseling another new convert: this time a young wife and mother who was distraught over the fact that though she desperately wanted to quit her smoking habit, nothing she had tried up to that point had worked. She simply could not find the motivation necessary to successfully resist the power nicotine had over her. Feeling completely desperate and ashamed, she confided to me that not even the idea of making this change for the sake of her kids had succeeded in helping her gain the strength necessary to break the unhealthy habit she was so weary of. She was thoroughly confused, and, as a young Christian, tempted to doubt the goodness and power of God in her life.

As I listened to her pour out her sense of frustration, I was beginning to feel a bit frantic. I was a young pastor (twenty-seven years old at the time), and frankly, it was not readily apparent to me what I had to offer her in terms of advice. Suddenly, I found myself saying to her, "You know, maybe you shouldn't worry so much about quitting this habit. Here's what I suggest you do: pray to Jesus, asking him to tell you if he wants you to make this change in your life. After all, as the Lord of your life, all you have and are belongs to him, including your body and your lifestyle. If Jesus speaks to your heart telling you that he wants you to quit this habit for him, then we'll have to assume that he will also provide you with the resources you will need to do so. But until then, just keep listening for some personal, definitive direction from the Lord."

It was only a week or so later that this young woman, beaming a broad grin, came back to see me. She explained that she had done what I suggested and had begun to pray, asking Jesus to reveal to her in a special, personal way what he wanted her to do with regard to her cigarette habit. The bottom line is that this young, new convert found that what she could not accomplish for the sake of her health, her husband or even her kids, she could do for Jesus. I submit that this is yet another case of prophetic edification taking place in our contemporary era.

One more story regarding this theme took place on a Sunday close to Christmas a few years ago. I had called for the congregation to leave their seats and file down to the front of the church. Gathered around the piano, filling in the space between the front row of pews and the platform and spilling into the church's aisles, the congregation was singing Christmas hymns as part of our worship service that Lord's Day.

Standing across from me was a young woman, a Christian worker named Dorothy. At some point during this special song service, I looked up and saw Dorothy, lost in worship, singing a song of devotion to the baby Jesus, her hands raised in humble adoration. Suddenly, I felt a strong impression to put my arm around Dorothy's shoulders and to whisper in her ear the words: "Dorothy, the Lord wants me to tell you that this is not my arm you're feeling around you right now; it's his arm. And he loves you very much."

Having obeyed this prompting, I noticed that Dorothy began to weep profusely. At the same time, the song service was now concluding and I had to return to my responsibility of leading the service.

Once the service had concluded and I had made sure that all the visitors and church members had been greeted upon their exit, I went back into the darkened sanctuary to retrieve my Bible from the pulpit. Sitting there all alone, praying but obviously waiting to speak with me, was Dorothy. I slid into the pew next to her and asked how she was doing. With her eyes filled with fresh tears she looked at me and said, "Why did you do what you did during the song service?"

Given the nature of this question, my first thought was that perhaps my actions had offended her in some way. Thus, I began to offer Dorothy an apology. She stopped me mid-sentence, however, saying: "No, what I want to know is what caused you to say and do what you did?"

A bit confused at this point, I explained to Dorothy that I had simply felt a strong impression from the Holy Spirit to speak and act on Christ's behalf.

At that, the two trails of tears running down Dorothy's cheeks were diverted as a smile formed on her face. Then even more tears filled her eyes. After a few moments, the lump in her throat relaxed enough for her to speak. She explained that the evening prior she had been sitting in her apartment all alone, feeling a bit sorry for herself. Unlike her two roommates who had gone on dates to Christmas parties, she did not have a boyfriend in her life. Emotionally weary and distraught, she had begun to pray saying: "Lord, I know it's wrong to feel this way. I know that I have you in my life and should be content with that. But, Lord, sometimes I just get so lonely. If I could physically feel your arms around me, if I could audibly hear your voice telling me you love me, then, maybe, I could be patient until I meet the person you have for me."

The very next morning, while worshiping Jesus with her eyes closed and hands raised, Dorothy suddenly felt an arm wrap around her shoulders and heard a voice whisper in her ear: "Dorothy, the Lord wants me to tell you that this is not my arm you're feeling around you right now; it's his arm. And he loves you very much."

I cannot say for sure that Dorothy, because of her emotional weariness, was on the verge of actual ministry burnout and that this experience of prophetic encouragement kept that from occurring. But neither can I say that it did not. Whether or not this experience of prophetic activity "saved" Dorothy for the kingdom cause, I know that it strengthened her faith and that of the hundreds of other disciples I have shared this story with over the years. Mark it down: prophetic edification can and does occur in our day.

PROPHETIC EQUIPPING

Both the Bible and church history seem to indicate that when God has his way, the process of spiritual formation eventually takes on an aspect of ministry formation as well. Broadly speaking, the ministry activity of *equipping* constitutes the third phase in the disciple's spiritual journey. After a person has been evangelized, and while they are being edified, they need also to be equipped for the specific ministry God has called them to. In particular, people need to acquire (1) a sense of ministry direction, (2) the requisite ministry skills and wisdom, and (3) the material and prayer support necessary for the successful completion of the task.[23]

Clearly there are institutionalized forms of equipping (preplanned and structured) that all evangelical believers should participate in, both as recipients and providers. But the phenomenon of prophetic equipping is a different sort of animal. I am referring here to the dynamic that occurs when one disciple equips one or more other disciples through prophetic means (i.e., equipping speech and actions that are prompted by the Holy Spirit and carried out in an impromptu, ad hoc manner).

Simeon again. I begin this brief survey of some biblical examples of prophetic equipping by observing that there is a sense in which the prophetic word Simeon directed toward Mary and Joseph served an equipping as well as edifying purpose (Lk 2:34-35). While it could not have been pleasant for this young mother and father to hear the prophetic message that their son would suffer terribly because of his prophetic career, and that before it was over their own hearts would be pierced with feelings of pain and sorrow, sometimes we need to hear the truth about our reality in order to be equipped to deal with it.

Ananias (of Damascus). Just as Simeon's ministry can be viewed as an example of both prophetic edification and equipping, so can that of Ananias in Acts 9:10-20. Luke tells us that Ananias received a special prompting from the Lord to find a recently blinded Saul of Tarsus and then pray for his healing, which he did. Obviously, regaining his eye-

---

[23]There is a sense in which the ministry of helping people both within and without the community of faith to survive can also take the form of prophetic equipping (see Gal 6:10). However, since these acts of compassion can also serve as means by which the gospel is proclaimed and people brought to faith in Christ, in this survey they were treated under the topic of prophetic evangelism. In this section of the survey the focus will be on equipping fellow Christ followers for the mission God as called them to.

sight was a practical help which enabled Saul/Paul to fulfill his own ministry vocation.

Praying for Peter's release from prison. We see something similar take place in the story of the Jerusalem church praying for the apostle Peter's deliverance on the eve of his execution (Acts 12:1-17). The text leads us to believe that this was a special, ad hoc prayer meeting, rather than a routine gathering.

From these and other passages there emerges an important missional principle: *whenever an evangelical believer obeys a special prompting to pray for someone involved in ministry, for whatever reason, the end result is prophetic equipping!*

One ministry's support for another. An amazingly profound example of prophetic equipping can be found in Acts 11:27-30:

> During this time some prophets came down from Jerusalem to Antioch. One of them, named Agabus, stood up and through the Spirit predicted that a severe famine would spread over the entire Roman world. (This happened during the reign of Claudius.) The disciples, each according to his ability, decided to provide help for the brothers living in Judea. This they did, sending their gift to the elders by Barnabas and Saul.

Members of one church obeying a prompting by the Holy Spirit to provide desperately needed material support to members of another church (or ministry). The equipping aspect of this prophetic activity is surely too obvious to miss.

Miscellaneous passages that reflect prophetic equipping in the book of Acts. Other passages from the book of Acts that reflect the phenomenon of prophetic equipping taking place either between the Spirit and the recipient disciple or between disciples include Acts 13:1-4, 6-12, 15:22-29, 16:6-10, 20:22-23, 21:1-6, 10-14, 23:11 and 27:21-26. Once again, I want to encourage an honest, judicious pondering of these passages. The cumulative effect may well be that we contemporary evangelicals will become a bit more sensitive than we have been in the past to promptings from the Spirit to speak or act in an equipping manner in someone's life.

ANANIAS OF DAMASCUS:
OUR PROPHETIC MINISTRY MODEL

In this section I will revisit something I alluded to in chapter one: my theory that, whether intended by Luke or not, the story of Ananias presented in Acts 9:10-20 actually provides the church of every age with a broad, overarching model or paradigm of what prophetic ministry in general looks like (or to put it differently, what a missionally faithful life in the Spirit might entail). In a nutshell I want to suggest that, based on the story of Ananias, Christ desires that all of his Spirit-filled followers, whether they self-identify as Pentecostals/charismatics or not, to possess the capacity to hear God's voice, receive ministry assignments, speak and act on Christ's behalf, make disciples and build up the church, defeating religious relativism in the process!

Now I consider it important to underscore once again at this point that the missional faithfulness constituted by this prophetic activity on our part mirrors the faithfulness of the Holy Spirit both to Christ's mission and his followers. It is not that the Spirit depends on us to achieve his mission, but that through our engagement in the prophetic activity prompted at the Spirit's initiative we are granted the privilege of participating in his mission. It is not that Ananias was using the Spirit to grow his church, but that the Holy Spirit was using Ananias to achieve God's purposes in the world.

This having been said, the question remains: Is this notion of a missionally faithful life in the Spirit really doable in our day? Though I will deal with this question in much more depth in chapters three and four, I will respond to it now in a preliminary manner by posing several questions, the chief of which is: *What are we evangelicals supposed to make of the experiences, biblical and contemporary, that we have looked at in this chapter?* On the one hand, I am convinced that the three kinds of prophetic ministry activities described in this chapter actually occur in our lives more often than we realize. How many of us who preach God's Word have *never* had the experience of beginning, mid-sermon, to speak with a passion and profundity that could not be attributed to our preparation? How many of us who routinely offer counsel to other believers have *never* had the experience of being somewhat surprised, even impressed, with the words of comfort, challenge, encouragement and exhortation that seemed to flow from a source deep inside of us—wisdom we did not know we possessed and that we feared we could not replicate? How many of us have *never* felt a special prompting to speak up in some sort of ministry meeting, reminding the group of some important biblical principle or sharing some strategic advice, the wisdom of which was immediately obvious to everyone at the table? How many of us have *never* had a strong impression that God wanted us to say or do something of ministry value to or for a particular person or in the midst of a particular situation? How many of us have *never* felt led of the Lord to lead out in prayer and praise, only to find ourselves speaking forth a psalm-like utterance that seemed to stream from a source other than the left side of our brain?

Really? *Never* a strong impression to share the gospel with someone in particular? *Never* a strong impression to provide some kind of special support for a particular missionary at a particular time? *Never* a strong impression to give more generously than usual in a particular offering? *Never* a strong impression to send a note of spiritual encouragement to someone in particular? *Never* a strong impression to be especially generous in Jesus' name to a particular homeless person requesting a handout? *Never* a strong impression to launch or partner with a ministry designed to alleviate human suffering in Christ's name? *Never* a strong impression to do what we could to make peace between estranged brothers and sisters in Christ, or to pursue such a reconciliation ourselves? *Never* a strong impression to pray, really pray, for someone we had not communicated with for a while?

It is hard for me to believe that any spiritually sincere evangelical believer reading this book has *never* experienced something of what I have just described. What if God really is behind at least some of these strong impressions to speak and act in Jesus' name? What if millions of evangelicals, concerned about the increasingly post-Christian ethos of our contemporary ministry context were to open themselves to the possibility that, like Ananias, this sort of thing could happen to them? What if the kind of prophetic activity I am describing here—obeying a significantly strong impression to humbly, gently speak and act in the name of the risen Christ—really is, at least some of the time, the work of the Holy Spirit? What kind of missional faithfulness would such a large-scale paradigm shift among evangelicals unleash in the Western world?

I want to conclude this chapter by quoting at length from Roger Stronstad's insightful volume *The Prophethood of All Believers*. Stronstad concludes this work by commenting on the contemporary relevance of its topic. In the process, he addresses some pungent words of admonition to all evangelicals, to those who are not Pentecostal or charismatic, and to those who are. These words of admonition warrant a full recitation. Stronstad writes:

> The church is to be a community of prophets. But from the post-apostolic period to the present it has not functioned as a prophetic community which is powerful in works and word. In fact, in too many places the Church views itself as a didactic community rather than a prophetic community, where sound doctrine is treasured above charismatic action. Indeed, the preaching and teaching of the word displaces Spirit-filled, Spirit-led and Spirit-empowered ministry. The Spirit of prophecy has been quenched and the gifts of the Spirit have been sanitized and institutionalized. The non-Pentecostal/non-charismatic church needs to recapture its prophetic heritage, to which it is either hostile or indifferent.
>
> As a prophetic community God's people are to be active in service. But all too often the Pentecostal, charismatic movements focus on experience, the emotion and the blessing more than they do on Spirit-filled, Spirit-led and Spirit-empowered service. This shift in focus from vocation to personal experience, from being world-centered to self-centered, renders the service of the Pentecostal, charismatic just about as impotent as the service of the contemporary non-Pentecostal, non-charismatic church. This focus on experience rather than on service is like selling one's birthright of Spirit-empowered service for the pottage of self-seeking experience and blessing.
>
> In the twentieth century there are many exceptions on both sides to these generalizations. But exceptions prove rather than falsify the rule. Therefore, in spite of the exceptions the above generalizations are sadly valid. The antidote to this malaise in which the Spirit of prophecy is

either quenched or misused is for the contemporary Church to recapture, both doctrinally and vocationally, the first-century reality which Luke reports. This reality is one in which all of God's people are prophets because the Lord had put his Spirit on them.[24]

These are strong words. But is the essential admonition valid? In particular, is it really possible, as Stronstad suggests, for groups of contemporary evangelical believers to once again begin to function as prophetic communities that can be used by the Spirit of mission to offer the people around them a compelling alternative to religious relativism?

I sincerely believe that such a thing is not only theoretically possible, it is actually occurring in places like Latin America, Africa and Asia. This is precisely the point I will attempt to make in chapter three, which will seek to understand the explosive growth currently occurring among Pentecostal and charismatic groups of believers living and ministering in the developing nations of the world. Then, in chapter four we will ponder the implications of this explosive growth for us evangelicals living in the industrialized nations of the West, exploring in some depth why, despite the cultural changes occurring here, such a missional faithfulness/hopefulness/fruitfulness might also be experienced by us.

---

[24]Stronstad, *Prophethood of All Believers*, pp. 123-24.

3

"THE SPIRIT BADE ME GO"

Missional Faithfulness and the
Global Growth of Pentecostalism

IT IS WELL KNOWN THAT THE segment of the church presently experiencing the greatest growth worldwide participates in what is known as the Pentecostal-charismatic renewal.[1] Religious statistician David Barrett has famously estimated that at mid-2000 the number of Pentecostal-charismatic believers was just shy of 500 million, approximately one fourth of the world's 2 billion Christians. If the current rate of growth among Pentecostals/charismatics continues, says Barrett, by mid-2025 their numbers will increase to over 800 million. By mid-2050 the figure will be well over 1 billion.[2]

The rapid global growth of Pentecostalism[3] was acknowledged in a

---

[1]In his book *The New Shape of World Christianity*, Mark Noll makes the point that one result of the amazing growth of Pentecostalism is that "Christians with more-or-less evangelical commitments are found almost everywhere on the globe." In other words, there is a sense in which the global spread of Pentecostalism has also widened the influence of evangelicalism. Says Noll, "Evangelicalism, in these terms, has become a world religion of great consequence" (Mark Noll, *The New Shape of World Christianity* [Downers Grove, Ill.: IVP Academic, 2009], pp. 42-43).

[2]David Barrett et al., *World Christian Encyclopedia* (New York: Oxford University Press, 2001), p. 4.

[3]Pentecostal scholar Cecil Robeck has observed that when speaking of Pentecostalism in a global context, we should actually speak of "Pentecostalisms" rather than Pentecostalism (Cecil M. Robeck, "Taking Stock of Pentecostalism," *Pneuma* 15, no. 1 [1993]: 45, cited in Veli-Matti Kärkkäinen, *Pneumatology* [Grand Rapids: Baker Academic, 2002], p. 89). See also Vinson Synan, *The Holiness-Pentecostal Tradition: Charismatic Movements in the Twentieth Century* (Grand Rapids: Eerdmans, 1997), pp. 282-85; and Amos Yong, *The Spirit Poured Out on All Flesh* (Grand Rapids: Baker Academic, 2005), p. 18. Therefore, for the sake of expediency, and

recent report commissioned by the Pew Forum on Religion and Public Life titled "Spirit and Power: A 10-Country Survey." The following excerpt from that report not only refers to the growth of Pentecostalism but also remarks on what makes the movement unique among other versions of the Christian faith:

> By all accounts, pentecostalism and related charismatic movements represent one of the fastest-growing segments of global Christianity. According to the *World Christian Database*, at least a quarter of the world's 2 billion Christians are thought to be members of these lively, highly personal faiths, which emphasize such spiritually renewing "gifts of the Holy Spirit" as speaking in tongues, divine healing and prophesying. *. . . Even more than other Christians, pentecostals and other renewalists believe that God, acting through the Holy Spirit, continues to play a direct, active role in everyday life.*[4]

THE SIGNIFICANCE OF GLOBAL PENTECOSTALISM

By and large the growth of Pentecostalism is an urban, Majority-World phenomenon. As of the year 2000, the three areas most highly impacted by the proliferation of this movement were Latin America (141 million), Africa (126 million) and Asia (135 million), as compared to North America (80 million), and Europe (38 million).[5]

Though Pentecostal theologian Veli-Matti Kärkkäinen has suggested that the significance of Pentecostal-charismatic missions has largely escaped the notice of non-Pentecostal-charismatic missiologists, an increasing number of scholars, not all of them Pentecostal, have made reference not only to the statistical *growth* of Pentecostalism, but its *significance* as well.[6] For example, in his widely read book *The Next*

---

following some scholarly precedent, I will use the term Pentecostalism in an umbrella-like manner that is meant to refer not only to Classical Pentecostals but to charismatic, neo-Pentecostal and neo-charismatic believers as well (see Allan Anderson, *An Introduction to Pentecostalism* [New York: Cambridge University Press, 2004], p. 14).

[4]"Spirit and Power: A 10-Country Survey," *Pew Forum on Religion and Public Life*, March 19, 2009, http://pewforum.org/Christian/Evangelical-Protestant-Churches/Spirit-and-Power.aspx, emphasis added. The report stipulates that the term *renewalist* is used to refer to Pentecostals and Charismatics collectively.

[5]Anderson, *Introduction to Pentecostalism*, p. 123. See also Yong, *Spirit Poured Out*, p. 19.

[6]Veli-Matti Kärkkäinen, "One Hundred Years of Pentecostal Missions: A Report on the Euro-

Christendom: The Coming of Global Christianity, Philip Jenkins refers to
an oft-cited assertion made by Harvard theologian Harvey Cox that
the Pentecostal expansion across the southern continents has been so
astonishing as to justify claims of a new Reformation.[7] Allan Anderson, a Pentecostalism scholar known for his willingness to view this
movement with a critical eye, nevertheless asserts that "the Pentecostal
movements of the world today have many lessons for the universal
church in its mission, and although we may look at some manifestations of Pentecostalism with amusement or even alarm, we ignore this
enormous factor of world Christianity at our peril."[8] He goes on to affirm the view of Cox that "religion itself has been 'reshaped' through
the 'rise of Pentecostal spirituality'" and suggests that "whatever our
opinion or particular experience of Pentecostalism . . . it is a movement
of such magnitude that Christianity itself will never be the same."[9]

So what is it about the Pentecostal-charismatic movement that accounts for this remarkable ministry impact? While I will not attempt
to conduct here a thorough analysis of Pentecostal-charismatic missions history or methodology, I will present a brief survey of the most
commonly cited explanations for the phenomenal growth of this movement in the Majority World. In addition to several explanations that
seem to center on the physical, spiritual, psychological and sociological benefits that are produced when a holistic version of the Christian
gospel is contextualized for hurting people living in the developing
nations of the world, a much more basic explanation, more theological
in nature, will be put forward—an elucidation more in keeping with
what we have discovered so far about the Holy Spirit's penchant for
using God's people to accomplish God's purposes in the world. In a
nutshell, the message of this chapter is that it is a grace-empowered,
Spirit-enabled, experience-driven embrace of a theological realism

---

pean Pentecostal-Charismatic Research Association's 1999 Meeting," *Mission Studies* 16, nos.
1-2 (2000): 207, cited in Roger Hedlund, "Critique of Pentecostal Mission by a Friendly Evangelical," *Asian Journal of Pentecostal Studies* 8, no. 1 (2005): 68-69.
[7]Philip Jenkins, *The Next Christendom: The Coming of Global Christianity* (New York: Oxford
University Press, 2007), p. 8.
[8]Allan Anderson, "Towards a Pentecostal Missiology," July 26, 2010, http://artsweb.bham.ac
.uk/aanderson/Publications/towards_a_pentecostal_missiology.htm.
[9]Anderson, *Introduction to Pentecostalism*, p. 279.

that veritably compels rank-and-file members of Pentecostal churches in the Majority World to speak and act toward their unchurched friends, neighbors, coworkers and family members in a prophetic, missionally faithful manner.[10]

However, before I commence this survey of proffered explanations for the global growth of Pentecostalism, I want to address another question, the answer to which will inform how we proceed with the survey itself. *Are we justified in referring to the ministry impact of global Pentecostalism as an expression of missional faithfulness?*

THE GLOBAL GROWTH OF PENTECOSTALISM AS AN EXPRESSION OF MISSIONAL FAITHFULNESS

As we shall soon see, Pentecostal communities have been careful to contextualize the gospel in such a way as to attract the attention of masses of hurting human beings around the world, especially in the global South. As was pointed out in this book's introduction, at the heart of the missional impulse is a pneumatological question that is contextual in nature: *What is the Holy Spirit up to in this or that ministry location, and how might/should we cooperate with him?* In the introduction we also took note of the fact that what the missional movement calls for is a culture-specific contextualization of the gospel that allows for people to be *formed by the gospel within their cultures.* One of the reasons why I believe it is appropriate to suggest that the phenomenon of global Pentecostalism, with all its imperfections, is an expression of *missional* faithfulness is due precisely to its commitment to contextualize the message of a holistic gospel to the various cultures that exist in the Majority World.

Support for this contention can be found in the writings of missiologist Allan Anderson, who has emphasized the fact that most of the people living on this planet take the spiritual world very seriously. Thus, says Anderson, Pentecostalism's "holistic worldview that does

---

[10]F. D. Bruner indicates that paying attention to Pentecostal explanations for their considerable missionary success can provide insight as to the nature of the movement as a whole (Frederick Dale Bruner, *A Theology of the Holy Spirit* [Grand Rapids: Eerdmans, 1970], p. 25).

not separate the physical from the spiritual"[11] rings much more true than does a highly rationalistic, more exclusively philosophical version of the Christian faith.[12] Anderson further underscores the importance of the holistic gospel Pentecostals proclaim in a contextually sensitive manner saying:

> Pentecostals responded to what they experienced as a void left by ratio-nalistic western forms of Christianity that had unwittingly initiated what amounted to the destruction of traditional spiritual values. Pente-costals declared a message that reclaimed the biblical traditions of heal-ing and protection from evil, they demonstrated the practical effects of these traditions and by so doing became heralds of a Christianity that was really meaningful. Thus, Pentecostalism went a long way towards meeting physical, emotional and spiritual needs of people in the Major-ity World, offering solutions to life's problems and ways to cope in what was often a threatening and hostile world.[13]

Furthermore, Anderson goes on to comment on the fact that Pente-costalism has demonstrated an "innate ability to make itself at home in almost any culture,"[14] allowing new believers to maintain the best as-pects of their own culture while embracing the good news concerning Jesus Christ. As a chief proponent of what we might call the "contextu-alization" explanation for Pentecostalism's global growth, Anderson believes that it is important to people living in the Majority World that the message of Christian missionaries not completely demonize every aspect of their native culture.[15] Therefore, more than once in *An Intro-duction to Pentecostalism* Anderson affirms the fact that Pentecostalism's "emphasis on 'freedom in the Spirit' has rendered the [various Pente-costal and charismatic] movements inherently flexible in different cul-tural and social contexts."[16] Though this obviously raises concerns about the problem of syncretism,[17] it has also "made the transplanting

---

[11]Anderson, *Introduction to Pentecostalism*, p. 211.
[12]Ibid., p. 212; see also pp. 216, 285.
[13]Ibid., p. 212; see also pp. 241-42.
[14]Ibid., p. 283.
[15]Ibid., p. 215.
[16]Ibid., pp. 201-2, 212-13, 215-16, 223-24, 283-84.
[17]Ibid., pp. 237-38. See also Walter Hollenweger, *Pentecostalism: Origins and Developments*

of their central tenets in the Majority World and among marginalized minorities in the western world more easily assimilated."[18]

Now, if it is granted that a Spirit-guided process of contextualizing the gospel for people of various cultures is at the heart of being missional, and that such contextualization is going on among Pentecostals in the Majority World, then this might suggest that the approach to ministry engaged in by Pentecostals/charismatics in the southern continents may be thought of as a strikingly fruitful contemporary form of missional faithfulness.

Though I will issue an important caveat to this assessment in due time, let us proceed now to a survey of some of the proffered explanations for the prolific expansion of Pentecostalism around the world.

THE *BENEFITS* PENTECOSTALISM DELIVERS

During the past two decades, not a few books, articles and scholarly papers have been written that explain the reasons for Pentecostalism's amazing growth, especially in the Majority World, in terms of the *benefits* that accrue to those who participate in its communities of faith. Some of these proffered explanations overlap a bit, the difference between them owing to whether the focus of the theory provider is on the physical, spiritual, psychological or sociological effect of the benefit being described. What follows is a brief survey of several of the major categories which these kinds of suggested explanations fall into.

The physical benefits. In addition to a prophetic preaching of the gospel, many Pentecostal communities are engaged in ministries designed to alleviate the physical suffering of the poor and oppressed. Allan Anderson begins a discussion of the widespread contemporary appeal of Pentecostalism with the assertion that "the reasons for crowds of people flocking to the new churches have to do with more than the power of the Spirit, although we may not disregard this important pneumato-

---

Worldwide (Peabody, Mass.: Hendrickson, 1997), pp. 132-41; and Yong, *Spirit Poured Out*, pp. 24-26; 46-54.

[18]Anderson, *Introduction to Pentecostalism*, p. 236. We will return to the phenomenon of a Spirit-led theological innovation ("fresh hearing of the gospel") that leads to methodological innovation (new ministry praxis) in chap. 4.

logical factor. The offer of a better and more prosperous life often gives hope to people struggling in poverty and despair."[19]

Anderson seems to be suggesting here that the flocking of many people to Pentecostal churches might have less to do with a desire for a spiritual experience and more to do with a desperate desire to experience some material, financial improvement in their lives.

It is true that in some quarters and among some groups, this focus on a more prosperous life takes the form of the preaching of a "prosperity gospel," also known as the "Word of Faith," the "faith message" and "positive confession." It must also be pointed out that not all Pentecostals embrace or promote such a prosperity gospel.[20]

It is also true, according to Anderson, that while in the past "Pentecostals have been accused of a spirituality that withdraws from 'worldly' issues like politics and the struggle for liberation and justice, and of proclaiming a gospel that either spiritualizes or individualizes social problems," in reality "Pentecostals in various parts of the world have always had various programmes of social action," and that "throughout the world today Pentecostals are involved in practical ways caring for the poor and the destitute, those often 'unwanted' by the larger society."[21]

This is essentially the same message we find in *Global Pentecostalism*, authored by Donald Miller and Tetsunao Yamamori. This book refers to the emergence in the last decade of a *progressive* Pentecostalism—groups of Pentecostals that are engaging their communities in acts of compassion and service.[22] According to these authors, "Progressive Pentecostals are confronting the AIDS pandemic in Africa, they are educating impoverished children around the world, and they are establishing health clinics and initiating programs for street children."[23]

In sum, this type of proffered explanation suggests that, given the severity of suffering present in many depressed locales around the

---

[19]Ibid., p. 280.
[20]Ibid., pp. 157-58, 159-60, 220-24, 262.
[21]Ibid., pp. 261, 276-77.
[22]Donald Miller and Tetsunao Yamamori, *Global Pentecostalism: The New Face of Christian Social Engagement* (Los Angeles: University of California Press, 2007), pp. 1-2, 66.
[23]Ibid., p. 2.

world, it makes sense to think that Pentecostalism's enthusiastic engagement in ministries that seek to meet basic physical needs such as food, clothing, shelter, health care and legal advocacy might be something the Spirit of mission is using to draw people into Pentecostal communities of faith where they might hear the gospel preached and experience the convicting, regenerating work of the Spirit in their lives.

Furthermore, as will be alluded to later in this chapter, not all of this relief work is done at a programmatic level. It is not uncommon for the Holy Spirit to prompt an individual member of a Pentecostal or charismatic church to do something specific in order to relieve the suffering of someone particular. Thus, it is not simply the reception of the food, clothing, shelter, health care, legal advocacy and so on that impresses the grateful beneficiary; it is the prophetic manner in which this personal relief work is carried out.

The spiritual benefits. The suffering of some living in the Majority World is not due to hunger or homelessness, but disease or demonization. Over against this type of suffering, the Pentecostal emphasis on supernatural signs and wonders (especially divine healing and deliverance from the demonic) is well known. Allan Anderson has asserted that the Pentecostal practice of praying for divine healing is "perhaps the main reason for its growth in the developing world."[24] He explains that "the main attraction of Pentecostalism in the Majority World is . . . the emphasis on healing and deliverance from evil. Preaching a message that promises solutions for present felt needs, the 'full gospel' of Pentecostal preachers is readily accepted."[25]

So, this type of explanation argues that it is because Pentecostal communities offer hurting people the hope of deliverance from the power of disease and the demonic that many desperate souls are brought into an environment where they can experience the convicting and regenerating ministries of the Spirit of Christ.

Furthermore, we must also keep in mind that the proclamation by Majority World Pentecostals/charismatics of the "full gospel" with

---

[24]Anderson, *Introduction to Pentecostalism*, p. 30.
[25]Ibid., p. 234.

signs following (e.g., healing and deliverance) not only occurs in church services and mass rallies held at stadiums, it happens also on a person-to-person basis, often as a result of a special prompting by the Holy Spirit. Again, anecdotes from the field related by missionaries of repute indicate how common it is for rank-and-file church members to feel led of the Lord to go to certain people and say or do certain things on Christ's behalf. This prophetic speech and action often creates opportunities for ministry conversations that result in conversions.

The psychological and sociological benefits. It is important to keep in mind, say the proponents of this type of explanation, that Pentecostalism makes use of egalitarian forms of prayer, worship and nurture that are ennobling to all adherents, especially those who have experienced social marginalization. Pentecostal theologian Frank Macchia suggests that the theological significance of the practice of glossolalia, or speaking in tongues, for many Pentecostals around the world is that "tongues allow the poor, uneducated, and illiterate among the people of God to have an equal voice with the educated and the literate."[26]

Likewise, social ethicist Murray Dempster has put forward the idea that the serious manner in which Pentecostals and charismatics treat the reception of spiritual gifts has an egalitarian effect on a congregation. His suggestion is that "through the Holy Spirit's charisms every member is made into an equally valued participant in the diversified Christian community" regardless of gender, age, socioeconomic status or race.[27]

In a similar manner, Walter Hollenweger, regarded by many as the doyen of Pentecostal studies, argues that the apparently spontaneous and enthusiastic worship of Pentecostals does in fact involve a liturgy, albeit an oral one that is memorized.[28] He explains that the value of an oral liturgy is that it allows for the "active participation of every member

---

[26]Frank Macchia, "The Struggle for Global Witness: Shifting Paradigms in Pentecostal Theology," in *The Globalization of Pentecostalism: A Religion Made to Travel*, ed. Murray W. Dempster, Byron D. Klaus and Douglas Petersen (Irvine, Calif.: Regnum Books, 1999), p. 18. See also Hollenweger, *Pentecostalism*, p. 272.

[27]Murray W. Dempster, "Evangelism, Social Concern and the Kingdom of God," in *Called and Empowered: Global Mission in Pentecostal Perspective*, ed. Murray W. Dempster, Byron D. Klaus and Douglas Petersen (Peabody, Mass.: Hendrickson, 1991), p. 29.

[28]Hollenweger, *Pentecostalism*, p. 270.

of the congregation" and legitimizes the effort of each person to render to God an expression of worship that is acceptable in his sight.[29]

Elaborating on the insights provided by Hollenweger, Allen Anderson makes a similar assertion: "Pentecostal liturgy has social and revolutionary implications in that it empowers marginalized people. It takes as acceptable what ordinary people have to give in their worship of God and thereby overcomes the social barriers of race, status and education."[30]

The same kind of leveling dynamic can be seen in the manner in which Pentecostals tend to engage in the activity of nurture. In *Pentecostal Formation*, Cheryl Bridges Johns describes the empowering effect of the charismatic catechetical process utilized among the oppressed, marginalized peoples of Latin America, especially Chile and Brazil.[31] In this model, a formal mentor-disciple relationship is deemphasized in favor of a charismatic group experience. In this charismatic group there really is no teacher-student relationship because the only teacher is the Holy Spirit. Everyone is entitled to belong, participate and experience truth as the Holy Spirit reveals it to them. This is a very liberating and validating experience for the poor, uneducated people of Chile.[32]

Though we might express concern that this egalitarian educational process allows for too much subjectivity when it comes to biblical interpretation (especially in an ecclesial climate where there might exist a tendency toward anti-intellectualism), it cannot be denied that belonging to and participating in a charismatic community of learners where one's own contributions to the collective learning process are taken seriously would be attractive to oppressed, marginalized people.

Thus, according to this explanation, socially marginalized people all around the world are experiencing within Pentecostal and charismatic churches empowering, ennobling forms of prayer, worship and instruction, and this is a primary reason why these hurting people are attracted to Pentecostal communities of faith where they can experi-

---

[29]Ibid., pp. 271, 273-74.
[30]Anderson, *Introduction to Pentecostalism*, p. 235.
[31]Cheryl Bridges Johns, *Pentecostal Formation: A Pedagogy Among the Oppressed* (Sheffield, U.K.: Sheffield Academic Press, 1993), p. 77.
[32]Ibid., p. 16.

ence the converting, regenerating, empowering work of the Holy Spirit in their lives.

Now, as legitimate as all of these benefit-focused explanations may be, there are other Pentecostal scholars who contend that such explanations, by themselves, cannot fully explain the prolific growth of Pentecostalism. According to some Pentecostal missiologists, a fully adequate explanation will have to account for Pentecostalism's amazing ability to see remarkable numbers of rank-and-file church members move past a preoccupation with the gospel's physical, spiritual, psychological and sociological benefits toward an enthusiastic missional engagement in the presentation of the kingdom of God to their local neighborhoods through prophetic evangelism, edification and equipping.

For this reason we must consider another type of explanation for the global growth of Pentecostalism—an explanation that focuses not on the *benefits* it provides but on the experience-supported *beliefs* it promotes.

PENTECOSTALISM'S EMBRACE OF A THEOLOGICAL REALISM

The description of Pentecostals/charismatics presented in "Spirit and Power: A 10-Country Survey" included these lines: "Even more than other Christians, pentecostals and other renewalists believe that God, acting through the Holy Spirit, continues to play a direct, active role in everyday life." What this description seems to suggest is that at the root of the phenomenal growth of Pentecostalism is a *theological realism:* the simple, basic belief that God is that ultimate reality out which all the physical (and virtual) realities around us derive their existence, and that his real presence is immediately accessible to his people.[33] It is this theological realism—this conviction that God, acting through the Spirit, is graciously, faithfully at work in their everyday lives—that empowers Pentecostals and charismatics to respond faithfully when the Spirit of mission bids their participation in the accomplishment of

---

[33]For a helpful discussion of theological realism and its relationship to worship, see John Jefferson Davis, *Worship and the Reality of God* (Downers Grove, Ill.: IVP Academic, 2010), pp. 21-25.

God's missional purposes through an engagement in prophetic activity. Another way to say this is that yet another explanation for the global growth of Pentecostalism is one that focuses on the fact that this movement provides its adherents with a unique set of experience-supported beliefs that together encourage an enthusiastic engagement in an aggressive form of evangelism through both gospel proclamation and social action within those adherents' homes, neighborhoods and places of work.

Following this trajectory, Pentecostal missiologist Grant McClung suggests that "since its inception, the Pentecostal Movement has had underlying theological assumptions which have formed the impulse for its missionary expansion."[34] McClung identifies these theological assumptions as the centrality of the Word and Spirit in the life of the Pentecostal believer, an eschatology that provides the Pentecostal believer with a sense of missional urgency, and the sense of call or destiny many Pentecostals possess.[35] These three assumptions, says McClung, "constitute the internal essence of the theological infrastructure of pentecostal missions" and are important aspects of "pentecostals' worldview and theology which have propelled them into continuous missionary outreach since the turn of the twentieth century."[36]

With apologies to McClung, I present not three but four specific experience-supported beliefs based loosely on his work, which I contend veritably impel many Pentecostal believers past a preoccupation with the self toward a missional engagement that is both faithful and hopeful. The power of these beliefs is due precisely to the fact that they are grounded in a firm Spirit-driven, experience-supported embrace of a rigorous theological realism that includes a conviction concerning the faithfulness of the Spirit of mission.

Taking the Bible seriously. First, because of their embrace of the idea that the Bible is God's Word, Pentecostal and charismatic believers tend to interpret it realistically and take it seriously as a guide for fruit-

---

[34]Grant McClung, "Truth on Fire: Pentecostals and an Urgent Missiology," in *Azusa Street and Beyond: 100 Years of Commentary on the Global Pentecostal/Charismatic Movement*, ed. Grant McClung (Gainesville, Fla.: Bridge-Logos, 2006), p. 78.
[35]Ibid.
[36]Ibid.

ful evangelistic ministry. Since they take the Bible seriously, Pentecostals are motivated to obey the Great Commission to make disciples of all nations, being careful to use the book of Acts as their manual for how to do so.[37] This willingness to take the Bible at face value has the effect of instilling within them a strong confidence in the idea that, because they are being faithful to the teaching of Scripture, they should expect to experience the same kind of missional success as that achieved by the earliest Christians.[38] For many Christian workers this is an exciting, ennobling proposition.

Furthermore, their *realist* approach to biblical interpretation has resulted in a determination among Pentecostals to proclaim nothing less than the "full gospel" they find in its pages—which includes healing, deliverance and the bestowal of spiritual gifts.[39] We have already seen that a gospel that is accompanied by supernatural signs and wonders is attractive to its *hearers*. The fact is that such a gospel is attractive to its *bearers* as well. Becoming involved (either programmatically or personally) in the fruitful proclamation of a message, the veracity of which is routinely authenticated in supernatural ways, can be a very affirming, exciting, existentially comforting, hope-producing experience.[40]

Embracing the in-filling of the Spirit. Second, because of their embrace of the idea that the in-filling of the Spirit produces an identifiable evidence in one's life, Pentecostal-charismatic believers tend to possess an innervating confidence in the fact that they have been empowered to be witnesses for Christ by the same missionary Spirit who launched the Christian movement two thousand years ago. Pentecostals believe that the Holy Spirit is at the heart of Christian mission. McClung writes, "Though some pentecostal theologians may move in other di-

---

[37]McClung, "Truth on Fire: Pentecostals and an Urgent Missiology," pp. 79-80, 147.

[38]See Chris Armstrong, "Embrace Your Inner Pentecostal," *Christianity Today*, September 19, 2006, www.christianitytoday.com/ct/2006/september/40.86.html.

[39]Paul A. Pomerville, *Pentecostalism and Missions: Distortion or Correction?* (Pasadena, Calif.: Fuller School of Intercultural Studies, 1982), p. 352, cited in McClung, "Truth on Fire: Pentecostals and an Urgent Missiology," p. 79.

[40]See my book *Defeating Pharisaism* for a discussion of how a need for spiritual certitude can also lead the Christian believer to adopt a pharisaical approach to his or her spirituality (Gary Tyra, *Defeating Pharisaism: Recovering Jesus' Disciple-Making Method* [Colorado Springs: Paternoster, 2009], pp. 70-74).

rections, pentecostal *missiologists* will contend that the Baptism of the Holy Spirit is primarily for ministry, especially for evangelism.[41] He goes on to explain the importance of each believer experiencing a "personal Pentecost":

> The Pentecostals have exploded into phenomenal growth around the world not only because they have reached the masses and the poor, or have concentrated upon the receptive, or have utilized the energies of the common man, or have done whatever else outside observers have marked as good methodology. The primary pentecostal distinctive in their theology has been their insistence upon the outpouring of the Holy Spirit personally into the life of each believer in a "personal pentecost."[42]

Why, as it relates to mission, is the experience of a "personal Pentecost" considered so important? Because of their theological realism many Pentecostals and charismatics are convinced that the experience of Spirit in-filling is not simply symbolic or metaphorical; it actually imparts spiritual power that motivates and enables effective witness (see Acts 1:8).[43] The simple truth is that the history of Pentecostal-charismatic missions seems to indicate that, when it comes to the issue of supernatural signs and wonders, expectancy does tend to precede experience. Furthermore, this history also suggests that to the degree a believer *experiences* what is perceived to be divine assistance while engaging in evangelistic ministry (e.g., prophetic guidance or inspiration), he or she will possess a heightened awareness that not only increases the believer's ability to recognize other missional opportunities when they present themselves, but will cause him or her to be more courageously willing to engage in them than the believer otherwise would have been. In other words, the faithfulness of the Spirit of mission enables a faithful, hopeful missional response.

---

[41]McClung, "Truth on Fire: Pentecostals and an Urgent Missiology," p. 82.

[42]Ibid., p. 81.

[43]Bruner writes, "The Pentecostal is persuaded that his historical success is due to this theological distinctive, the experience of the Holy Spirit in power. It is from this spiritual center that Pentecostalism understands itself and its mission. The Pentecostal groups in Brazil, for example, are reported to have affirmed that 'their growth is due to the power of the Holy Spirit enabling them to witness and testify with power. This . . . is the secret of church growth'" (Bruner, *Theology of the Holy Spirit*, p. 26).

Compelled by a sense of eschatological urgency. Third, because of their embrace of the ideas that the return of Christ is imminent and that eternal punishment awaits those who fail to confess Christ as Lord in this life, Pentecostal-charismatic believers have historically felt compelled by a sense of eschatological urgency to become involved in missional activities. McClung reminds us that from the earliest days of contemporary Pentecostalism (i.e., ever since the outpouring of the Holy Spirit at Azusa Street in 1906) the adherents of this movement have interpreted such passages as Joel 2:28-32 in such a way as to be convinced that the church is now living in the last days.[44] Further, fueled by an embrace of premillennial dispensationalism, many if not most Pentecostals and charismatics have held the belief that the return of Christ could happen at any moment.[45] Since *many* Pentecostals and charismatics also hold to an exclusivist rather than inclusivist or universalist view of salvation (i.e., since they believe that only those who confess Christ as Lord will be saved), they have felt a keen responsibility under God to "reach the lost" while there is still time to do so. Whatever one thinks of these eschatological and soteriological positions, it cannot be denied that historically they have served to motivate many Pentecostal-charismatic believers toward a faithful, hopeful missional engagement.

A special sense of call. Finally, because of their embrace of the idea that they have been divinely and uniquely commissioned to proclaim the "full gospel" to lost and hurting people around the world, Pentecostal-charismatic believers have tended to manifest a remarkable willing-

---

[44]McClung, "Truth on Fire: Pentecostals and an Urgent Missiology," p. 83.

[45]Ibid. It is also true, however, that not all contemporary Pentecostals and charismatics are dispensational in their eschatology. My personal sense is that many Pentecostals and charismatics have been influenced by the historical premillennialism advocated by scholars such as George Ladd (see Robert G. Clouse, ed., *The Meaning of the Millennium: Four Views* [Downers Grove, Ill.: InterVarsity Press, 1977], pp. 17-40). Furthermore, Pentecostal theologian Frank Macchia has advocated a nuanced perspective that differentiates between an eschatology that he believes has tended to promote a social passivity (dispensationalism) and one that encourages the church to engage in ministries of social transformation that present to the world a foretaste of the kingdom of God to come. In the process, he expresses a desire for Pentecostals to "rediscover the eschatological fervour " that historically has not only inspired much Pentecostal soul winning but social action as well (Frank Macchia, "The Struggle for Global Witness," pp. 23-24).

ness to do this very thing despite the cost and inconvenience such ministry involvement has brought their way. Many observers of Pentecostalism have taken note of the fact that the movement has demonstrated an extraordinary ability to get the rank-and-file church member involved in missional ministry. For example, according to missiologist Paul Pomerville, church growth specialists have identified as the number one reason for their remarkable growth the unique ability of many Pentecostal churches to mobilize the laity toward an involvement in aggressive evangelism.[46]

How do we explain this unique ability Pentecostal and charismatic churches possess to motivate their members toward a vigorous missional ministry involvement? Could it be that something prophetic is going on?

Grant McClung is eager to point out that this success at ministry mobilization is not primarily due to great human leadership but to the very ethos of the movement—a shared sense among Pentecostals and charismatics that they possess *a special call* to do everything necessary to win the world for Christ.[47]

A special sense of call. It is not hard to see that such a sense of divine commissioning would motivate any believer toward an enthusiastic missional engagement.

Some questions I want to pose at this point are: Does this *special sense of call* or commissioning occur among Pentecostals and charismatics only at a collective level, or is there a personal aspect to it as well? Does this call function merely in a general manner, or can it sometimes be quite specific? In other words, *could it be that within Pentecostal-charismatic churches around the world it is not uncommon for individual church members to occasionally experience a particular call to engage in prophetic ministry (speech or action) in a particular way to particular people with the result that everyone involved experiences a meaningful demonstration of the reality that Jesus is Lord?* These are questions that will occupy us for the remainder of this chapter.

---

[46]Paul A. Pomerville, *Introduction to Missions: An Independent-study Textbook* (Irving, Tex.: ICI University Press, 1987), pp. 95-97, cited in Anderson, "Towards a Pentecostal Missiology."

[47]McClung, "Truth on Fire: Pentecostals and an Urgent Missiology," p. 85.

PROPHETIC ACTIVITY AND THE
GLOBAL GROWTH OF PENTECOSTALISM

Not only do I believe that some form of prophetic activity (hearing the voice of God, receiving a ministry assignment from him, and then speaking and acting toward others in his name) is involved in each of the corporate benefit-producing ecclesial dynamics previously referred to in this chapter,[48] it is my contention that yet another reason why Pentecostalism is growing so rapidly around the world is that more than a few rank-and-file Pentecostal believers have been willing to follow the personal leading of the Spirit of mission to speak and act prophetically into the lives of lost and hurting people living in their communities. Is there any evidence to support this thesis? There is, and it comes to us via several sources.

Demographic evidence. Statistical support for the thesis I am putting forward is provided by Margaret Poloma and John Green who, though their research was conducted among Pentecostals living in the developed rather than developing world, have concluded on the basis of it that *there is indeed a causal connection between prophetic activity and benevolent action on the part of the Pentecostal believer.* In *The Assemblies of God: Godly Love and the Revitalization of American Pentecostalism* these sociologists of religion write:

> Our statistical analysis suggests that commonly experiencing prophecy is by far the leading descriptor of a person who acknowledges being an instrument of divine healing. In short—and relevant to our thesis on Godly love—our findings imply that spiritual experiences involving divine-human interaction may be facilitators of benevolence, including effective prayer for the healing of others. . . . In short, *divine collaborators who hear the voice of God and respond to it are also the most likely to be functioning as God's instruments of healing in the church. . . .*
>
> Benevolent action (at least for pentecostals) is frequently accompanied by experiences of the divine that appear to empower the believer as suggested in sociologist Pitirim Sorokin's concept of "love energy." This pattern is evident in our exploration of healing rituals and experiences

---

[48]For example, see Yong, *Spirit Poured Out*, p. 40, where the author refers to the ennobling effect of woman prophesying in Pentecostal churches located in Latin America.

reported in this chapter. Through the use of multiple regression analysis, we have been able to describe demographic traits and aspects of spiritual experiences as they relate to healing, specifically to benevolent acts of healing prayer. Our findings clearly point to the special role that prophecy—hearing the voice of God and responding to it—plays in the healing process.[49]

In other words, the extensive research conducted by Poloma and Green indicates a connection between the benevolent actions of Pentecostals toward other people (i.e., missional engagement) and the dynamic of prophecy, which is described by Poloma and Green as "hearing the voice of God and responding to it."

Evidence from the literature devoted to global Pentecostalism. Quite independent of but in harmony with the research just cited, some Pentecostalism scholars have forthrightly addressed the fact that the special sense of missional call associated with the movement functions not only corporately but individually as well. For example, in a paper titled "Towards a Pentecostal Missiology for the Majority World," Allen Anderson states:

> Pentecostals place primary emphasis on being "sent by the Spirit" and depend more on what is described as the Spirit's leading than on formal structures. People called "missionaries" are doing that job because the Spirit directed them to do it, often through some spiritual revelation like a prophecy, a dream or a vision, and even through an audible voice perceived to be that of God.[50]

Furthermore, this call to missionary service is not limited to full-time professionals. According to Pentecostal scholar John Michael Penney, the narrative that depicts the coming of the Spirit in Acts 2 functions for Pentecostals and charismatics as a "normative paradigm for every Christian to preach the gospel."[51]

---

[49]Margaret M. Poloma and John C. Green, *The Assemblies of God: Godly Love and the Revitalization of American Pentecostalism* (New York: New York University Press, 2010), pp. 141-42.

[50]Allan Anderson, "Towards a Pentecostal Missiology for the Majority World," *Asian Journal of Pentecostal Studies* 8, no. 1 (2005): 31.

[51]John Michael Penney, *The Missionary Emphasis of Lukan Pneumatology* (Sheffield, U.K.: Sheffield Academic Press, 1997), pp. 11, 15, cited in ibid., p. 32.

Going further still, Anderson explicitly indicates that this Pentecostal-charismatic sense of call to missional ministry "was not only a collective experience of the Spirit" but an "individual experience that each Christian had with the Holy Spirit."[52]

We have already taken notice of Pentecostalism's success at mobilizing its lay adherents toward an enthusiastic and ambitious involvement in missional activities. Pentecostal missiologists Byron Klaus and Loren Triplett attribute the movement's successful "minimizing of the clergy/laity barrier" to an emphasis on "the whole body as ministers supernaturally recruited and deployed." Putting my own spin on the argument put forward by Klaus and Triplett, allow me to suggest that the following syllogism is at work in Pentecostalism as a whole: since (1) the Holy Spirit supernaturally recruits and deploys members of Christ's body to function as Christian ministers, and since (2) the Holy Spirit graciously speaks to all believers equally, regardless of education, training or worldly rank, therefore (3) each Spirit-filled member of Christ's body is capable of ministering on Christ's behalf.[53] Notice in this line of reasoning the importance attached to the individual church member's ability to hear God's voice and to receive a ministry call/assignment from him as a result (i.e., prophetic capacity).

Even more evidence of this type is available to us via an unpublished academic paper titled "The Spirit Bade Me Go: Pentecostalism and Global Religion" by Margaret Poloma, professor emerita of sociology at the University of Akron. After giving careful consideration to some of the more theologically and sociologically nuanced explanations for the growth of Pentecostalism that have been put forward by Pentecostal scholars, Poloma states: "The blend of a biblical mandate, a personal call, and experiential empowerment has touched many thousands who have taken off for foreign lands within

---

[52]Pomerville, *Introduction to Missions*, p. 97, cited in Anderson, "Towards a Pentecostal Missiology for the Majority World," p. 31.

[53]Byron D. Klaus and Loren O. Triplett, "National Leadership in Pentecostal Missions," in Murray A. Dempster, Byron D. Klaus and Douglas Petersen, *Called and Empowered: Global Mission in Pentecostal Perspective* (Peabody, Mass.: Hendrickson, 1991), pp. 226, cited in Anderson, "Towards a Pentecostal Missiology for the Majority World," p. 39.

the past century as Pentecostal missionaries."[54]

Poloma's view seems to be most influenced by the findings of Pentecostal missiologist Grant McClung, who, after "scanning the field of Pentecostal literature," identified as a major reason for the proliferation of Pentecostalism worldwide the belief that "the Holy Spirit is personally active, living in and directing his servants in the world."[55] Thus Poloma devotes a significant portion of her essay to an examination of a case study she believes illustrates this particular Pentecostal-charismatic dynamic—a rigorous embrace of theological realism. The case study focuses on Loren Cunningham and his ambitious though controversial founding of a very effective interdenominational missionary-sending organization—Youth With a Mission (YWAM)—on the basis of a vision he received from the Lord. (Hence, the title of Poloma's paper—"The Spirit Bade Me Go: Pentecostalism and Global Religion.")[56]

The full story of how YWAM was launched is related by Cunningham in a book titled *Is That Really You, God?*[57] The cover of this popular work presents the reader with two subtitles. One is "The Youth With a Mission Story." Another more prominently displayed subtitle is "Hearing the Voice of God." Indeed, the book is replete with anecdotes that illustrate in a compelling manner the thesis of both Poloma's paper and this chapter—that a major reason for the spread of Pentecostalism over the globe is an ability and willingness on the part of many of its adherents to hear and obey the special, personal promptings of the Spirit of mission to engage in missional ministry.

---

[54]Margaret Poloma, "The Spirit Bade Me Go: Pentecostalism and Global Religion," *Hartford Institute for Religion Research*, August 11-13, 2000, http://hirr.hartsem.edu/research/pentecostalism_polomaart1.html.

[55]Grant McClung, "Missiology," in *Dictionary of Pentecostal and Charismatic Movements*, eds. Stanley M. Burgess, Gary B. McGee and Patrick H. Alexander (Grand Rapids: Zondervan, 1988), p. 607.

[56]It should be noted that Poloma's intention behind the use of this story seems also to have been to illustrate what anthropologist Karla Poewe describes as the "experiential, idealistic, biblical, and oppositional" characteristics of the global culture that is charismatic Christianity (see Karla Poewe, *Charismatic Christianity as a Global Culture* [Columbia: University of South Carolina Press, 1994]).

[57]Loren Cunningham, *Is That Really You, God?* (Grand Rapids: Chosen Books, 1984).

Evidence in the form of expert testimony. Yet another source of evidence for the premise behind this chapter is the credible testimony provided by those who either have firsthand experience with life on the mission field, or who oversee those who do.

For example, during a conversation with George O. Wood, general superintendent of the Assemblies of God, that took place on October 15, 2010, I presented to him the premise that underlies this chapter and asked his opinion regarding it. Responding immediately in the affirmative, he referred to several major "fields" that were opened up to Pentecostal missionary activity as a result of a believer sensing a prophetic prompting to take the full gospel to those lands.[58]

According to Lance Pittluck, pastor of the Vineyard Christian Fellowship of Anaheim, California, and a member of the national board of Vineyard Churches USA, a similar dynamic lies behind the worldwide proliferation of Vineyard churches. In a personal interview conducted on October 30, 2010, Pittluck explained that John Wimber's original vision was simply to see ten thousand Vineyard churches planted within the United States. It was due to a prophetic call experienced by John and Eleanor Mumford during a two-year internship at the Anaheim Vineyard that the first overseas Vineyard church was planted in London, England. Out of that one church, approximately one hundred other Vineyard churches have been established in the United Kingdom, many if not most of them due to Vineyard church members experiencing promptings of the Spirit to start new churches in new locations. Thus began the international Vineyard church movement. Today there are approximately fourteen hundred Vineyard congregations spread across sixty countries. When asked how common it is for rank-and-file Vineyard church members in these various churches to experience the phenomenon of being prompted by the Spirit of mission to speak and act into the lives of others in a missional manner, Pittluck indicated that this dynamic is quite common since

---

[58]Subsequently, Dr. Wood had Darrin Rodgers, director of the Flower Pentecostal Heritage Center, editor of the Assemblies of God *Heritage* magazine, and coeditor of the *Society for Pentecostal Studies Newsletter* provide detailed information regarding these ministry incidents in an email sent on October 20, 2010.

that was the whole idea behind [John] Wimber's original concept of power evangelism: that average people could be with their friends and family, get a prophetic word, get an insight and end up praying for them and ministering to them. . . . It was the idea that God is still speaking today and that God could speak to us about our neighbor or give us a word of knowledge or prophetic insight or whatever.

Pittluck went on to affirm that this kind of prophetic activity—so much at the heart of the Vineyard ministry ethos—is indeed one of the biggest reasons for the growth of the Vineyard movement worldwide.

Doug Petersen is the Margaret S. Smith Distinguished Professor of Intercultural Studies at Vanguard University of Southern California. In 1977, Petersen cofounded Latin America ChildCare (LACC) and served as its international coordinator and president for twenty-three years. LACC, an international relief organization, provides food, medical care and education for over 100,000 impoverished children in Latin America and the Caribbean. Petersen is also the founder of the international linguistics school CINCEL (Centro de investigaciones y estudios lingüísticos) in San José, Costa Rica. In an interview conducted on October 21, 2010, I explained the premise of this chapter and asked Dr. Petersen to provide his take on it. After commenting on the difference between the kind of prophetic activity involved in sensing a call to take the gospel to a certain part of the world, and a prompting to engage in a specific ministry activity to a particular person, Petersen affirmed that both types of prophetic activity are common in Latin American Pentecostal churches, the latter type especially prevalent among rank-and-file believers. This is due, he says, to the fact that the preconversion worldview of these believers is so very "comfortable with the supernatural." Thus, when these folks read the Bible, they bring to it a "preunderstanding" that causes them to simply expect to experience the same kinds of signs, wonders and miracles they read in its pages. There is an expectation on their part that just as God broke into the lives of the biblical characters, providing them with ministry instructions in a prophetic manner, he will do the same in their lives as well.

Essentially echoing Petersen's observations is the testimony provided by Dr. Greg Austring, associate professor of intercultural studies at

Vanguard University. Austring spent ten years as a missionary to Guatemala, serving as the coordinator of the Latin American ChildCare ministry in that country. In the course of an interview conducted on October 21, 2010, Austring stated that as he witnessed the effectiveness of various Guatemalan national LACC school directors and pastors, it became apparent to him that these leaders were being guided not simply by their training but by prophetic promptings provided by the Holy Spirit, a fact which these directors were quick to bear witness to themselves. Furthermore, says Austring, while rank-and-file believers in Guatemala are always careful to defer to the ministry authority of their national and local church leaders, it is not at all uncommon for them to testify to having been instructed by the Holy Spirit to speak and act into the lives of others, or to have been on the receiving end of such prophetic ministry.

Dan Campbell, a veteran missionary who spent fifteen years planting churches and starting Bible schools in Argentina, Venezuela and Ecuador, is now pastoring an Assemblies of God church in San Juan Capistrano, California. A personal friend, Dan and I were having coffee on the morning of September 15, 2010, when I explained to him the thesis of this book as a whole and this chapter in particular. When asked to comment on this thesis, Dan not only offered an affirming response, he began to eagerly relate story after story which serve to verify the accuracy of my premise. What follows is an account of just one of many such stories related by a missionary with impeccable ministry credentials. What makes this particular story interesting is the way it shows the Holy Spirit prompting and enabling the planting of a church in a new region, while at the same time effecting prophetic missional ministry to a particular hurting family. Says Pastor Dan:

> I had felt the Lord's leading to plant a new church in Tandil, Argentina. After several failed attempts to make a scouting trip to this target city, I and a national worker named Ricardo finally made it there. We drove around town, praying, looking, and listening.
>
> After and hour or so, Ricardo said, "I think a man I met several years ago in Tres Arroyos moved here."
>
> The problem was that all Ricardo could remember was the man's

first name: Oscar. So, I'm thinking to myself, *What are the chances of us finding one man in a city of 150,000—a man we're not completely convinced actually lives here?* Still, since it was our only real option at that point, we prayed and asked the Holy Spirit to somehow, someway guide us to him.

We drove for some time through residential neighborhoods and finally stopped at a kiosk to ask for directions. Ricardo asked the proprietor: "Is there a family close by that moved here from Tres Arroyos? I believe the man's name is Oscar."

The newspaper seller thought for a moment and said, "I think that may be the family that lives in that house." Amazingly, he then pointed to a house just half-way down the block!

We said thank you to the man and drove the short distance to the house he'd pointed too. All the while I'm thinking: *This is nuts! We don't know for sure that the man, whom Ricardo thinks was named Oscar, actually moved here. We're just shooting in the dark!*

Before I could ask Ricardo how he thought we should proceed, I discovered that he was already out of the car and striding toward the house's front door. He waited for me to catch up before he knocked on the door, however, since he thought that I should be the one to explain to "Oscar" why we were there!

The door opened, and after looking us over suspiciously, the man standing there asked us in a somewhat brusque manner what we wanted. I introduced Ricardo and myself to him, and explained that we were looking for a man named Oscar who had moved there from Tres Arroyos. "Might that be you?" I asked.

Rather than respond to my query, he simply shot back: "Who sent you?" To which I repeated my introduction.

Again, he asked rather sternly, "Who sent you?"

For the third time I introduced Ricardo and myself to the fellow, but this time added that we had been led of the Lord to start a church in Tandil, and that that was why we were there.

At this point the fellow's facial expression changed and he invited us into his home. He told us that though he didn't remember meeting Ricardo, his name was Oscar, he was from Tres Arroyos, and that he and his family had moved to Tandil during the time frame to which Ricardo had referred.

Oscar then proceeded to tell us his story. Since moving to Tandil he had not been able to find a church, and had been working sixty-plus hours a week in order to take care of his family, his wife having recently been diagnosed with cancer. The doctors in Tandil had done everything they could for her and had suggested she be taken to Buenos Aires to see a specialist.

Having arranged to take a few days off work, Oscar took his wife to Buenos Aires. Because of the seriousness of her condition, the specialist put her in the hospital immediately. What was supposed to have been short stay turned out to be over a month long. At the end of that time the doctors had instructed Oscar to take his wife home to die. There was simply no hope.

The night they returned home to Tandil, Oscar had prayed, "God if you really care about us, send someone to see us!" That was the night before Ricardo and I showed up at his door. All of a sudden I understood why he'd kept asking us, "Who sent you?" I also realized that we weren't in Tandil that day simply to scout out the territory for a new church plant.

God did some special things in all of us through this divine appointment. Yes, he did indeed heal Oscar's wife despite her dire diagnosis. But he also taught me a valuable lesson about hearing his voice and being guided by the Holy Spirit as I continued in the ministry of church planting.

Today there is a thriving church in Tandil. Oscar, his wife and three daughters were the beginning of that work.[59]

In *A Theology of the Church and Its Mission: A Pentecostal Perspective*, Melvin Hodges includes a passage evidently designed to encourage his readers to believe that, *with the help of the Holy Spirit*, missional success can be achieved in any context regardless of the obstacles that might stand in the way. This passage illustrates the belief among Pentecostals and charismatics that the work of the Holy Spirit is absolutely crucial to missional faithfulness.

Against this gloomy background we dare to proclaim anew that

---

[59]The initial meeting with Dan Campbell took place on September 15, 2010. A subsequent email providing a written draft of the story presented here was sent by Campbell to me on October 20, 2010.

Christ is Lord and Saviour. We dare to believe that the Holy Spirit in His church is mightier than all the forces in the world combined. As long as the Church is in the world we can expect the Holy Spirit to guide and empower it. The task Jesus gave the Church to preach the gospel to every creature and to all nations is still with us and must be carried out. But this task must be fulfilled in the power of the Holy Spirit, for it is the Holy Spirit who imparts life; it is the Holy Spirit who provides the motivation—the love of God shed abroad in our hearts. It is the Holy Spirit that calls men [and women] both to accept Christ and afterwards to serve Him. This same Holy Spirit imparts gifts and ministries and the power with which to perform the tasks. *He gives wisdom and vision for the work of God far beyond the capacities of the human intellect.*[60]

While I wish that Hodges would have included in this quote an even more specific reference to the Spirit's empowering of *prophetic speech and action*, he does go on to say:

No man or any one group of men is wise enough to lay out the strategy that is required to reach the almost 3 billion people still unevangelized. Jesus Christ is the Head of the Church and the Lord of the harvest. *The Holy Spirit is able to impart to each one the personal direction that will enable him to cooperate with the divine strategy.*[61]

We have seen that there are apparently many reasons why the Pentecostal-charismatic version of the Christian faith is advancing in such a prolific manner all over the world. I have suggested in this chapter that the ministry impact of this movement can and should be considered a contemporary expression of the kind of missional faithfulness exhibited by the first followers of Christ. Rooted in a rigorous embrace of a theological realism and a bedrock conviction that the Spirit of mission is faithful, many Pentecostal and charismatics are offering a faithful and hopeful response to the personal direction provided them by the Holy Spirit toward an engagement in missional ministry.

Now the question is: Is it possible for evangelicals to manifest a con-

---

[60]Melvin L. Hodges, *A Theology of the Church and Its Mission: A Pentecostal Perspective* (Springfield, Mo.: Gospel Publishing House, 1977), p. 172, emphasis added.
[61]Ibid., p. 173, emphasis added.

textually sensitive missional faithfulness here in the post-Christian West? If so, how might this be accomplished? What would a missional faithfulness that takes prophetic speech and action seriously look like in our ministry context(s)? It is toward an answer to these crucial questions that we now turn our attention.

4

"MEN OF ATHENS!"

Becoming More Missionally Faithful in the West

JUST A FEW YEARS AGO *Christian History* magazine published an article titled "The Rise of Pentecostalism," which took the form of an interview with prominent Pentecostalism scholar Walter Hollenweger. The lead-in to this article ran: "It's not tongues but a different way of being a Christian."[1]

A different way of being a Christian. I have been arguing in this book that a missional pneumatology is the way forward for all evangelicals—Pentecostals-charismatics and non-Pentecostals-charismatics—to increase their missional faithfulness. In support of this thesis I have pointed out that both the Old and New Testaments seem to teach that when the Spirit of mission comes upon God's people in an empowering manner something missionally significant occurs: the impartation of prophetic capacity—a new ability to hear God's voice, receive ministry assignments from him, and speak and act into people's lives on his behalf. In addition, I have endeavored to demonstrate the connection between prophetic activity and the remarkable missional faithfulness of the earliest Christians as portrayed in the book of Acts. I have further argued that the phenomenon of prophetic activity among rank-and-file church members is a big reason for the global growth of Pentecostal-charismatic Christianity, especially in the Majority World. All the

---

[1]"The Rise of Pentecostalism: Christian History Interview—Pentecostalism's Global Language," *Christian History*, April 1, 1998, www.christianitytoday.com/ch/1998/issue58/58h042.html.

while, I have been honest about the fact that to embrace this pneuma-tological paradigm—to open oneself to the possibility that on any given day God's Spirit might choose to use us the way he did the disciple Ananias in Acts 9:10-20—may indeed amount to our having to learn a "different way of being a Christian."

Admittedly, this is a lot to ask, especially of those non-Pentecostal-charismatic evangelicals who are not used to such an experiential ap-proach to the Christian faith, and of the many Western Pentecostal-charismatic evangelicals who, truthfully, may not really be taking the phenomenon of prophetic speech and action very seriously either.[2] In other words, for nearly all evangelical believers living in the West, we are talking about a paradigm shift of monumental proportions.

The truth of this statement is underscored by the fact that the idea of learning a "different way of being a Christian" also appears in vari-ous forms in the literature devoted to the missional church movement.[3] Much of the missional church argument centers on the need for Chris-tians and congregations (mainline Protestant and traditional evangeli-cal) to move away from traditional, attractional, *institutional* ways of doing church. This move is called for, say many missional authors, due to the fact that most traditional approaches to ministry are still rooted in a "Christendom" way of thinking of the church's relationship to cul-ture[4] that has been overly influenced by certain aspects of modernity,

---

[2]Margaret Poloma and John Green refer to Max Weber's theory regarding the routinization of charisma, suggesting that it has had application in the history of American Pentecostalism. See Margaret M. Poloma and John C. Green, *The Assemblies of God* (New York: New York Univer-sity Press, 2010), p. 2.

[3]For example, Roxburgh and Boren refer often to the need for a "new imagination" (pp. 21, 53, 67, 68), a "new way of reading Scripture" (p. 39), and the need to "learn new skills to be mis-sionaries" (Alan J. Roxburgh and M. Scott Boren, *Introducing the Missional Church* [Grand Rapids: Baker, 2009], p. 77). Guder et al. speak of the need for the church to gain a "new vision" (Darrell Guder, ed., *Missional Church: A Vision for the Sending of the Church in North America* [Grand Rapids: Eerdmans, 1998], p. 77). Frost and Hirsch speak of the need for a "paradigm-busting imagination" (p. 7), as well as "a whole new set of skills and assumptions" (Michael Frost and Alan Hirsch, *The Shaping of Things to Come* [Peabody, Mass.: Hendrickson, 2003], p. 81). In *Breaking the Missional Code*, Stetzer and Putnam begin a chapter titled "Emerging Strategies" with the sentence: "Innovation is a good thing" (Ed Stetzer and David Putnam, *Breaking the Missional Code* [Nashville: Broadman & Holman, 2006], p. 108).

[4]According to many missional authors, a Christendom orientation occurs when a congregation, failing to recognize the post-Christian condition of its ministry context, and the marginaliza-tion of the church within it, still thinks of Christianity as the "official" religion of its society,

chief of which are its preoccupation with rationality as the final arbiter of truth and the promotion of an unhealthy, unbiblical, unbalanced individualism.[5] As a result, too many traditional evangelical churches are still attempting to do ministry in an exclusively attractional/institutional manner—"if you build it, they will come."[6] It is over against a traditional, attractional, *institutional* way of doing church that the need for a more *missional* model is presented.[7] Alan Roxburgh and Scott Boren write:

> The church is God's missionary people. There is no participation in Christ without participation in God's mission in the world. The church in North America to a large extent has lost this memory to the

and as a result does not recognize the need to adopt a missionary posture toward it. For example, see Guder, *Missional Church*, pp. 3, 5, 6-7. See also Frost and Hirsch, *Shaping of Things to Come*, pp. 13-21, 30; and Douglas John Hall, "Metamorphosis: From Christendom to Diaspora," in *Confident Witness—Changing World*, ed. Craig Van Gelder (Grand Rapids: Eerdmans, 1999), pp. 67-79.

[5] See Guder, *Missional Church*, pp. 21-23, 25; Roxburgh and Boren, *Introducing the Missional Church*, p. 60; and Walter C. Hobbs, "Faith Twisted by Culture: Syncretism in North American Christianity," in *Confident Witness—Changing World*, ed. Craig Van Gelder (Grand Rapids: Eerdmans, 1999), pp. 96-98, 103-5.

[6] See Roxburgh and Boren, *Introducing the Missional Church*, pp. 17, 81. See also Frost and Hirsch, *Shaping of Things to Come*, p. 19; and Stetzer and Putnam, *Breaking the Missional Code*, p. 65. Missional authors will also speak of postmodernity as an aspect of our cultural context that needs to be taken into consideration, but the emphasis tends to be more on how to contextualize ministry for those who have embraced postmodernism versus any sort critique of how it has overly influenced traditional ways of doing ministry. Thus in most discussions of this type, it is the influence of modernity that must be overcome by way of the missional endeavor. This explains why, though Roxburgh and Boren are careful to distinguish between the missional and emergent movements, the two movements are so often confused. The common denominator is a laudable commitment to do ministry in an increasingly postmodern context (see Roxburgh and Boren, *Introducing the Missional Church*, pp. 53-54). For their part, Stetzer and Putnam also want to point out this distinction. However, they go on to express more concern over the tendency of some (not all) in the emerging movement who, in the attempt to reach the emerging generations, are willing to revise the ministry message itself as well as the method (see Stetzer and Putnam, *Breaking the Missional Code*, pp. 187-91).

[7] It should be borne in mind that in *Worship and the Reality of God* theologian John Jefferson Davis engages in a discussion of the kind of churches that will constitute the "next evangelicalism" and suggests that, going forward, evangelical churches functioning in our post-Christian environment should strive to be earmarked by the attributes *deep*, *thick*, *different*. In the process Davis seems to be describing a version of a missional church that, while committed to taking seriously its call to local mission, also maintains a strong commitment to historic theological orthodoxy and an ancient-modern approach to worship. This would seem to suggest a blending of missional and traditional-attractional (though not institutional) approaches to ministry (see John Jefferson Davis, *Worship and the Reality of God* [Downers Grove, Ill.: IVP Academic, 2010], pp. 25-32; see also note 14 of this chap.).

point that mission is but a single element in multifaceted, program-matic congregations serving the needs of its members. The gospel is now a religious message that meets the needs of self-actualizing indi-viduals. But the North American church is being invited by the boundary-breaking Spirit to discover once again its nature as God's missionary people. *This will mean going against the stream of most church life at this moment in time.*[8]

In other words, the advocates of the missional church are pleading with the rest of the evangelical world to realize that we are now living in an increasingly postmodern, post-Christian world. We live in Athens, not Jerusalem. As a result, a different way being both a Christian and the church is required!

Okay, but different how?

In this chapter my goal is to identify in necessarily broad strokes how some of the primary spokespersons for the missional church movement are attempting to answer this very question, and in the process to sug-gest some ways that the dynamic of prophetic activity is crucial to a missional approach to being the church in a post-Christian ministry context.[9]

Exploring some of the more prominent works devoted to the theme of missional church, several words keep coming to mind: *incarnation, imagination, innovation, contextualization* and *representation*. These, and other words like them, translate in the literature into two crucial missional ministry dynamics. At the risk of greatly oversimplifying things, I want to suggest that the goal of missional communities is (or should be) to engage in a faithful *representation* of the reign of God in-carnated into a particular ministry location by means of whatever meth-odological innovations are the result of an imaginative engagement in the process of ministry *contextualization*.

So the two main ministry dynamics are *contextualization* and *repre-sentation*. However, many missional church authors suggest that once

---

[8]Roxburgh and Boren, *Introducing the Missional Church*, p. 45, emphasis added.
[9]My primary dialogue partners in this endeavor will be missional leaders such as Lesslie New-bigin, the multiple authors of *Missional Church*, the several authors of *Confident Witness—Changing World*, Roxburgh and Boren, Frost and Hirsch, and Stetzer and Putnam.

Christ's followers follow his lead and "pitch their tents" in their respective neighborhoods in an *incarnational* manner,[10] a careful engagement in a missional ministry contextualization will require an *imaginative* dialogue with both the Scriptures and the cultural context that will likely lead to an adoption of theological as well as methodological *innovations*. This is an important part of the missional discussion. Aware of the perennial need to guard against a theological accommodation to the zeitgeist (cultural ethos) at work in any age or geographical locale, some evangelicals will tend to view with grave suspicion just about any talk of theological innovation being effected on the basis of a consideration of the cultural realities at work in a ministry context.[11] To some degree I can identify with this concern to "contend for the faith that was once for all delivered to the saints" (Jude 3).

That said, my goal in this chapter is to provide some biblical support for the two main ministry dynamics referred to—*contextualization* and *representation*—and to indicate how the prophetic activity described in the previous chapters can help those of us living in the post-Christian West to accomplish these crucial ministry dynamics in a manner that is both missionally faithful and hopeful.

PROPHETIC ACTIVITY AND AN IMAGINATIVE MINISTRY CONTEXTUALIZATION

Michael Frost and Alan Hirsch provide their readers with this rather formal definition of what it means to contextualize the gospel:

> Contextualization, then, can be defined as the dynamic process whereby the constant message of the gospel interacts with specific, relative human situations. It involves an examination of the gospel in light of the respondent's worldview and then adapting the message, encoding it in such a way that it can become meaningful to the respondent. Contextualization attempts to communicate the gospel in word and deed and to establish churches in ways that make sense to people within their

---

[10]See Roxburgh and Boren, *Introducing the Missional Church*, p. 32.

[11]Many evangelicals continue to struggle with the idea that in addition to Scripture, tradition and culture constitute actual *sources* for the doing of theology. See Stephan Bevans, "Living Between Gospel and Context," in *Confident Witness—Changing World: Rediscovering the Gospel in North America*, ed. Craig Van Gelder (Grand Rapids: Eerdmans, 1999), pp. 142-43.

local cultural context. It is primarily concerned with presenting Christianity in such a way that it meets peoples' deepest needs and penetrates their worldviews, thus allowing them to follow Christ and remain in their own cultures.[12]

There is a sense in which ministry contextualization is what being missional is all about. While an embrace of this dynamic is not limited to the missional movement, the literature devoted to the missional church clearly indicates that the practice of contextualization lies at its very heart. For example, Roxburgh and Boren speak of the importance of contextualization to missional life:

> Each of our contexts is unique; each has its own particular intermixing of cultural interactions. The gospel, therefore, must always be understandable in the language and thought patterns of that context. Specific forms of missional church, therefore, will be constructed locally. The primary need is for local strategies of engagement with the people in the neighborhoods, which is why it is so important for churches to become skilled in listening to their own setting. Missional life emerges from the kind of listening that connects us with what God might be up to in a particular context.[13]

For my part, it is precisely this enthusiastic emphasis on contextualization that arouses my interest and elicits my qualified support for the missional movement.[14]

---

[12]Frost and Hirsch, *Shaping of Things to Come*, p. 83.

[13]Roxburgh and Boren, *Introducing the Missional Church*, p. 87. See also Richard Mouw, "The Missionary Location of North American Churches," in *Confident Witness—Changing World*, ed. Craig Van Gelder (Grand Rapids: Eerdmans, 1999), pp. 3-15.

[14]I speak here of a "qualified" support due to the fact that I share the concern of some evangelicals, both without and within the missional church movement, that some expressions of the missional movement have tended to neglect the disciple-making dimension and the importance of belonging to the church, focusing instead almost exclusively on its social action component. Furthermore, I am also concerned that reading some missional authors can give the impression that if a church spends any significant amount of effort conducting worship or teaching gatherings to which the unchurched are invited in the hope that they might experience the convicting, regenerating work of the Holy Spirit, this is an indication that the church is de facto still rooted in an "attractional" versus "missional" ministry paradigm. In other words, the impression given by some missional works is that we must choose between being missional and conducting worship or teaching events to which the unchurched are invited to attend. To their credit, Frost and Hirsch will sometimes contrast missional with *institutional* instead of attractional. This slight change in nomenclature rightly portrays the reality that a church can conduct an "attractional" event to which the unchurched are invited without at the

To some degree, my appreciation of the practice of ministry contextualization stems from my own work as a pastor/church planter. In the course of my three-decade-long ministry as the primary leader-teacher in a couple of established churches and one church plant, I came to recognize how important it is to communicate the gospel in a way that allows people to fully grasp its meaning for life both now and in the age to come. Indeed, while the ministry of the local church involves much more than preaching and teaching, there is a sense in which effective preaching and teaching—something I refer to as "prophetic" preaching and teaching—always involves a serious engagement in the ministry art of contextualization—a prayerful interaction with the cultural context, the biblical texts and the Holy Spirit.

This concept of prophetic preaching is something I will return to later in this chapter. But for now let me hasten to add that beyond my personal experience as the leader of a local church, my embrace of ministry contextualization is also based on a recognition of the support it receives from a thoughtful reading of the New Testament.[15]

Doubtless, most readers of this book are aware of the famous passage in which the apostle Paul seems to be referring to his practice of ministry contextualization:

> Though I am free and belong to no man, I make myself a slave to everyone, to win as many as possible. To the Jews I became like a Jew, to win the Jews. To those under the law I became like one under the law (though I myself am not under the law), so as to win those under the law. To those not having the law I became like one not having the law (though

---

same time defining itself in institutional terms, i.e., "as an institution to which outsiders must come in order to receive a certain product, namely, the gospel and all its associated benefits" or as a sanctified space "into which unbelievers must come to encounter the gospel" (Frost and Hirsch, *Shaping of Things to Come*, pp. xi, 12). Stetzer and Putnam also caution against an overreaction in this regard, allowing room in their missional paradigm for a church to conduct attractional events while still seeking to impact its community in an incarnational manner. In point of fact, Stetzer and Putnam not only presume attractional worship gatherings but suggest that inviting the unchurched to experience them is key to both evangelism and disciple making (see Stetzer and Putnam, *Breaking the Missional Code*, pp. 65, 102-7, 145-52). In other words, a church can do attractional events without buying hook, line and sinker into an institutional ecclesiology, and can conduct some "attractional" gatherings while still functioning in an essentially missional (noninstitutional) manner within its community.

[15]See Frost and Hirsch for a similar though longer discussion of the biblical support for the practice of contextualization (Frost and Hirsch, *Shaping of Things to Come*, pp. 84-88).

I am not free from God's law but am under Christ's law), so as to win those not having the law. To the weak I became weak, to win the weak. I have become all things to all men so that by all possible means I might save some. I do all this for the sake of the gospel, that I may share in its blessings. (1 Cor 9:19-23)

This passage serves as strong biblical support for the concept of ministry contextualization, suggesting as it does that Paul was in the habit of altering his basic ministry approach in sensitivity to the sociocultural context of each ministry location.

More support for the practice of ministry contextualization can be found in the book of Acts, where we discover that though the gospel message itself seems not to have changed from location to location in the apostle's missionary travels, the homiletical method used to deliver it certainly did. Apparently, Paul was in the habit of varying the manner of communicating the gospel, depending on the degree to which the people in each location were committed to the authority of the Hebrew Scriptures. So, the sermon Paul delivered in the synagogue located in Pisidian Antioch (Acts 13:13-41) abounds with references to the Old Testament, while the one directed at the Athenian philosophers gathered at the Areopagus (Acts 17:22-31) is completely void of biblical references, but contains an allusion to an idea put forward by several Greek philosopher-poets (Acts 17:28).[16] It made a difference whether the apostle was in Asia or Athens, not in terms of his ultimate message but with regard to his method.[17] Though both of Paul's sermons culminated with a bold announcement of Christ's resurrection (Acts 13:37; 17:31), the rhetorical route to that sermonic denouement differed dramatically. We should be careful to note as well that the texts under consideration seem to imply that Christian disciples were made as a result of both preaching events (Acts 13:43; 17:34). Because of the faithfulness of the Spirit of mission, disciples can be made in any sociocultural context, even Athens!

Going beyond this more familiar biblical support for the concept of ministry contextualization, Roxburgh and Boren have put forward a

---

[16]See I. Howard Marshall, *Acts*, Tyndale New Testament Commentaries (Downers Grove, Ill.: InterVarsity Press, 2008), p. 289.

[17]See Stetzer and Putnam, *Breaking the Missional Code*, pp. 94-95.

couple of other observations. First, in a section titled "The Missional God: Jesus as a Contextual Theologian," these missional authors point out that

> John tells us in his Gospel, "The Word became flesh and dwelt among us" (John 1:14 NKJV). Eugene Peterson paraphrases this verse, "The Word became flesh and moved into the neighborhood" (Message). John uses *Word* to communicate a radical message: the Word is Jesus and the Word came to earth and showed us who God is. Jesus' way of being a theologian was to embody God in a local setting. He came to earth not in an ideal time, an ideal way, or with an ideal plan. He did not come to all people at all times in some kind of universal way of the mystics or philosophers. He came in a very particular way to a particular people at a particular time in history. He moved into the neighborhood of Galilee and demonstrated there who God is.[18]

The implication is that just as Jesus' incarnational approach to ministry was contextually particular, so should ours be.[19]

Another move in support of ministry contextualization is made by Roxburgh and Boren when they suggest that the composition of the New Testament as a whole was itself an exercise in ministry contextualization. In support of this bold thesis they argue that many of Paul's letters (especially his letters to the Ephesians and the Corinthians) were attempts to address the particular issues at work in each ministry location, and to do so in such a way as to equip the letters' recipients to "awaken to what was happening around them as well as to ask how God might be calling them to shape their lives in that context."[20] Based on this observation, and making use of a hospitality/table-setting metaphor, Roxburgh and Boren assert that the New Testament is about "ordinary men and women waking up to their neighborhoods and figuring out how to be the kinds of cooks who set the gospel table using local ingredients,"[21] and that

---

[18]Roxburgh and Boren, *Introducing the Missional Church*, p. 94. See also Guder, *Missional Church*, pp. 13-14.

[19]See Guder, *Missional Church*, p. 14; and Frost and Hirsch, *Shaping of Things to Come*, pp. 35-41.

[20]Roxburgh and Boren, *Introducing the Missional Church*, p. 98.

[21]Ibid., p. 97.

Paul and the other New Testament writers were continually dong this kind of theology. They were not trying to be abstract and difficult. They were awake, listening to their neighborhoods and the communities where these little households of God were springing up, and they kept asking, "What kind of table does God want us to set in the name of Jesus in the midst of these particular sounds, smells, and sights?"[22]

The proponents of the missional movement insist that a contemporary engagement in the process of ministry contextualization, in order to qualify as missional, must involve an *imaginative* dialogue between the scriptural text and the cultural contexts. The purpose of this conversation is to help us discern what God is already up to in this ministry location so we can cooperate with it.[23] Sometimes, this process of theological discernment, if engaged in *imaginatively*, will lead to new, *innovative* ministry approaches designed to reach people who, in terms of what comprises the target audience of most traditional churches, are not the usual suspects.[24]

So, a new focus on some new people living nearby that utilizes some new methods of getting the gospel to them: is that all there is to the kind of innovation that comes to mind when we read many missional books? Not quite, for many missional authors will speak of the need for traditional evangelicals to experience a "fresh hearing of the gospel."[25]

I am convinced that a careful examination of most missional works will assure most evangelicals that references to the possibility of theological innovation and use of the phrase "a fresh hearing of the gospel" need not signify a move away from the core components of historic Christian orthodoxy. These exhortations seem rather to suggest that a pedestrian, populist understanding of the gospel that makes it all about personal sin management, that promotes the concept of cheap grace and that serves to produce nominal, consumerist, spectator-oriented church members unwilling to engage in any sort of disciple making, social action or creation care must be reevaluated in light of

---

[22]Ibid., 99.
[23]Ibid.
[24]Frost and Hirsch, *Shaping of Things to Come*, pp. 42-43.
[25]Guder, *Missional Church*, p. 86.

not only the sensibilities at work in our post-Christian ministry context but also what the Bible actually has to say about the kingdom (or reign) of God.[26]

With this I am in hearty agreement.

At the same time, I will press on to offer a minor but profoundly important *enhancement* to the process of theological or methodological innovation as it is presented in these missional works. The proposed enhancement is this: *that which is more or less implied in these works—that the Holy Spirit will speak to us through our imaginative dialogue with the biblical text and cultural context—needs to be made more explicit.*[27] In other words, given what we have learned about the prominence of prophetic activity among the earliest Christians and those who are currently ministering in the Majority World, *the process of ministry contextualization should be said to involve a conversation with three entities not two: the biblical text, the cultural context and the Spirit of mission!*

A biblical example of prophetic activity precipitating a new ministry method (praxis). The Bible would seem to support this call for a greater emphasis on the role of the Spirit in the process of ministry contextualization. One of the principal biblical texts illustrative of the concept of a theological innovation leading to new ministry praxis (practice) is the story presented in Acts 10 of Peter overcoming his ethnocentrism and provincial understanding of the gospel in order to become the first of Jesus' apostles to preach the gospel to a Gentile audience. A close look at Acts 10 will show that Peter's engagement in this new ministry praxis was the result of his having arrived at a new or fresh understanding of the gospel: that it was actually intended by God to function as good news for Gentiles as well as the Jews. Christian believers may take this insight for granted now, but in Peter's time and place this unheard of theological position would have been fiercely resisted by just about all of his fellow Jewish church members, including his apostolic peers! And yet Peter courageously acted on this new theological insight into

---

[26]Ibid., pp. 86-97; Roxburgh and Boren, *Introducing the Missional Church*, pp. 45, 70.

[27]Roxburgh and Boren do refer at least once to the fact that the end result of building relationships with people in a ministry context is that we will "hear all the clues about what the Spirit is calling us to do as the church in that place" (Roxburgh and Boren, *Introducing the Missional Church*, p. 85).

the nature of the gospel and boldly preached the gospel to Cornelius and his household. This was a game-changing move on Peter's part. The history of the Christian movement was altered because of it. Surely this is an example of the kind of imaginative ministry contextualization that many missional authors would advocate.[28]

And yet another important fact to be noted about this story is that it contains a plethora of references to the dynamic of prophetic activity— the Holy Spirit speaking to or through human beings on behalf of the kingdom of God. To be more specific, the Acts 10 passage reveals that this new understanding of the gospel came to Peter not as he dialogued with the biblical text and the cultural context, but as he interacted with the Spirit of mission.[29] Moreover, it is also important to keep in mind that this interaction with the Spirit was not the result of any missional initiative on Peter's part; the Holy Spirit initiated this important prophetic encounter (Acts 10:13, 15, 20)! Finally, we must also keep in mind that the two things indicating to Peter that God was indeed at work in this ministry context and should be cooperated with—which emboldened Peter to not only preach the gospel to Gentiles but to baptize them as well—were likewise incidents of prophetic activity: Cornelius's prior conversation with an angel (Acts 10:3-7), and Peter's sermon being interrupted by this group of Gentiles "speaking in tongues and praising God" (Acts 10:44-46).[30]

---

[28]See Lesslie Newbigin, *The Gospel in a Pluralist Society* (Grand Rapids: Eerdmans, 1989), p. 124.

[29]Interestingly, as George O. Wood points out when conducting tours of the Holy Land, this interaction with the Spirit took place while Peter was in Joppa, a sea-coast town famous for being the site from which the prophet Jonah, another Jew who struggled with the idea that God's mercy extended to Gentiles, attempted to flee to Tarshish.

[30]Of course, it may be asked at this point if the concept of theological innovation based on such things as prophetic activity and observations of what God is *apparently* up to in a certain ministry context might not open the door to theological and ministry accommodation, perhaps even heterodoxy in terms of both belief and practice. This concern was addressed by the late Ray Anderson in his book *The Soul of Ministry: Forming Leaders for God's People*. According to Anderson, before we break with long-established theological and ministry tradition, we must be able to point not only to the sovereign activity of the Spirit in people's lives, but also to *a theological antecedent presented in sacred Scripture*. Anderson asserts that the story told in Acts 10 of Peter breaking with tradition to baptize Gentiles into the church illustrates this dynamic. The story told in Matthew 12:1-8 of Jesus allowing his disciples to pick and eat grain in an apparent violation of the Jewish sabbath is another. Both of these stories indicate, says Anderson, the Bible's own awareness that new ministry structures are sometimes required when it becomes apparent that a ministry response that is faithful to the heart of God requires it in this

Thus, it is my contention that the story related in Acts 10 does more than support the concept of an experience of theological innovation/illumination that leads to methodological innovation; it also supports my contention that the Holy Spirit should be expected to play a much more explicit role in such a process than the missional literature tends to allow for.[31] *A genuine missional faithfulness calls for evangelicals to be open to the possibility of occasional experiences of prophetic activity that may indeed lead to the kind of ministry contextualization the missional movement seems eager to promote.*

---

particular circumstance. In other words, the "ministry structures" we find presented in Scripture should not be considered sacrosanct—as ends in themselves—but as means to a greater end—the actualization of the will or reign of God. So, as we read the biblical narrative, we should be careful to look past the specific ministry structures we find promoted there, attempting to zero in on the big picture, the *telos*, ultimate purpose or inner logic of what God is really up to in people's lives. If we find ourselves in a ministry context such as Peter did in Acts 10 or Jesus himself did in Matthew 12 where it becomes apparent that an innovative ministry structure (a new wineskin) is required in order for the message of God's astounding grace and offer of new life through Christ (the new wine) to be manifested in this situation, we have not only the freedom but also the responsibility to engage in a new ministry praxis (see Ray Anderson, *The Soul of Ministry* [Louisville: Westminster John Knox, 1997], pp. 17-24, 124-28). Still, it may be that Anderson's use of the term *innovation* will remain problematic for some evangelicals concerned that the concept of theological innovation will open the door to the practice of theological accommodation because it can sound like we are talking about the possibility of a new revelation or a new truth rather than a new understanding of truths previously revealed in Scripture. In response I make the observation that since Anderson very clearly referred to the requirement of a theological antecedent observable in Scripture, some of us might prefer to think in terms of an experience of theological *illumination* (rather than innovation) that leads to new ministry praxis. The illuminating work of the Spirit is something Jesus told his disciples to expect (e.g., see Jn 16:13-15) and that Paul refers to in his writings (e.g., 1 Cor 2:9-16). Furthermore, in the case of the theological innovation illustrated in Acts 10, the inner logic of God's saving concern for Gentiles as well as Jews is present as a theological antecedent in both the Old Testament Scriptures and the Gospels (e.g., see Gen 17:4; 22:18; Ps 2:8; 86:9; Is 42:1, 6; 49:6; Mt 8:5-12; 28:19; Jn 10:14-16). Thus, perhaps it is possible to think of the Spirit *illuminating* previously revealed theological truths to Peter and the Jerusalem church rather than "new truth" being arrived at by them via an "innovative" process. In other words the new ministry praxis stemmed from a spiritual illumination rather than a theological innovation. For their part, Guder et al. suggest that because of the work of the creating and inspiring Spirit of God, "neither the church nor its interpretive doctrine may be static. New biblical insights will convert the church and its theology" (Guder, *Missional Church*, p. 12). It should be noted that the emphasis here seems to be on new insights into previously revealed truth rather than the revelation of truths that are entirely new.

[31]To the person who might want to minimize the importance of this story to Christian history, arguing instead that it was the apostle Paul's embrace of the idea that the gospel is also for the Gentiles that had the greatest effect on the movement as a whole, I would point out that it is reasonable to presume that the manner in which Paul was first introduced to this concept was likewise an experience of prophetic activity: Ananias received it from the Lord and then passed it on to Saul (Paul) (see Acts 9:15-16).

Contemporary examples of prophetic activity precipitating new ministry praxis. Though the biblical support is primary, a second justification for a greater emphasis on the role of prophetic activity in the ministry contextualization process is that contemporary examples of this dynamic are readily available. For example, in *Introducing the Missional Church* we read of a retired white couple that, inspired by their church's new commitment to becoming more missional (i.e., having experienced a fresh hearing of the gospel), moved closer to their church's building even though the neighborhood around it was now "primarily Black-American." Wanting to impact the neighborhood for Christ, the wife (Mary) began a journey down the main street, speaking to shopkeepers about ways the church might be of help to the community. When one shopkeeper "unceremoniously told her to leave and not come back," she was understandably shaken. But as she and her small group prayed about this situation, so the story goes, "God gave Mary a new imagination." In other words, in some way or another, the Spirit spoke to this woman, providing her with an innovative approach to building relationships with her new neighbors. As Roxburgh and Boren report it, this retired couple routinely walked down the main street with garbage bags, picking up litter along the way. As time passed, the members of the community began to nod in acknowledgement of what this retired couple was doing. A full year later, the shopkeeper who had been so rude to Mary invited her in for some coffee. A conversation began that eventually turned into a coalition of community members, out of which there eventually emerged a plan to develop housing within the neighborhood. Roxburgh and Boren cite this story to indicate how ordinary church members can engage in an imaginative process of ministry contextualization. I refer to this story because the methodological innovation it depicts is reported to have come into focus as a result of an experience of prophetic activity.

Furthermore, as the story related in the first pages of this book indicates, I have had my own experiences of a Spirit-empowered engagement in ministry contextualization. One particularly interesting incidence of this phenomenon occurred several years ago when my wife Patti and I sensed the Holy Spirit leading us to plant a new church.

This was a bold decision on our part that required both of us to acquire "tent-making" jobs to make ends meet (we had two kids living at home at the time).

I had been working as an adjunct professor at a Christian liberal arts university for several years prior to this ministry move. In addition to continuing this part-time work at the university, I did what was necessary to earn the emergency credential California requires of anyone wanting to function as a substitute teacher in one of its public schools. In this way I not only began a brief but memorable career as a substitute high school teacher but also put myself in a situation where a prophetic encounter with the Holy Spirit would precipitate a very innovative engagement in missional ministry.

Introvert that I am, it did not take me long to figure out that arriving at a new school every day in order to face five or six large classes of high school students, many of whom had little or no respect for substitute teachers, was not a comfortable experience. At the same time, it was genuinely frustrating to be around so many young people who desperately needed Christ, and yet, because of church-state separation constraints, to not be able to initiate the kind of ministry conversations that would enable me to speak plainly of him.

So I prayed—hard. I remember praying very specifically *asking God to give me a strategy* that would enable me within the first few minutes of each class session to build a rapport with a new group of students, and that despite the legal constraints would enable me to generate any ministry conversations with these public high schoolers that the Spirit of mission knew needed to happen.

How does this story end? Without going into too many details I can report that within minutes of saying this prayer, I began to conceptualize a strategy that would prove to be successful at (1) humanizing me in the eyes of the students, (2) beginning each session on a positive, fun and humorous note, (3) getting the high school students thinking and talking enthusiastically about a controversial, provocative, intellectually stimulating theme, and (4) eliciting from the students questions regarding my other careers as a college professor and a church planter, and, most importantly, my Christian worldview. It was genius and worked like a charm (so to speak). I ended up serving as a substitute teacher in a public high school for only half a year, but in that time I was able to speak and act into the lives of thousands of high school students in the name of Christ, offering pastoral counsel to many, material support to a few and actually praying with one student in between class sessions as he surrendered his life to the reign of God. But, then again, what should we expect? This unique missional strategy was from God—the Spirit of mission—as a result of an honest-to-goodness experience of prophetic activity that enabled a powerful engagement in ministry contextualization.

Hence, my call for a greater emphasis on the role of prophetic activity in the missional ministry contextualization process. I would like to think that Lesslie Newbigin would agree with this attempt at an enhancement. The following quote by the doyen of the missional church movement concludes his essay "Contextualization: True and False." In this brief excerpt we find Newbigin weighing in on some issues related to that imaginative dialogue that must take place for a missional contextualization of the gospel to occur. In the process he not only gives the nod to the primacy of Scripture over the cultural context, he also strongly emphasizes the role of the Holy Spirit working prophetically in the lives of everyone involved. He writes:

> Of course it is always required of us that we listen sensitively to both the desires and the needs of people, and that we try to understand their situation. But neither these desires and needs, nor any analysis of their situation made on the basis of some principles drawn from other sources than Scripture, can be the starting point for mission. The starting point is God's revelation of himself as it is witnessed to us in Scripture. The dynamic of mission is the presence of God the Holy Spirit with power to convict the world and to bring home the truth of the gospel to each human heart. True contextualization happens when there is a community which lives faithfully by the gospel and in that same costly identification with people in their real situations as we see in the earthly ministry of Jesus. When these conditions are met, the sovereign Spirit of God does his own surprising work.[32]

---

[32]Newbigin, *Gospel in a Pluralist Society*, pp. 153-54.

PROPHETIC ACTIVITY AND A FAITHFUL REPRESENTATION OF THE REIGN OF GOD

As the Newbigin quote indicates, the ultimate goal of a properly contextualized missional ministry is a faithful *representation* of the kingdom of God to a particular ministry neighborhood. With this thought in mind, Roxburgh and Boren have much to say about the need for a missional community to function in its ministry context as a "contrast society" that embodies God's dream for the world.[33] In order for this to occur, say Roxburgh and Boren, the church must not only allow its self-perception to be shaped by the "contrast story" we find in Scripture—a story of God's concern for the redemption not only of individual souls but for a more just world,[34] it must also adopt certain "contrast practices" (such as hospitality, radical forgiveness, the breaking down of social and racial barriers, and self-sacrificial love) made possible by and evidenced through both a personal and communal engagement in the classic disciplines of the Spirit.[35] Roxburgh and Boren go on to indicate that "when God's people adopt God's practices, people outside the church will take notice."[36]

In all likelihood, the idea that by living as a contrast society the church will gain a hearing in a post-Christian culture is dependent on Lesslie Newbigin's discussion of the nature of church's mission in his *The Gospel in a Pluralist Society*. In this work Newbigin famously observes that while the mission of the church is often viewed today as a burden or obligation or duty, in the New Testament era mission seems rather to have begun "with a kind of explosion of joy."[37] This is why, observes Newbigin, we do not find in the pages of the New Testament very many exhortations for church members to be careful to engage in mission or reminders of their duty to do so.[38]

---

[33]Roxburgh and Boren, *Introducing the Missional Church*, pp. 101-11. We hear something of the same message and call in James Davison Hunter's *To Change the World* when the author asserts: "A theology of faithful presence means a recognition that the vocation of the church is to bear witness to and to be the embodiment of the coming Kingdom of God" (Hunter, *To Change the World*, p. 95).

[34]Roxburgh and Boren, *Introducing the Missional Church*, p. 104.

[35]Ibid. pp. 104-8

[36]Ibid., p. 105.

[37]Newbigin, *Gospel in a Pluralist Society*, p. 116.

[38]Ibid., p. 119.

Furthermore, Newbigin insists that preaching in the New Testament era was not viewed as a lecture forced on uninterested ears but rather as a response to a question continually being put to the church by those in the community: "What is going on among you Christians?" This ministry-generating question was prompted by the "new reality" that onlookers saw taking place in the life of the church. [39] That "new reality," asserts Newbigin, was (and is) the resurrected Jesus himself, and in him, the kingdom of God come near. [40] In other places, Newbigin indicates more precisely that the "new reality" at work in the church is the presence in it of Christ's Spirit, the *arrabōn* or foretaste of God's coming kingdom made possible "because of what Jesus has done, because of his incarnation, his ministry as the obedient child of his Father, his suffering and death, his resurrection, his ascension into heaven, and his session at the right hand of God."[41]

A slightly different tack is taken by one of the contributors to *Confident Witness—Changing World*, who avers that

> we are not called to be so much an alternative society, or a countercultural community, as a *parallel community* of God's family. The problem with defining the mission of the church as an alternative society, or a countercultural community, is that its mission usually becomes something that is over against the world. One has to ask the question, "Alternative to what, or countercultural to what?" The answer to this question leads us into defining our priorities over against those of the world. In many cases it even leads us into using the tactics and methods of the world to try to achieve our agenda. How often, in the history of the church, have we seen so-called alternative societies or countercultural communities defining themselves *over against* something, rather than *living for* something.[42]

This emphasis on living *for* rather than *over against* something leads us to the discussions of missional vocation, witness and community that

---

[39]Ibid., pp. 116-17. See also Dan Devadatta, "Strangers but Not Strange: A New Mission Situation for the Church (1 Peter 1:1-2 and 17-25)," in *Confident Witness—Changing World*, ed. Craig Van Gelder (Grand Rapids: Eerdmans, 1999), pp. 117, 118.

[40]Newbigin, *Gospel in a Pluralist Society*, p. 133.

[41]Ibid., p. 120.

[42]Devadatta, "Strangers but Not Strange," p. 116.

are contained in what continues to be one of the most influential books on the missional church ever published—*Missional Church: A Vision for the Sending of the Church in North America.* In this book we find a thoughtful, accessible and compelling call for evangelical churches to function as a contrast society that manifests that new reality by endeavoring to faithfully represent to our respective communities the reign of God.

Missional Church seems reluctant up front to offer a definition of the reign (or kingdom) of God, except to say that it centers in God's mission to restore all creation. The various tantalizingly vague descriptions provided early on in the discussion imply that the reign of God centers in his mission to restore that which was lost as a result of the Fall—a sense of shalom between humans and God, humans and themselves, humans and other humans, and humans and nature.[43] It seems that the authors of this work prefer to allow a more nuanced understanding of the reign of God to emerge gradually as the manner by which missional communities are to represent God's kingdom are discussed. This crucial discussion is introduced this way:

> In what forms should this representation take place? Just how does a community of people go about representing the reign of God among its neighbors near and far? The most likely location for an answer to these questions is the mission of Jesus. His mission, after all, represents the most direct and complete expression of God's mission in the world. Therefore, the church's own mission must take its cues from the way God's mission unfolded in the sending of Jesus into the world for its salvation. In Jesus' way of carrying out God's mission, we discover that the church is to represent God's reign as its community, its servant, and its messenger.[44]

As this quote indicates, the authors of *Missional Church* ground their understanding of what is involved in representing the reign of God in three dynamics present in the life and ministry of Jesus. Thus, they issue a call for churches in the post-Christian West to engage in three

---

[43]See also Hunter, *To Change the World*, pp. 228-30.
[44]Guder, *Missional Church*, p. 102.

ministry means: *community*, *service* and *proclamation*.[45] It is my contention that these three ministry means that were at work in the life and
ministry of Jesus were also at work in the life and ministry of his first
followers, as indicated in the book of Acts. However, when I treated
these same three ministry means in chapter two, I referred to them as
edification, *equipping* and *evangelism*.

With this thought of a thematic parallel in mind, it is interesting to
note that a contributing author to *Confident Witness—Changing World*,
after asserting the need for contemporary churches to get back to the
basics, identifies these three basic ministry dynamics as (1) a renewed
commitment to preach and teach the truth of the Word of God, (2) a
renewed commitment to communal discipleship, and (3) a renewed
commitment to be the place that equips people for ministry.[46] It should
be noted that this view of the ministry agenda of the missional church
also corresponds nicely with my identification of the early church's involvement in *prophetic evangelism*, *edification* and *equipping*.

Tacit support for the attribution of a *prophetic* dynamic to the ministry agenda of the missional church, however it is conceived, can be
found in the fact that, as we have seen, Newbigin seems to ground the
representational ministry of the church not only in the incarnational
life and work of Jesus but also in the person and work of the Holy
Spirit, the *arrabōn* (foretaste) of God's kingdom made possible by the
life and work of Jesus.[47] Thus, there is a sense in which the "new reality" at work in the church—that is, its ability to represent to the world
the presence of the risen Christ and his coming kingdom—is connected
to the Spirit-empowered prophetic activity taking place in and through
the members of the church, Christ's body.

So, in the pages that follow, my aim will be to demonstrate how the
dynamic of prophetic speech and action can enhance the ability of missional churches to effect the kind of *community*, *service* and *proclamation*
that, according to the authors of *Missional Church*, constitute a faithful representation of the reign of God to our post-Christian ministry context.

[45]Ibid., n. 29.
[46]Devadatta, "Strangers but Not Strange," pp. 121-24.
[47]Newbigin, *Gospel in a Pluralist Society*, p. 120.

The call to community. According to the authors of *Missional Church*, just as Jesus in his incarnation and ministry willingly submitted himself to a set of covenant obligations so that in everything he could represent fallen humanity as a whole, and Israel in particular, so Jesus is now represented by the New Israel, the church. The significance of this is that

> before the church is called to do or say anything, it is called and sent to be the unique community of those who live under the reign of God. . . . It is the harbinger of the new humanity that lives in genuine community, a form of companionship and wholeness that humanity craves.[48]

In other words, job one for a missional church is to do its best to model before the world the unity and mutuality that was present in the world before the Fall (see Gen 2:24-25) and that will occur once again in the restoration (Is 2:4). Until then,

> Jesus seeks our oneness with one another "so that the world may believe" that he indeed has been sent by his Father (John 17:21). The church's love and unity holds significance for the world as the visible basis of the gospel's power and legitimacy. In fact, the church is itself the promise of the gospel. The universal invitation to believe the gospel includes the invitation to enter the reign-of-God-produced community of the new humanity.[49]

It should not be too difficult to conceive how the dynamic of prophetic edification can and will enhance the ability of missional churches to represent to those around them a foretaste of God's kingdom community.[50] Remember the story related in chapter two of the

---

[48]Guder, *Missional Church*, p. 103.

[49]Ibid., p. 104.

[50]In *Breaking the Missional Code* Stetzer and Putnam actually prescribe four rather three key ministry dynamics that should make up the ministry agenda of the missional church: evangelism, community, experience and service. It should be noted that in their treatment of the dynamic of "experience," they essentially suggest that churches can represent the kingdom of God to the unchurched by inviting them to witness for themselves "the life that takes place within the Christian community" (Stetzer and Putnam, *Breaking the Missional Code*, pp. 83-86). I contend that the dynamic of prophetic edification as described in chap. 2 of this book constitutes the kind of community "experience" that will prove to be winsome and compelling to those invited to "taste and see" for themselves what the kingdom is like (Ps 34:8; 1 Pet 2:2-3). Indeed, this is one of the lessons we learned from our study of the

Spirit of God prompting me to communicate on Christ's behalf an edifying, hope-producing message of love, concern and affirmation to a church member named Dorothy? I am absolutely convinced that such experiences of community-building prophetic edification are more common than many realize; and yet they still occur less frequently than the Spirit desires.

This potentially controversial conviction is based on several theological, pneumatological and ecclesiological observations: First, many theologians view the Holy Spirit as the eternal personification of the eternal love that exists between the eternal Father and the eternal Son. Second, along with this, many theologians have sought to ground the practice of ecclesial community in the eternal community of love that is our trinitarian God.[51] Third, that the Holy Spirit is all about love is indicated by such passages as Romans 5:5, where we read that God has poured out his love into our hearts by the Holy Spirit, and Galatians 5:22, which indicates that love is the first of the fruits that the Spirit desires to produce in the lives of Christ's followers. Fourth, while some might want to interpret 1 Corinthians 13 as a call from Paul to privilege love over the prophetic gifts referred to in 1 Corinthians 12, I would aver that a careful read of 1 Corinthians 14 will indicate that what Paul was advocating in the pericope made up of these three chapters is the twin ideas that love should be the manner in which the prophetic gifts are exercised (see 1 Cor 14:39), and that a concern to edify others should be the goal of their execution (see 1 Cor 14:4-5). The combination of these four theological, pneumatological and ecclesiological observations lends support to the conclusion that *since love is so very integral to who the Spirit is and what he is about, it should not surprise us to discover him encouraging church members to speak and act toward others in the loving, edifying ways.*

All of this leads me to pose the crucial question: What if more evangelical church members were in the habit of taking seriously the promptings produced by the Spirit to speak and act toward one another

---

Pentecostal-charismatic church in chap. 3.
[51]See, e.g., Stanley Grenz, *Theology for the Community of God* (Grand Rapids, Eerdmans, 1994), p. 27.

in loving, edifying ways? What kind of message concerning the coming kingdom would such spiritually alive, loving communities of faith send to the world around them?[52]

The call to service. The authors of *Missional Church* are careful to explain that a primary manner in which Jesus manifested the reality and nature of the reign of God was by "exercising its authority over brokenness, domination, oppression, and alienation."[53] In particular, it was by way of "his healings, exorcisms, calming of storms, feeding of the multitudes, and raising the dead to life" that Jesus revealed to his contemporaries what God is like and what he "fully intends to bring about at the world's consummation, when all that creation was envisioned and imagined to be is made finally true." These authors say, "The actions of Jesus show forth the horizon of the coming world of shalom—peace, justice, and joy in the Holy Spirit."[54]

Missional Church goes on to suggest that at the heart of everything Jesus did as a servant was a "compassionate response to human need,"[55] and that these many responses were integral to the message he preached.[56] Therefore, the church, if it faithfully represents the reign of God to its contemporaries, will be led by the Spirit to offer compassionate responses to the human need it witnesses in the world. In a particularly powerful passage, these authors explain:

> Our responses may be small and personal: a cup of cold water, a warm blanket, or a visit with cookies and cakes. They may be bold: "Rise up and walk," or the expulsion of evil spirits in the name of Jesus. They may engage the complexities of corporate modern living: pressuring governments and corporations for the sake of the disadvantaged or the ravaged earth, lobbying for just laws, solidarity with oppressed peoples,

---

[52]Though the authors of *Missional Church* are careful to include a section devoted to "The *Koinonia* of the Holy Spirit," which has much to say about the cruciality of the Spirit to Christian community, I am unable to find any references in it to the kind of prophetic activity I have referred to. There is, however, a reference to a Spirit-enabled deliberative process that requires "open conversation in which we listen for the Spirit in the midst of communal dialogue" (see Guder, *Missional Church*, p. 174).

[53]Ibid., p. 104.

[54]Ibid., p. 105.

[55]Ibid.

[56]Ibid., p. 106.

initiatives to cease hostilities among nations, care for marginalized peoples and the creation, or compassionate remolding of socioeconomic structures. Whatever our responses may be, they bring wholeness and dignity to the world and thereby provide a taste of a future in the reign of God under the rule and authority of Christ's lordship. These are signs that invite people to "enter and taste more, to eat and be full."[57]

The idea presented in this passage—that the church's servant responses to human need may be either small and personal, or bold and big—will, I hope, bring to mind a couple of observations I made in chapter two: (1) missional, prophetic acts of compassion can be *spectacularly miraculous* (such as exorcisms and physical healings) or *subtly miraculous* (such as a sacrificial sharing of one's resources with those in need, or a willingness to be reconciled with previously estranged entities), and (2) in the book of Acts (and to a lesser degree in Luke's Gospel) Luke seems to present to us several stories that portray Spirit-filled disciples engaging extemporaneously in acts of compassion (both spectacular and subtle) that are obviously the direct result of a special, in the moment, prophetic prompting to do so.

The following story (related to me by Dan Campbell, the Southern California pastor referred to in chap. 3) illustrates the kind of prophetic equipping (act of compassion) that can result when church members are encouraged to believe that they can be used by God in an Ananias-like manner. According to this remarkable but true story:

> A young man named John (not his real name) had just left our Wednesday evening Bible study. Sitting in his car he prayed, "Lord, we studied tonight about your speaking to Samuel. Do you still speak to people today? If you'll speak to me, I'll try to obey."
>
> On the way home, John passed a convenience store when he heard a loud voice in his head saying, "Buy a gallon of milk!" He slammed on his brakes, pulled over and asked, "Is that you, Lord?"
>
> "Buy a gallon of milk," the voice in his head repeated. This is crazy, he thought. But if it's the Lord, I will obey. Besides, I can always use the milk.
>
> John bought the milk and started home when he heard the voice

---

[57]Ibid., p. 106.

again, "Turn down this street and stop." He did so reluctantly, all the while asking himself, *Am I going crazy?*

Again, the voice prompted him, "Take the milk to that house." The small row house was dark; it was late and the occupants appeared to be asleep.

Reluctantly, John knocked on the front door. Through a window in the door he saw another interior door opening from a lighted room within the home. A man walked down a hallway, opened the front door and simply stood there staring at John. Trembling, John said to the man, "I don't know why, but I felt like I should bring you some milk."

The man grabbed the milk and ran back down the hall shouting in Spanish. A young woman carrying a baby came to the door with tears streaming down her face. She explained in broken English, "We had no money to buy milk for our baby, so I prayed and asked God to send an angel with some milk. Are you an angel?"

John explained his strange urge to bring milk to their house. Then, before he left, he gave them all the money in his wallet to help them buy the groceries they so desperately needed. He left praising God and thanking him that he does still speak today if we will only listen for his voice![58]

I am convinced that the Holy Spirit really is able and willing to prompt acts of compassion that possess this kind of particularity because many years ago, when my wife and I were just a young, impressionable ministry couple, we were the recipients of an act of compassion that was delivered in a prophetically powerful and particular manner.

During our first pastorate Patti alerted me one day to the fact that our property tax payment would soon be due. The problem was that we had no money set aside to pay this bill. So early one Sunday morning I knelt in prayer, asking God to somehow provide the funds necessary to keep this tax payment from becoming delinquent.

Just a few hours later, the morning worship gathering I was presiding over was interrupted near its conclusion by the members of the church's official board. That Sunday turned out to be some sort of national pastor appreciation day, a fact that I can honestly say had completely escaped

---

[58]From an August 11, 2010, email from Dan Campbell of San Juan Capistrano.

my notice. The members of the board called for Patti to join me at the front of the church and then announced to the congregation that, as a token of appreciation, the church was going to underwrite our participation in an upcoming minister's retreat conducted by our denomination.

Standing there in front of the congregation I was doing the math in my head. The amount of money the board had allocated for this retreat would very nearly enable us to pay our property tax bill. Immediately, I knew what I would do: after the day's festivities were over (which included a pot luck celebration replete with skits, testimonies and special music in our honor) I would pull the board aside, explain our predicament to them and get their permission to redirect the church's generous gift toward the payment of our tax bill.

I never got the chance. Midway through the celebration I went to my office to retrieve something Patti needed for one of our kids. As I returned to the fellowship hall, I was met in the hallway by one of our parishioners. She pulled me aside, looked into my eyes, smiled and then pressed a folded check into my hands. She then said, "The Lord spoke to me, letting me know that you and Patti have a need for this." When I unfolded the check I discovered that it represented the precise amount of our property tax bill.

Honestly, this is a true story. There had been no prior conversation between this woman and either Patti or me about our need. This is a genuine account of a church member acting boldly on a holy hunch, functioning prophetically in an equipping servant-like manner. I can verify that this prophetic activity on the part of a church member, coming as it did early in our pastoral career, tremendously strengthened our respect for the priesthood of the laity, our confidence in God's ability to provide for those committed to full time kingdom service, and our own ability to engage in generous acts of compassion toward those in need.

Again, I want to ask: What if more evangelical church members were in the habit of taking seriously the promptings produced by the Spirit to speak and act toward those inside and outside the family of believers in loving, equipping ways (see Gal 6:10)? How many more missionally effective acts of servant-like compassion might be generated? A missionally faithful and hopeful response to the human need all around us can be effected by a recovery of the dynamic of prophetic speech and action.

The call to proclamation. The authors of *Missional Church* go on to point out that Jesus did not simply engage in acts of compassion, he also endeavored to "put into words what was true about his presence and his deeds," to interpret the significance of what people were seeing and experiencing in his ministry.[59] Ultimately, the message of Jesus' preaching ministry was this: "These things you see and hear mean that the reign of God has come among you. Receive it. Enter it."[60]

Placing the emphasis on Jesus' preaching as an interpretation of the meaning and purpose of his actions (rather than viewing his actions as signs demonstrating, illustrating and testifying to the veracity and validity of his preaching), *Missional Church* calls for churches to realize that though the main items on their ministry agenda should be the cultivation of community and engagement in acts of service, these representational ministry dynamics remain "anonymous, ambiguous, and subject to misreading" unless the signature of Jesus is added by means of preaching. These influential missional authors explain that "verbalizing the gospel of Jesus removes the ambiguity. It also renders the reign of God accessible. By it the reign of God is opened to the participation of the whole world. Our words become the way to say of it all, 'It's free! This community is open! You are welcome!' "[61]

While *Missional Church*'s discussion of representation through proclamation definitely centers on the need to invite people to enter into the Christian community rather than into a personal relationship with God through faith in Christ, its authors do concede that Christian proclamation can and should do both.[62] Thus, I deeply appreciate the strong stance the authors of this influential work take on the importance of proclamation, as well as community and service. Toward this end they state unequivocally that

---

[59]Guder, *Missional Church*, p. 106.
[60]Ibid., p. 107.
[61]Ibid.
[62]Ibid., pp. 136-37.

Proclamation is inevitable if our being and doing signify anything at all about the presence of God's reign. If in our being the church, the world *sees* God's reign, and by our doing justice, the world *tastes* its gracious effect, then the call to all on the earth to receive and acknowledge that reign begs to be expressed. That is why Jesus said it is necessary that his followers preach repentance and the forgiveness of sins in Christ's name to all the nations, so that all the nations may hear (Lk 24:47; cf. Rom. 10:14-17).[63]

As I endeavored to indicate in chapter two, we know for a fact that the first followers of Christ took this call to proclamation very seriously. Much of the reign-of-God-representing prophetic activity we see occurring in the book of Acts was both evangelistic and sermonic in nature.

It is my contention that there is such a thing as *prophetic preaching* and that its practice can greatly enhance the ability of evangelical churches and missional communities to represent the reign of God as its messenger. Such preaching occurs within the church, I will suggest, when the theme of the sermon is due to a special prompting of the Spirit, when the study of the pertinent biblical text(s) seems to possess an unusually insightful quality, when the dynamic of serendipity occurs during the acquisition of illustrative material, and when the Holy Spirit seems to "speak through" the preacher during the preaching event, articulating sermonic content the preacher had no intention nor natural capacity to deliver, and then impresses this especially profound content upon the minds and hearts of those listening in an especially powerful manner.

It stands to reason that such preaching will often be highly effective. I suspect there are not very many preachers or teachers reading this book who do not know what I am talking about. People from my faith tradition refer to this experience as the "anointing." While needing to be, as John Stott urges, cautious in this use of this term, we must be careful not to lose it either.[64] The "anointing" refers to something real, precious and valuable that can be missed if those of us engaged in

---

[63]Ibid., pp. 107-8.
[64]John Stott, *Baptism and Fullness* (Downers Grove, Ill.: InterVarsity Press, 1975), p. 70.

preaching and teaching ministries allow a routinization of charisma to occur in our lives through a failure to keep going to the Spirit for help every time we open their mouths for God.[65]

Furthermore, it has been my experience that this kind of anointed sharing concerning Christ and his kingdom can occur outside the four walls of the church as well as within (as the story of my missional ministry to some neighborhood kids hanging out in a local park indicates), and need not be limited to the delivery of a sermon or homily per se (as the story of my missional ministry to my neighborhood friend presented in the opening pages of this book will attest). Finally, I am also committed to the idea that the dynamic of prophetic preaching can be engaged in by rank-and-file church members as well as professional clergy (as my analysis of the growth of Pentecostalism in the Majority World has shown).

So one more time I want to ask: What if more evangelical church members in the West were in the habit of taking seriously the promptings produced by the Spirit to speak and act toward those outside the church building in such a way as to generate ministry conversations that allow for an anointed sharing of the good news concerning Christ and his kingdom? When *genuinely* led and empowered by Christ's Spirit, this kind of representational proclamation ministry, combined with the church's engagement in community and service, will always be effected in a humble, loving, Christlike and, therefore, compelling manner.[66] As a result, we have every reason to believe that a recovery of prophetic activity can enhance the evangelical church's ability to represent the reign of God via proclamation to a post-Christian society in a missionally faithful and hopeful manner.

Incarnation, imagination, innovation, contextualization, representation: *a different way of being a Christian*. The authors of *Missional Church* believe that because of the work of the creating and inspiring Spirit of God,

---

[65]See note 2 of this chapter.

[66]"We need to hear about the Spirit, because one of the most important things the Bible has to say about the Spirit is that the Spirit forms us into the image of Jesus Christ" (James V. Brownson, "Hearing the Gospel Again, for the First Time," in *Confident Witness—Changing World*, ed. Craig Van Gelder [Grand Rapids: Eerdmans, 1999], p. 139).

neither the church nor its interpretive doctrine may be static. New biblical insights will convert the church and its theology; new historical challenges will raise questions never before considered; and new cultural contexts will require a witnessing response that redefines how we function and how we hope as Christians.[67]

This seems to suggest that the agenda of the missional church is profoundly shaped by the Spirit of God providing new insights into the biblical text. These insights may, in turn, have the effect of leading us toward a different way of being a Christian. At the very least, they can lead toward a different way of being the church!

Could it be that the importance of prophetic speech and action to Christian witness is an example of a new biblical insight that might positively impact the life of many missional communities?

The purpose of this chapter has been to examine the reasons why evangelicals living in the West can believe that the kind of missional faithfulness modeled by the first followers of Christ, and observable in the global growth of Pentecostalism, can be effected in our post-Christian context. We have learned that the Holy Spirit has a penchant for involving God's people in the fulfilling of God's mission. It is my contention that a recovery of the biblically supported and historically validated dynamics of prophetic speech and action can enhance our ability to live missionally effective lives in our own ministry context. Yes, it will require a paradigm shift, but we can do this. We evangelicals have always been about the mission. And now we have a missional pneumatology that can greatly assist our endeavor to form missional churches and missionally faithful church members.

In chapter five we will focus on the practical steps evangelical church leaders, denominational leaders and academics must take in order to encourage rank-and-file church members to offer the Holy Spirit a missional faithfulness. My hope is that something presented in this final chapter will resolve any lingering doubts regarding the advisability of our doing so.

---

[67]Guder, *Missional Church*, p. 12.

5

"A Man Named Ananias Came to See Me"

Encouraging Missional Faithfulness Among the Evangelical Rank and File

THE FOLLOWING MINISTRY ACCOUNT illustrates the kind of prophetic missional ministry that can result when evangelical church members living in the industrialized West are encouraged to believe that they can be used by God in an Ananias-like manner.

In *Living Faith: Willing to Be Stirred as a Pot of Paint*, Helen Roseveare, an English physician who served for two decades as a medical missionary in Zaire, relates a powerful and fairly well-known story which demonstrates the kind of prophetic partnerships that can exist between church members back home and the missionaries they send to the field. According to the story, Roseveare had been endeavoring to save the life of a woman experiencing premature labor. Though the woman died, her newborn baby and its two-year-old sister survived. With no neonatal technology at her disposal, Roseveare called for an assistant to fill the mission's only hot water bottle so that it could be used to keep the baby warm during the chilly nights that often occur in that equatorial region. Unfortunately, after a short while the assistant came back and sheepishly reported that the hot water bottle had burst. What to do now? Roseveare arranged for the baby to be placed as safely near the fireplace as possible, and for someone to sleep between it and the door to protect it from drafts.

The next day, while Roseveare was saying prayers with some of the orphaned children associated with the mission, she referred to the tiny premature baby clinging to life and her two-year-old sister who was distraught over losing her mommy. Having also mentioned the burst hot water bottle, she suggested the children pray for God's hand of protection and comfort to be at work in these two lives.

Roseveare was somewhat alarmed, however, when, during the prayer time, an orphaned girl named Ruth boldly and specifically asked God to provide a new hot water bottle for the sake of the baby, and to do so that very afternoon! Furthermore, Ruth's importunate prayer went on to say that, while he was at it, God might also provide a new dolly for the two-year-old sister so she could know how much Jesus loves her. Though a mature Christian of many years, Roseveare blushed at the audacity of the prayer and, frankly, worried a bit about what effect a public prayer such as this might have on the faith of all the children should it prove to be nonperforming. Roseveare explains that though she fully believed that can God can do anything, this particular prayer request seemed to require a logistical impossibility. The most likely source of a new hot water bottle would be a parcel from the members of her church back home in England. She had been in Africa four years up to that point and had never received such a parcel. Furthermore, even if a parcel were to arrive on that particular day, Roseveare wondered, who would think to include a hot water bottle in a package going to someone living near the equator?

However, later that afternoon, while Roseveare was engaged in the training of some nurses, news came to her that there was a car at the front door of the mission. By the time she got to that place in the compound, says Roseveare, the car had gone. But sitting there on a porch was a twenty-two pound parcel. The excited orphanage kids gathered around as Roseveare carefully opened the package and revealed its contents: clothes for the kids, materials for bandages, a box of dried fruit. Then, to her utter surprise, Roseveare pulled out of this unexpected parcel from home—a new hot water bottle!

At this, Ruth, came forward exclaiming that if God had sent the hot water bottle, he must also have sent the dolly too. She reached in and, sure enough, retrieved from it "a small, beautifully dressed dolly." Ruth then asked if she could go with Roseveare to give the dolly to the little two-year-old girl "so she'll know that Jesus really loves her."

Roseveare concludes this amazing account of prophetic equipping this way:

> That parcel had been on the way for five whole months, packed by my old GCU [Sunday school] class, the leader had heard and obeyed God's prompting to send a hot water bottle, even to the equator, and one of the girls had put in a dolly for an African child—five months earlier in answer to the believing prayer of a ten-year-old to bring it "That afternoon!"[1]

This poignant story introduces the main question that will serve as the focus of this final chapter: *What will it take for even more rank-and-file evangelical church members living in the West to become able and willing to behave in an Ananias-like manner: hearing God's voice, receiving ministry assignments from him, prophetically speaking and acting in people's lives, making a difference in the world as a result?*

The material presented in this chapter will be more suggestive than exhaustive, and will not provide a technical discussion of how to effect change in local congregations. My goal is simply to indicate a few first steps that might be taken by local church leaders, denominational officials and members of the academy toward the end of encouraging larger numbers of evangelicals to embrace the missional pneumatology—that is, to recover the ability of the earliest Christians to live missionally faithful lives in the power of the Spirit, offering a persuasive alternative to religious relativism as they do so. Throughout this discussion I will make repeated references to the need for this recovery of prophetic activity to occur in a manner that is neither weird (i.e., superspiritual or off-putting) nor motivated by a perverse desire to either attract attention to the self or exercise control over others.

---

[1]Helen Roseveare, *Living Faith: Willing to Be Stirred as a Pot of Paint* (Fearn, U.K.: Christian Focus, 2007), pp. 56-58.

THE ROLE OF LOCAL CHURCH LEADERS

Clearly, the leaders of local churches, both lay and professional, exercise the greatest degree of immediate influence on the believing and behaving of rank-and-file church members. There are actually quite a few things such leaders can do to increase the number of evangelicals in the West who routinely engage in missional prophetic activity without it becoming weird or perverse in the process. It goes without saying that local church leaders can and should keep reminding church members of the need to be missionally engaged, while modeling for them what a lifestyle earmarked by a missional faithfulness and hopefulness looks like. That said, here are a few other things local church leaders can do.

Missional faithfulness and prophetic activity. Local church leaders can help church members become convinced of the connection between missional faithfulness and prophetic activity. Assuming that the members of our churches are sufficiently motivated toward a missional engagement with the world around them, the next big hurdle is to help them recognize the crucial role prophetic speech and action can play in this regard. It is my hope that this is where the exegetical treatments found in first two chapters may be useful.

Historically, evangelicals are people of the Book. If they can be convinced, truly convinced, that a certain belief or behavior is prescribed in Scripture, they tend to be willing to embrace it regardless of whether it comports with the plausibility structures operative in the surrounding culture. This is one of our strengths as a movement. It needs to be leaned into.

I have rehearsed in many churches, classrooms and conversations the biblical foundation for the idea that prophetic capacity (Spirit-inspired speech and action) should be viewed as an inevitable result of in-filling experiences with the Holy Spirit, and that this kind of prophetic activity best accounts for the phenomenal growth of the early church despite the fact that its surrounding culture embraced religious relativism. The response to this message has been overwhelmingly affirmative. This initial "field testing" of my thesis leads me to believe that a series of thoughtfully prepared teachings based on the first two chapters of this book can have the effect of persuading significant numbers of missionally concerned evangelical church members that it is God's will for them, à la Acts 1:8, to experience a supernatural empowerment to live more missionally faithful lives in the power of the Spirit.

Philosophical presuppositions, theological positions and psychological perspectives. Local church leaders can help church members deal with the philosophical presuppositions, theological positions and psychological perspectives that can have the effect of impeding an engagement in missional ministry in general and prophetic activity in particular. An increasing number of evangelical theologians feel that the contemporary evangelical church in the West has allowed itself to be too influenced by modernism and the Enlightenment project that birthed it. For instance, the late Stanley Grenz expressed a concern about a radical individualism that seems to permeate many evangelical congregations.[2] By itself, such a radical individualist mindset, along with the consumerist mentality that often accompanies it, will obviously prove deleterious to the kind of missional activity we want to see our church members engage in.[3]

Another issue that concerns some theologians is the way many evangelicals, due to an embrace of a hyper-rationalism, have tended to turn Christianity into primarily an intellectual exercise.[4] This dynamic is reinforced when Christians adopt a hard foundationalist epistemology, which essentially holds that such foundational truths as the existence of God and the inspiration of the Bible are rationally provable. When a person begins the Christian journey with a near exclusive focus on the rationality of some foundational truths, it can lead to a hyper-rationalistic approach to everything else.

The problem is that modernism ends up denying the concept of the miraculous because individual miracles cannot be rationally proved nor empirically verified under controlled conditions. Alas, succumbing to

---

[2] Stanley Grenz, *Revisioning Evangelical Theology: A Fresh Agenda for the 21st Century* (Downers Grove, Ill.: InterVarsity Press, 1993), pp. 15-16.

[3] For a scalding critique of the way contemporary church leaders have allowed church members to "maintain a consumer, or client, relationship to the church," see Dallas Willard, *The Divine Conspiracy: Rediscovering Our Hidden Life in God* (San Francisco: HarperSanFrancisco, 1998), p. 301.

[4] Stanley J. Grenz and John R. Franke, *Beyond Foundationalism: Shaping Theology in a Postmodern Context* (Louisville: John Knox Press, 2001), p. 34.

the hyper-rationality of modernism, there are not a few evangelical Christians who are not convinced that miracles really can happen today. Obviously, such a perspective will impede any sort of openness to the experience of prophetic activity we see in the book of Acts.

Reinforcing this dynamic are those theologies that relegate certain workings of the Spirit (especially those involving any sort of prophetic encounters with God) to the biblical era only. Indeed, not a few evangelicals have been taught that any kind of supposed prophetic activity occurring today is surely of demonic rather than divine origin. Obviously, church leaders who are convinced that the Spirit desires to effect today the same kind of prophetic activity we see in the book of Acts will need to address these kinds of philosophical and theological issues in a deft but resolute manner.[5]

Finally, yet another issue that must be taken into consideration is the fact that some evangelical church members are less able at a psychological level to deal with the ambiguity and resulting loss of control that is involved in an Ananias-like lifestyle. Ananias had his day interrupted by an unexpected encounter with God that sent him off on a somewhat

---

[5]I want to recommend once again the excellent book John Jefferson Davis, *Worship and the Reality of God* (Downers Grove, Ill.: IVP Academic, 2010). In this book Davis issues a strong call for evangelical churches located in post-Christian North America to adopt (and practice) a theological realism that is rooted in an ontology of *"trinitarian supernaturalism."* This philosophical understanding of reality is that the eternal, triune God is that which is most real, that to which all physical and virtual realities in our universe owe their existence. Furthermore, because this view embraces the concept of the supernatural, it insists that the universe is an open system in which miracles are possible. Among other things, this means that Christians are justified in taking seriously the possibility of interacting with a *real presence* of God during their times of corporate worship. (I would add that this view also supports the conviction that we are justified in taking seriously the ministry promptings delivered to us by means of the third person of the Trinity, the Holy Spirit, whether or not these ministry promptings occur during the course of a formal worship gathering.) According to Davis, such an ontology, in contradistinction to the ontology of modernity (*scientific materialism*) and of postmodernity (*digital virtualism*), is required if the worship occurring in evangelical churches is going to be renewed (see ibid., pp. 21-25, 197-98) and better equipped to present the "absolute truth of the Bible and the Christian faith" in a compelling manner to people living in an increasing post-Christian, religiously pluralistic ministry context (ibid., pp. 19-20). Toward this end, Davis boldly calls for the evangelical church in the West to unsaddle itself from theological views "that can handcuff the Holy Spirit in the life of the church and blind it to where the Spirit may be working dramatically in the world today." Davis is speaking here of the view known as "cessationism" (ibid., p. 30), which holds that some of the manifestations of the Holy Spirit, especially the prophetic gifts referred to in 1 Corinthians 12–14, ceased once the New Testament canon was fully composed.

scary mission. For people who crave certainty and control, and who abhor ambiguity, reading this story can have an unsettling effect. While I am convinced that to some degree all of us crave a sense of certitude and control, I have found that some people are less able to tolerate ambiguity than others. Though this is not the place for a thorough discussion of the possible reasons for a pronounced inability to live with ambiguity, it should be pointed out that church leaders committed to encouraging missional prophetic activity will need to be sensitive to the fact that some of their church members will require extra care in this regard. We must help these church members see that God has apparently chosen to allow us to live in a world that is filled with paradox and ambiguity, perhaps for the express purpose of creating the need for prayer as well as study and ritual. Sensitive to their psychological predisposition against the experience of ambiguity and loss of personal control, we will need to exercise patience, coaching rather than cajoling these church members into a more experiential life in the Spirit.

We will also need to do our best to provide skittish church members with an ecclesial environment that assuages at least some of their anxieties. Such an environment will be one that is marked by two things: (1) a sense that some biblical and theological discernment is occurring as church members are encouraged to speak and act prophetically in a missional manner, and (2) that some accountability structure is in place that provides safeguards against abuse. The next several suggestions for local church leaders wanting to promote a missional faithfulness through prophetic activity in their churches address these two vital ecclesial needs.

Recognizing problems. Local church leaders can help church members recognize that missional prophetic activity does not have to be weird, should never replace the diligent study of Scripture or set one Christian up to control others. It can be weird; I will be the first to admit it. I have seen church members and leaders abuse the dynamic of prophetic activity in such a way as to promote their own ideas and agendas, or to exercise control over others. I also know that it is possible for church members and leaders to so focus on the phenomenon of prophetic activity that they neglect the diligent and disciplined study of

Scripture. This is why, when speaking on the theme of a missional pneumatology in churches, I am only half joking when I encourage church members to beware of anyone who has had business cards printed that bill the bearer as some sort of prophet, and to avoid becoming involved with any community of believers that fails to recognize that the quality of any prophetic experience should be tested against the clear teaching of Scripture.[6]

Then again, we must also go on to remind jaded church members of the need to beware of the swing of the proverbial pendulum. It is possible to overreact to the abuse of prophetic activity and miss genuine workings of the Holy Spirit in the process. Surely this is why the apostle Paul wrote the church members in Thessalonica saying: "Do not put out the Spirit's fire; do not treat prophecies with contempt. Test everything. Hold on to the good" (1 Thess 5:19-21).

Achieving a sense of balance in the Christian life is seldom easy but always necessary. The good news is that I have found that most evangelicals understand the need for balance and will respond well to repeated exhortations to pursue it in their own walk with Christ, especially when the outcome promises to be a greater missional faithfulness. Thus I am led to believe that we can help our church members see the importance of not allowing a few negative examples to keep the church as a whole from experiencing a genuine empowerment for ministry that comes from the Spirit of mission.[7]

Biblically informed discernment. Local church leaders can provide church members with a biblically informed method by which they can

---

[6]See Clark Pinnock, *Flame of Love* (Downers Grove, Ill.: InterVarsity Press, 1996), p. 134; Gordon Fee, *God's Empowering Presence* (Peabody, Mass.: Hendrickson, 1994), pp. 251-53; Christopher J. H. Wright, *Knowing the Holy Spirit Through the Old Testament* (Downers Grove, Ill.: IVP Academic, 2006), p. 81.

[7]It is toward the end of a *balanced* approach to prophetic ministry that evangelical theologian Clark Pinnock writes these words of admonition: "It is wrong for churches to suppress this gift [prophecy]. The community that silences its prophets is in danger of becoming a Spiritless place. Outwardly things may run smoothly, but inwardly the Spirit is rebuked. Prophecy is a charism that belongs to church life and should not be a rare occurrence. Like tongues, it arises from encountering God and from listening. Teaching is of crucial importance, but the prophets must also be heard. A climate of listening must be formed among God's people" (Pinnock, *Flame of Love*, pp. 134-35). Furthermore, for a thorough and helpful discussion of how local churches can utilize structures and dynamics of discernment that will enable them to hold fast to the good while letting go of that which is not, see ibid., pp. 241-45.

discern between ministry promptings genuinely produced by the Spirit of mission and those that are not. In his account of the process by which he was led of the Lord to become the president of World Vision U.S., Richard Stearns alludes to some prophetic edification he received from one of his friends, Bill Pryce. According to the story, every time Bill, a fundraiser for World Vision, prayed about who the next president of the worldwide relief organization should be, God kept telling him it was going to be Richard Stearns, who was at that time happily serving as the president and CEO of Lenox (the fine china company). What makes this story especially relevant to our discussion is that Bill Pryce was certain that God was speaking this prophetic word to his heart.[8]

Actually, this is an issue that I have been asked about numerous times over the years. Good-hearted church members want to know how they can discern when a "prompting" to speak or act prophetically into someone's life is genuinely from the Spirit or is something they have concocted themselves. Not knowing how to make such a determination has caused many evangelical church members (even those attending Pentecostal-charismatic churches) to simply ignore all ministry promptings altogether. While this is understandable in light of what the Bible has to say about those who "prophesy lies" (see Jer 5:30-31; 14:13-15; 23:25-32; 27:10, 15; Lam 2:14) and "prophesy out of their own imagination" (Ezek 13:17), it can also lead to missed ministry opportunities and a sense of guilt for not having obeyed the voice of the Lord.[9]

I am convinced it does not have to be this way. Church leaders can provide their parishioners with a biblically informed method to determine whether they should act on an internal prompting to speak or act prophetically into someone's life, or ignore such a prompting without feeling any guilt in the process.

First, keeping the paradigmatic story of Ananias in view, I suggest

---

[8]Richard Stearns, *The Hole in Our Gospel* (Nashville: Thomas Nelson, 2009), pp. 30-31.

[9]We should keep in mind that these passages were prompted by a specific historical situation: out of a desire to remain in good stead with their contemporaries, certain "prophets" in ancient Israel spoke "prophetic" words promising peace and safety when, in reality, divine discipline was in the offing. This clarification notwithstanding, the practice of deliberately delivering prophetic words to others that God has not actually authorized obviously should be avoided.

that we do what Ananias did with his prompting experience—take any hesitancy we are experiencing to the Lord in prayer and then see what happens. I believe it is safe to say that if a prompting to engage in prophetic ministry is truly from God, it will be important to the kingdom cause and thus will persist over time despite our initial feelings of ambivalence toward it. Indeed, as in the case of Ananias, it is likely that the more we pray about a genuine ministry prompting, the more we will become ultimately convinced of its kingdom import and be filled with a sense of peace about proceeding with it. If this peace does not come to us straightaway, we should keep praying until it does (it need not take long) or until the "haunting" dynamic dissipates altogether, indicating that the origin of the call was not the Spirit after all.

Second, I have come to view with suspicion those occasions when the Spirit's prompting seems to be urgent or frenetic—to either act now or never, allowing us virtually no time for discerning prayer or reflection. This kind of ministry scenario—which is often accompanied by a sense that if we do not act in haste at this very moment some irreparable, eternal harm to someone will result—seems to lack biblical precedent and strikes me as being inconsistent with Christ's own orderly, unhurried, unflappable, poise-maintaining approach to interpersonal ministry.

Third, keeping not only the story of Ananias and Saul but also the personality of the Holy Spirit in mind, I suggest that because the Spirit of mission is a Spirit of *love* and a Spirit of *hope* (Rom 5:5; 15:13, 30; Gal 5:22-23), we can safely assume that it is never inappropriate to behave toward others in a loving, hope-producing manner. Neither is it ever inappropriate, with an encouraging, edifying motive in place, to communicate to someone the message that the risen Christ knows them, cares for them, wishes good things for them, is there for them and the like. I am not saying that we should in a willy-nilly manner go around telling people that God has told us to say such and such to them if we have not genuinely sensed such a specific prompting to do so. But given the facts that the Spirit of mission is also the Spirit of love and hope, and that so many human beings are so very needy of an experience of both of these dynamics, it should not surprise us if we often sense the Spirit's prompting to communicate through speech or action to a particular person or group of persons the message that because the risen Christ knows them, cares for them and is the Lord of all things despite all appearances, they can hold onto hope despite any adversity or anxiety they are presently experiencing. I am also saying that we can deliver this message with a fair amount of confidence that it is indeed the will of the Spirit of mission to do so. In other words, when trying to discern whether a prompting to communicate to someone the message of Christ's strong, enduring, unconditional love for him or her is actually from the Holy Spirit, our default should be to assume that it is, rather than that it is not. Given the biblically sound and basic nature of the message, and the ubiquity of the need, when experiencing a prompting to deliver such a message to someone, we should rarely feel the need for some sort of confirming sign to do so.

On the other hand, if for some reason we fail to deliver such a message, or do so and then wonder later if this prompting was truly from the Spirit, I suggest that we evangelicals need to allow the powerful promise presented in Romans 8:28 to assuage any anxiety that arises in our hearts: "And we know that in all things God works for the good of those who love him, who have been called according to his purpose."

Fully recognizing the potential for this passage to be abused—to justify all sorts of sinful behavior on the basis of God's ability and commitment to make things turn out okay in the end (see Rom 3:8; 6:1)—and fully aware of those passages previously cited that warn against "prophesying lies," I nevertheless believe the promise contained in Romans 8:28 carries with it an important implication for our current discussion: Given the sovereignty of God and his commitment to cause all things to work for good for those who belong to him and are genuinely endeavoring to please him, we can engage in missional prophetic activity in a supremely hopeful manner. We can speak and act toward others in his name, confident that even if we do commit a prophetic faux pas, inadvertently communicating a message to someone as having come directly from the risen Christ when it really did not, God is able to cause even our missional mistakes to ultimately work for the good of everyone involved. This is one of many occasions in our spiritual journey when a rigorous embrace of a theological realism and a bedrock conviction regarding the faithfulness of the Spirit are revealed. Our engagement in missionally prophetic ministry can and should be informed by our confidence in the fact that God is both sovereign and good.

Once church members recognize that there is a biblically informed method by which they can evaluate whether a ministry prompting is genuinely from the Holy Spirit—a method that will allow them to ignore some promptings without incurring guilt, and to obey others with the same result—many of them experience a new sense of freedom to engage in this kind of missional behavior.

Furthermore, it is my habit to encourage church members to avoid using overly dogmatic language when engaging in prophetic activity. Instead of prefacing every instance of prophetic speech with a bold "Thus says the Lord," all one has to say is "You know, I could be wrong, but I have this strong impression that I am supposed to tell you something that I suspect might be from the Lord. Are you open to hearing it and then evaluating for yourself whether it could be from God?" I have found this approach to prophetic ministry to be a more honest portrayal of my sense of certainty regarding most ministry promptings, more winsome in its effect on those to whom I am endeavoring to minister, and it enables me to act on more ministry promptings than I would were I required to boldly state "Thus says the Lord."

Accountability structure. Local church leaders can provide church members with an accountability structure that will increase the likelihood that their engagement in prophetic activity will be for the right reasons and in ways that are missionally faithful. The suggestion that preceded this one assumes that the motive for engaging in missional prophetic activity is genuinely benevolent and altruistic in intent. This is of crucial importance since Scripture plainly teaches that God is aware of our true motives and that they matter much to him (Prov 16:2; 21:2). Because these passages also suggest that a person's true motives can remain unknown even to themselves, church leaders who want to proactively steer their congregants away from the kind of prophetic activity that ends up being self-serving rather than Christ-honoring can and should encourage them to become accountable to other members in their Christian community with regard to any prophetic ministry activity they engage in. Indeed, it is my contention that *it is incumbent on church leaders to actively help church members evaluate whether their intention when speaking or acting prophetically is genuinely to honor Christ and bless the other, or rather, to draw attention to themselves or to exercise a measure of control over another human being.*

Toward this important end, church leaders might go so far as to insist that church members not consider it spiritually safe (or acceptable) to engage in prophetic ministry unless they are part of small group that can provide some accountability in this regard by routinely posing such accountability questions as (1) Have you recently sensed the Holy Spirit prompting you to speak or act into someone's life on behalf of Christ? (2) Did you obey this prompting, endeavoring to speak and act in a Christlike manner (i.e., doing your best to imitate Jesus' thoughtful, gentle, compassionate and merciful ministry style)? (3) Did you obey this prompting with a selfless rather than selfish motive (i.e., making sure before you acted that you did not stand to gain anything from the encounter)? (4) Did you obey this prompting by being careful to point the person(s) to the loving lordship of Christ (see Acts 9:17, 20)? (5) What was the result?

If the goal is to enable prophetic ministry among rank-and-file evangelical church members that is truly missionally faithful and not simply weird, church leaders should assume the responsibility to proactively cultivate an ecclesial environment that maintains a delicate but important balance between Word and the Spirit, reason and experience, freedom and responsibility, the individual and the group, and a commitment to community and to mission. The best way to do this is to encourage individual charismatic missional activity while also holding church members accountable to the Scriptures and fellow believers.[10] I am convinced that it is possible to encourage this kind of accountability

---

[10]See chap. 10 of my book *Defeating Pharisaism* for a discussion of the fruitful way John Wesley made use of accountability questions in his disciple-making method (Gary Tyra, *Defeating Pharisaism: Recovering Jesus' Disciple-Making Method* [Colorado Springs: Paternoster, 2009], pp. 219-45).

in a way that has the effect of encouraging rather than discouraging genuine prophetic ministry.

Assuming that church leaders are exercising their due diligence toward the cultivation of an ecclesial environment marked by the presence of a thoughtful, biblically informed discernment process and structures that provide a degree of accountability, several other steps can be taken to encourage rank-and-file believers to become missionally engaged through prophetic speech and action.

Routinely gather for prayer. Local church leaders can encourage church members to routinely gather for prayer with other like-minded believers eager to experience ongoing empowerment from the Holy Spirit to live missionally faithful lives for Christ. In *Christianity 101* Gilbert Bilezikian writes: "Every instance of the intervention of the Holy Spirit reported in the New Testament indicates that he cooperates actively in situations where he is expected and wanted."[11] Likewise, a case can also be made for the idea that throughout the history of the church the *charisms* (gifts) of the Spirit (including prophetic activity in general) are manifest whenever groups of spiritually hungry believers have gathered in prayer, seeking a deeper communion with God that would draw them out of themselves and free them to participate in what God is doing and to be more responsive to the prompting of the Spirit in every life setting.[12] Thus, it would seem that a biblically informed (see Acts 1:14) and historically verified way of seeking a recovery of prophetic activity in contemporary evangelical churches is to encourage church members to gather in small groups in order to pray for spiritual empowerment as well as discernment.

I realize that a prevalent fear among church leaders is that things can become weird or unwieldy when church members start meeting together in small groups seeking more of God. To some degree, church leaders may need to become a bit more willing to live with this ambiguity and entrust some outcomes to God rather than trying to control all

---

[11]Gilbert Bilezikian, *Christianity 101* (Grand Rapids: Zondervan, 1993), p. 109.

[12]Many scholars have produced historical surveys that indicate the occurrence of spiritual gifts at various times in the history of the church. See, e.g., Cecil M. Robeck, *Charismatic Experiences in History* (Peabody, Mass.: Hendrickson, 1986); and Allan Anderson, *An Introduction to Pentecostalism* (New York: Cambridge University Press, 2004), pp. 19-38.

aspects of congregational life. On the other hand, there is nothing to say that church leaders cannot be proactive about making sure that each of these small groups of praying, seeking church members is supervised by a mature, responsible leader who, though committed to spiritual renewal, is also able to guide the group as per Titus 1:9.

Stories of reputable believers. Local church leaders can expose church members to the ministry stories of reputable believers that seem to reflect authentic occasions of prophetic activity leading to missional faithfulness. Despite the famous observation made by Mark Twain that "there is nothing more annoying than a good example," the fact is that there is tremendous power in a trustworthy testimony. Hence, when we hear stories of prophetic evangelism, edification and equipping taking place not only in the book of Acts, and not only on the mission field, but in our own communities, we become more inclined to think that this might actually happen to us as well. Church leaders who are serious about wanting to encourage church members to open themselves up to an experience of prophetic activity can be proactive about including credible stories of such missional ministry in sermons and teachings; exposing the congregation to special speakers (including career missionaries) who can share credible accounts of such activity; recommending books, blogs and magazine articles that relate such stories; and providing opportunities for church members to share with one another the exciting details of their own missional experiences. Through these various means it is possible to create a church culture that takes missional prophetic activity seriously.

Engage in spiritual life practices. Local church leaders can encourage church members to engage in certain spiritual life practices that will tend to make them more sensitive to ministry promptings provided by the Spirit of mission. While we never want to fabricate a prophetic ministry assignment, there are certain things Christ followers can do to put themselves in a place where it is more likely they will, like Ananias, genuinely hear the Holy Spirit's prompting to engage in such an endeavor. For example, church leaders can encourage their congregants to supplement their formal study of the Bible with the daily practice of reading Scripture in a prayerful, existential manner. This means that in addition to reading the Bible to sense how the original author hoped his original readers would respond to this or that passage, we are also open to the dynamic of the Holy Spirit, at times, impressing on us a sense that this or that passage is meant for us in a special way. Perhaps the Holy Spirit wants to use a particular passage to provide us with a special sense of encouragement, a special challenge or exhortation or a special word of wisdom or instruction. Again, this does not have to be weird. And clearly the astute Christ follower understands that the Holy Spirit, who inspired the original biblical author to write the biblical passage in the first place, will never use the passage to encourage him or her to believe or behave in a way contrary to the biblical author's originally intended meaning. That said, this existential method of Bible reading, performed regularly, will help church members develop the habit of prayerfully approaching each day open to the idea that the Holy Spirit desires to interact with Christ's followers in existentially meaningful ways.

With this thought in mind, church leaders can also encourage church members to cultivate the habit of continually asking God throughout each day: What are you up to in this situation? Is there something I'm supposed to say or do here? In another book I encourage readers to engage in a daily pursuit of Christ's empowering presence.[13] The idea is that through the agency of the Holy Spirit, it is possible to cultivate an ongoing, moment-by-moment mentoring relationship with the risen Christ. Given the commitment of the Godhead to mission, the assertion that practicing the presence of God should have a missional thrust to it should come as no great surprise. Therefore, my suggestion is that a missionally minded Christ follower should develop the habit of inwardly conversing with Christ throughout the day, inquiring how he or she should respond to this or that situation or interpersonal encounter. Again, the goal is not to fabricate ministry assignments but to increase our sensitivity to any genuine promptings generated by the Spirit of mission.

Descriptions of Christian discipleship. Local church leaders can win

---

[13]Gary Tyra, *Christ's Empowering Presence: The Pursuit of God Through the Ages* (Colorado Springs: Biblica Publishing, 2011).

the hearts of church members with tantalizing descriptions of what the life of Christian discipleship can be like when it involves the phenomenon of prophetic activity. In an article titled "Rethinking Evangelism" Dallas Willard advocates for an approach to evangelism that includes a necessary commitment to kingdom discipleship. Speaking to the issue of how we might interest post-Christians in a biblical concept such as the kingdom of God, Willard writes:

> The real question is, How do you do "evangelism-discipleship?" My short answer: You ravish people with the blessings of the kingdom. You make them hungry for it. That's why words are so important—we must be wordsmiths. You use words to ravish people with the beauty of the kingdom. It's the beauty of the kingdom that Jesus said was causing people to climb over each other just to get in. People become excited like the pearl-purchaser—they will give everything to get in.[14]

I am struck by the profound nature of the basic idea that words are powerful, especially when anointed by the Holy Spirit, and can be used to inculcate within people an interest in something they may not have given much thought to before. In the same way that Christians can pique the interest of post-Christians with tantalizing descriptions of life in the kingdom, church leaders can inspire church members with tantalizing descriptions of what Christian discipleship can be like when it has room within it for prophetic activity.

On the one hand, I am convinced that too many church-going evangelicals are bored. On the other hand, I am equally convinced that it does not have to be this way. In *Traveling Light*, Eugene Peterson writes:

> The word "Christian" means different things to different people. To one person it means a stiff, upright, inflexible way of life, colorless and unbending. To another it means a risky, surprise-filled venture, lived tiptoe at the edge of expectation. . . . If we get our information from the biblical material, there is no doubt that the Christian life is a dancing, leaping, daring life.[15]

---

[14]Dallas Willard, "Rethinking Evangelism," *DallasWillard.org*, September 4, 2010, www.dwillard.org/articles/artview.asp?artID=53. This article originally appeared in the winter 2001 issue of *Cutting Edge* magazine.

[15]Eugene Peterson, *Traveling Light: Modern Meditations on St. Paul's Letter of Freedom* (Colorado

The key to re-inspiring church-goers in their walk with Christ is not simply to exhort them to read their Bibles more, or to expose them to more stirring worship services, or to encourage them to take on an increased responsibility with regard to a ministry program conducted by their church. The key is to have them embrace the idea that Christian discipleship is an exciting, unpredictable adventure that God's Spirit might interrupt at any time, prompting them, as he did Ananias, to engage in prophetic missional ministry in the name of the risen Christ. This can happen. The leaders of evangelical churches can learn how to woo their congregants toward a more missionally effective life in the Spirit. The question is: Will we try?

THE ROLE OF DENOMINATIONAL OFFICIALS

Having addressed the role local church leaders can play in encouraging prophetic activity among the evangelical rank and file, let's do the same with regard to denominational officials. As someone who has served as the senior pastor for three denominationally affiliated churches over thirty-two years, I can attest to the fact that there are certain things denominational officials can do to inspire the leaders of local churches to engage in the important activities described previously.

Focus on the kingdom. Denominational officials can encourage church leaders to focus on the kingdom, not just the denomination. Whether or not it is true that we are currently functioning in a post-denominational era, I believe that it is time for the adherents of all evangelical denominations to ask themselves some searching questions. Chief among them: Is it possible that that some aspects of our traditional approach to ministry are hindering rather than helping our ability to be missionally faithful in an increasingly post-Christian ministry context?

Many religious organizations possess a tendency to make an idol of their distinctive teachings and traditions, viewing them as not only important but indispensable. Jesus confronted this same tendency in his interactions with the Pharisees (see Mt 15:1-9). In order to encourage a

---

Springs: Helmers & Howard, 1988), cited in Charles Swindoll, *The Grace Awakening* (Nashville: Thomas Nelson, 1996), pp. 82-83.

greater number of evangelical church members to become open to the kind of missional prophetic ministry illustrated by the stories in this book, *it may be necessary for local church leaders to deemphasize some denominational distinctives that are not at the heart of the gospel itself.* Because some church leaders may be reluctant to do this out of fear that they might incur ecclesiastical censure as a result, what is needed are some bold, forward-thinking denominational officials who, due to their knowledge of God's Word and a radical concern for the advance of the kingdom, are willing to encourage their church leaders to take a serious look at a more missional pneumatology even if it means becoming more ecumenical and less denominational in the process.

Incarnational and attractional approaches. Denominational officials can encourage church leaders to utilize an incarnational as well as attractional approach to ministry. Church leaders tend to focus on worship service attendance statistics as the primary metric indicating ministry success. Most pastors feel more or less good about themselves depending on how many people were in church last weekend. When pastors gather at denominational conferences, the conversation may eventually get around to the difference each church is making in its neighborhood, but initially church leaders ask each other about the raw numbers of bodies, budgets and buildings. Since this is so, is it any wonder that so many evangelical churches are myopically attractional in their approach?

It may be that this tendency among pastors to focus on numbers is not something denominational officials have much control over, at least not directly. Still, when the ministry success stories heralded by the denomination center on statistical growth, local church leaders receive a certain message: the quickest way to get noticed in this organization is to get as many people as possible into a church service each week!

It does not have to be this way. Taking a longer, larger, more missional view of things, denominational leaders can encourage local churches leaders to engage in ministries that are both incarnational and attractional in orientation. Making a difference in the neighborhood in Christ's name will not only advance the cause of Christ's kingdom, it will likely result in the statistical growth of member churches as well, especially if this missional ministry is prophetic in nature, pointing post-Christians to a version of the Christian faith that is experiential as well as intellectual, and humble rather than arrogant.

Leaders functioning in the power of the Spirit. Denominational officials can emphasize the need for constituent church leaders to function in the power of the Spirit, at the same time easing pastoral concerns about things "getting out of hand." Perhaps the dynamic impeding prophetic activity in a specific ecclesial setting is a theology of ministry that does not acknowledge the need for charismatic activity in the life of the congregation. A church leader may possess a number of natural talents that seem to predict ministry success. Furthermore, his or her training may have been impeccable. This innate giftedness and quality preparation can cause a leader to conclude that all the church needs to be effective is for him or her to work a little harder, do a little more. In such situations it may fall to the denominational official to find ways to communicate to gifted and well-prepared church leaders that there is a power source that must be tapped into if the local church is to fully emulate the style and experience the success modeled by the churches in the book of Acts. Wise and courageous is the denominational official who can and will fulfill this responsibility in a deft manner.

Furthermore, I am convinced that it is possible to encourage missional prophetic activity without things "getting out of hand." It has been my experience that some serious teaching based on the apostle Paul's counsel presented in 1 Corinthians 12–14 is sufficient to keep overeager church members from hurting rather than helping others in the name of the Lord. Nevertheless, evangelical church leaders should be assured that, as they entrust their congregations to the care of the Spirit (being careful to provide good biblical training and accountability structures in the process), should things genuinely get out of hand and some church members need to be lovingly but firmly confronted, the church leaders will have the support and assistance of the denomination.

Inspire pastors. Denominational officials can inspire pastors with tantalizing descriptions of what local church life can be like when a partnership with the Spirit of mission is more than rhetorical! We have already noted that Christians can pique the interest of post-Christians with tantalizing descriptions of life in the kingdom, and that church leaders can inspire church members with tantalizing descriptions of what Christian discipleship can be like when it makes room for prophetic activity. In the same way, denominational officials can and should learn to inspire church leaders with tantalizing descriptions of what church life can be like when a body of believers is empowered for ministry by the same Spirit of mission that turned the world upside down in the earliest decades of church history. It is my belief (hope) that even prophetically wary evangelical church leaders can be emboldened to embrace this missional pneumatology when skillful and passionate denominational leaders cast the vision before them of church members living and growing each day in the power of the Spirit.

THE ROLE OF THE MEMBERS OF THE ACADEMY

The academy gets little respect in some quarters, especially among evangelical groups that do not require an accredited educational degree for ordination. The most common complaint seems to be that, for a variety of reasons, the ministry formation occurring in the classroom cannot help but be impractical.

My own seminary experience was immensely helpful overall. Thus, I know it can be done. Ministry-bound students can experience within the academy a theological education that emphasizes both theory and praxis, and as a result is both inspirational and practical.[16]

My goal in the next couple of pages is to indicate how the members of the academy—Christian college, university and seminary—can well serve the evangelical movement as it relates to the topic of the missional pneumatology. Obviously, academicians need to inculcate within their ministry-bound students the concept of missional ministry in general and the dynamic of missional prophetic activity in particular. And an

---

[16]One of my former students recently told me that he had responded to a critique of his alma mater saying: "It's true that my ministry training didn't teach me how to address every situation I'm now experiencing in the local church. How could it have? What it did, however, was help me become the kind of person who possesses the wisdom and basic tools necessary to figure out how to address every situation I'm now experiencing in the local church." This, in my opinion, is some high praise for a well-balanced ministry education!

adequate training of future church leaders must include the preaching, teaching and leadership skills required to successfully encourage congregants to live in an Ananias-like manner. Given these truths, the brief discussion that follows will focus on a couple of less obvious but no less important theological and practical matters.

Recognizing a false antithesis. Professors of Christian theology and ministry can teach their students how to recognize a false antithesis and to always look for a mediating position instead. My experience is that even though balance is crucial to the Christian life, most Christians, even Christian leaders, follow the trajectory of the proverbial pendulum from one extreme position to the other. A nuanced, balanced, tension-embracing position between two eccentric perspectives is often the one we should strive to maintain. While there is such a thing as a true antithesis (e.g., see Mt 21:23-27), in our wonderfully complex world, the correct answers to many of life's most profound questions are not either-or but both/and.[17] For example: God is both one and triune at the same time; Jesus is both fully God and fully human; the kingdom of God is both already and not yet; worship should involve both the head and the heart; the goal of Christian ministry is both believing and beloving; our resource for ministry is both the Word and the Spirit. The presence of such paradoxical realities in Christian orthodoxy and orthopraxy are nearly endless.

A *false* antithesis occurs when someone attempts to steer people toward a position by presenting only two options: a pathetic caricature of the opposing view and a winsome portrayal of his or her own. This kind of argumentation occurs in discussions of topics ranging from parenting to politics, and especially in theology. Regardless of the actual topic, the message of the false antithesis usually goes something like this: "Since the opposing view is so ridiculously conservative (or liberal), only a fool (or demon) will disagree with me!"

In these types of discussions—when an antithesis is presented in a dogmatic manner—it is imperative that we think deeply and biblically

---

[17]Frost and Hirsch lend some support for the idea that we should often be on the lookout for mediating both-and solutions to vexing questions and problems (see Michael Frost and Alan Hirsch, *The Shaping of Things to Come* [Peabody, Mass.: Hendrickson, 2003], p. 27).

to locate, if possible, a mediating alternative, a *both/and* rather than an *either-or* position. And lest we disparage this move as a cowardly compromise, the truth is that the mediating alternative is actually a positive position that requires courage to hold since (1) it will come under fire by critics on both sides, and (2) often requires the embrace of an intellectual paradox with all the psychological ambiguity and existential discomfort such a move usually entails. But as Ray Anderson, my theology mentor in graduate school, used to say to mitigate a tendency toward either a pride- or fear-based theological dogmatism, "a *little* ambiguity never hurt anyone!"[18]

This concept of the mediating alternative relates to the issue at hand as that which will enable us to see through false antitheses that will otherwise cause us to conclude that

- Christ's followers must take their missional ministry cues from either the Word or the Spirit
- the reception of the Spirit is about either conversion-initiation or charismatic empowering
- prophetic activity involves either speech or action
- church members either should be encouraged to exercise prophetic gifts or frequently warned of their potential for abuse
- prophetic activity takes place either inside churches or out in the streets
- churches must choose to approach ministry in either an incarnational or attractional manner[19]
- the means of missional ministry is either gospel proclamation or social action
- our missional response to the Spirit can either be faithful or hopeful (in terms of fruitfulness)

---

[18]Anderson attributed this quote to Charles Suhor, deputy executive director of the National Council of Teachers of English, who formulated the law when he discovered "The universe is intractably squiggly" (cited in Paul Dickson, *The Official Rules* [New York: Dell, 1981], p. 226). For more on this, see my discussion of the root causes of Christian pharisaism in Tyra, *Defeating Pharisaism*, pp. 68-73.

[19]See n. 14 in chap. 4.

These are just a few of the binary options related to missional faithfulness that beg for a mediating, tension-embracing, alternative position. It is my contention that the skillful, artful, missionally faithful pastor is the one who (1) has learned that when it comes to theology and ministry, false antitheses abound, (2) recognizes and avoids these spurious arguments, always on the lookout for a mediating alternative, and (3) is teaching his or her parishioners to do likewise. This will require a theological education that helps students develop the habits of (1) thinking deeply and biblically about everything they read and hear, and (2) always being wary of dogmatic arguments that allow for only two eccentric, mutually exclusive positions. In other words, it is never too early to begin training future ministers how to, as Jesus put it, "stop judging by mere appearances, and make a right judgment" (Jn 7:24).

Model cardinal components. Professors of Christian theology and ministry can model for their students some of the cardinal components of missional faithfulness. Perhaps the biggest reason why my seminary education had such a profoundly positive effect on me was that I had professors who not only taught me valuable theological principles but modeled them for me as well. As a result of their example, it has been my goal as a pastor and professor to pass this legacy on to my parishioners and students. This modeling needs to happen everywhere evangelicals are trained for ministry, especially with regard to two aspects of missional faithfulness: prophetic activity and a humble orthodoxy.

We can model for our students the practice of prophetic speech by carefully praying over both the preparation and presentation of each lecture we deliver. Scripture teaches us to "pray in the Spirit" (see Rom 8:26-27; 1 Cor 14:15; Eph 6:18; Jude 20), and I have found that doing so prior to my preparation and presentation activities greatly increases the likelihood that I will end up writing and saying things that I did not know I knew. In other words, classroom lectures can be just as "anointed" as any Sunday sermon. Be aware: I am not talking about the style of delivery (emotion, gesticulation, tone of voice, etc.), but the content. The Holy Spirit can speak through us to our students in a prophetic manner, driving important, biblically grounded truths into the depths of their hearts in such a way as to become a permanent part of their theological and ministry paradigms.

Likewise, we can model what it means to act prophetically when we follow up on one of those innate hunches we sometimes have that an individual student needs some special attention: a word of encouragement or counsel, or perhaps some material resources. I am fairly certain that the popularity of some Christian professors is due not only to their intellect and pedagogy, but also their ability to prophetically re-present Christ to their students, both in and out of the classroom.

Furthermore, as was noted in the previous chapter, a contextually sensitive approach to ministry here in the West must recognize the increasing influence of postmodernism. One of the entailments of the postmodern turn is an aversion to strident truth claims articulated in an arrogant, overly dogmatic manner. Thus, another aspect of the missional faithfulness that can and should be modeled by Christian professors for their students is a commitment to a modest (rather than overreaching) epistemology and the humble orthodoxy that results from it. If the ultimate goal is to encourage rank-and-file church members, many of whom are still steeped in a hard philosophical foundationalism, to engage in missional ministry that is winsome rather than off-putting to the post-Christians who inhabit our ministry context here in the West, we must ask: Where will this new commitment to a more humble epistemology and orthodoxy come from?[20] The answer is that unless it comes from the model presented to them by the leaders

---

[20] *Epistemological foundationalism* is the idea that epistemological certainty is possible because our knowledge rests on a foundation of indubitable first order truths that can be "proved" through rational argument. Evangelical philosopher Nicholas Wolterstorff explains that the goal of foundationalism is "a body of theories from which all prejudice, bias, and unjustified conjecture have been eliminated. To attain this, we must begin with a firm foundation of certitude and build the house of theory on it by methods of whose reliability we are equally certain" (Nicholas Wolterstorff, *Reason Within the Bounds of Religion* [Grand Rapids: Eerdmans, 1993], p. 28; see also Stanley J. Grenz and John R. Franke, *Beyond Foundationalism* [Louisville: John Knox Press, 2001], pp. 23, 30). For a concise but helpful treatment of the major barriers to reaching unchurched/unreached people in our post-Christian ministry context, see Ed Stetzer and David Putnam, *Breaking the Missional Code* [Nashville: Broadman & Holman, 2006], pp. 82-83). Regarding *humble apologetics*, I have in mind an epistemological postfoundationalism or "critical realism" which contends that while all knowledge is indeed conditioned by our historical and cultural context, it is still possible to reach beyond these contexts to arrive at a "sufficient, good enough" knowledge of the world around us (see Kevin J. Vanhoozer, *The Drama of Doctrine* [Louisville: Westminster John Knox, 2005], pp. 286, 304; see also John G. Stackhouse, *Humble Apologetics* [New York: Oxford University Press, 2002], p. 104).

of their churches, who in turn had it modeled for them by their theological mentors, it probably will not. While it is often true that in the academy "pomposity happens!" the members of the Christian academy can and should model what it means to hold and offer to others an orthodoxy that is humble rather than haughty and hostile. Through our example, we evangelical professors can communicate the message that while there is such a thing as Christian dogma, not every doctrine is something we must argue about. Moreover, we can and should demonstrate for our students a capacity to disagree with others without resorting to derisive and dismissive comments (ad hominem arguments) in the process.[21]

In these ways professors of Christian theology and ministry can help steer their students away from a fighting fundamentalism on the one hand and an orthodoxy that is too accommodating on the other. I could be wrong, but I suspect that the future of the evangelical movement in the West hinges on the next generation of evangelical leaders getting this right. How will the church members they eventually lead be able to offer a persuasive alternative to the religious relativism all around them if they have no ability to gain a hearing among their post-Christian peers or if these Christians have embraced religious relativism themselves? This places a lot of responsibility on the shoulders of future Christian leaders and, ultimately, on those who are training them now.

I began this chapter with a ministry account that illustrates what the dynamic of missional prophetic activity looks like when engaged in by the members of evangelical churches. I then went on to suggest some things that local church leaders, denominational officials and members of the Christian academy can do to increase the number of rank-and-file church members who embrace a missional pneumatol-

---

[21]In *Humble Apologetics* Stackhouse includes a chapter that provides a number of "guidelines for apologetic conversation." It is instructive that the first two guidelines call for the adoption of an attitude of humility on the part of the apologist: "First, Listen and Understand," and then "Offer, Don't Demand" (Stackhouse, *Humble Apologetics*, pp. 161-67). I recommend the entire chapter for those who want to explore at more depth what contemporary Christians must do in order to gain a hearing among an increasing number of members of our increasingly postmodern, post-Christian society. Ibid., pp. 161-205.

ogy and the prophetic activity that is at its heart. In the process, my goal has been both to inspire hope and allay fears. I trust that I succeeded sufficiently to encourage others to at least experiment with a missional pneumatology, giving it an opportunity to make a difference in our world for Christ.

Imagine to what the world would look like if millions of evangelicals were to engage in the kind of prophetic evangelism, edification and equipping described in this book!

Conclusion

IN THE COURSE OF WRITING this book I have been asked many times by friends, colleagues, students and church members to summarize what it is about. My most basic response to such queries is that the book "explores the relationship between prophetic speech and action, and the missional faithfulness of evangelical Christians."

Toward this end, in chapter one we examined the support which both the Old Testament and New Testament provide for the dynamic connection between an in-filling experience with the Holy Spirit and the phenomenon of prophetic activity (prophetic speech and action). In chapter two the focus was on the connection between prophetic activity and the amazing missional faithfulness manifested by the earliest Christians. We discovered that the book of Acts makes it clear that the prophetic evangelism, edification and equipping engaged in not only by apostles and deacons but rank-and-file disciples like Ananias (of Damascus) caused the church to blossom despite the hostile environment it was planted in.[1] Chapter three focused on the phenomenal growth of the Pentecostal-charismatic movement worldwide, once again demonstrating a dynamic connection between missional faithfulness and prophetic activity on the part of ordinary church members. In chapter four we examined what a missional faithfulness might look like in the post-Christian West—how the endeavor to form missional churches might be enhanced by a recovery of the dynamic of prophetic speech and ac-

---

[1]Frederick Dale Bruner is careful to point out that Ananias was neither an apostle nor a bishop (see Bruner, *A Theology of the Holy Spirit* [Grand Rapids: Eerdmans, 1970], p. 190).

tion. Finally, in chapter five we discussed some of the most basic steps that might be taken by local church leaders, denominational officials and members of the academy to increase the numbers of rank-and-file church members who are actually living an Ananias-like life—one that is earmarked by occasional, Spirit-directed engagements in prophetic ministry to others.

I am convinced that an embrace of a missional pneumatology can make a huge difference in the lives of individual Christ followers, local churches and the world as a whole. Think about it: what *would* the world be like if more evangelical believers were responding to strong impressions provided by the Spirit of mission to

- share the gospel with particular people at particular times in particular ways

- provide particular kinds of support for particular missionaries at particular times

- give more generously than usual in particular offerings

- send notes of spiritual encouragement to particular people both within and outside the church family

- be especially generous in Jesus' name to particular homeless people requesting a handout

- launch or partner with particular ministries designed to alleviate human suffering in Christ's name

- make peace between particular brothers and sisters in Christ estranged from one another

- pray for some particular person they had not communicated with for a while

The possibility that the Holy Spirit might press us into service with this kind of particularity on any given day makes the Christian life exciting rather than boring. The dynamic of prophetic activity can cause churches in the West to exhibit the same kind of missional faithfulness that is occurring in the Majority World, where the phenomenon is much more common. The manifested presence of the risen Jesus that occurs whenever one of his followers obeys a genuine prompting by the Holy Spirit to speak and act prophetically into someone else's life puts to the lie the notion that he is simply one among many paths to God.

Earlier in this work I made reference to Youth With a Mission (YWAM), a dynamic missionary organization founded by Loren Cunningham as a result of a prophetic encounter he had with the Spirit of mission. I recently came across a magazine article that draws attention to the fact that YWAM is currently celebrating its fiftieth anniversary. The article says,

> Listening to God's voice and obeying Him, Cunningham says, is the key to YWAM's phenomenal impact. Last year, 26 young YWAMers in Nigeria were praying and felt God telling them to witness to a group of vicious militants known for murder, rape and occult practices. Thinking they might have the wrong idea, the young missionaries returned to prayer, listening patiently for God's voice. The word came back loud and clear: Go!
>
> So the YWAMers, most in their late teens, moved into the militant's camp and started serving them, doing menial chores and telling them about Jesus. In the past year, hundreds have surrendered their weapons and come to Christ. "They're broken . . . they're crying out to God," Cunningham says, "all because 26 young people listened to God's voice and obeyed."[2]

This story powerfully illustrates the possibility of contemporary Christ followers living their lives in an Ananias-like manner: that is, hearing God's voice and receiving ministry assignments from him that call for them to prophetically speak and act into hurting people's lives, with the result that lives are changed, disciples are made and the church is built up.

What is it, we may ask, that enabled these young people to boldly respond to what they sensed to be a prompting of the Spirit of mission when the stakes were so high? While I obviously cannot speak for them with any degree of authority, I suspect that their answer would be that the faithfulness of God's Spirit elicits and makes possible a

---

[2]Julian Lukins, "Man (and 2.5 Million Youth) With a Mission," *Charisma*, September 2010, p. 37.

missional faithfulness on the part of God's people. At least that has been my experience.

St. John of the Cross wrote about the experience he referred to as the "dark night of the soul." My version of this painful but ultimately beneficial spiritual experience occurred back in the early 1980s and lasted for eighteen months. I had been under a lot of stress, doing my best in my mid-twenties to pastor a small, somewhat dysfunctional church while also hurrying my way through an M.Div. degree and endeavoring to be a responsible husband and father. Then, on top of the physical, emotional and intellectual stress I was already wrestling with, I experienced a medical problem that, given my family's medical history, had the effect of thrusting me into a season of psychological and spiritual desolation. During the next year and a half I remained fully functional in terms of all my responsibilities. However, my spiritual life was like a guitar string tightened to the point of breaking. There were times during this ordeal when I began to wonder if God was there, and if he was, if he really cared.

Then I had an experience of the faithfulness of the Spirit that has profoundly affected my walk with Christ ever since. It was late on a Saturday night. I had just finished cleaning the church and was kneeling at the altar in prayer, desperately seeking some relief from a pervasive sense of anxiety, which had recently increased a great deal. It just so happened that I had been studying in seminary the theology of John Calvin and the doctrine of the double decree. At that spiritually precarious time in my life, on top of everything else I was wrestling with, I applied this doctrine to my life in the worst possible way,[3] with the result that, in addition to a phobic anxiety regarding my physical well-being, I began to be plagued by worry concerning my spiritual well-being.

While this may sound completely irrational and theologically naive to anyone reading this now, at the time it was very real. So, there I was, in an empty, dimly lit church, literally kneeling at an altar and crying out to God for some sort of word of assurance that he loves me and had

---

[3]See Karl Barth's warning in this regard in his *Church Dogmatics* 2/2, trans. G. T. Thomson and Harold Knight (Peabody, Mass.: Hendrickson, 1957), pp. 12-14.

chosen me to be part of his elect. While praying, I sensed that I was supposed to pick up my Bible and read Deuteronomy 7:6. Please trust me when I say that I had no awareness at that time (at least consciously) of what this passage had to say. Still, in obedience to this prompting by the Spirit, I turned to the designated passage and read these words: "For you are a people holy to the LORD your God. The LORD your God has chosen you out of all the peoples on the face of the earth to be his people, his treasured possession."

Out of all the verses in the Bible, I heard a voice in my heart telling me at that critical time to turn to and read this particular passage. What are you supposed to do with an experience like this, an experience that so dramatically and profoundly demonstrates the faithfulness of the Holy Spirit to those he indwells? What are we supposed to do with a God like this, a God so faithful that he is willing, at just the right time, to effect a personal encounter with one of his children, and to do so in a way that would leave him marked, in a good way, for the rest of his life? I want to suggest that the only appropriate response to such a God is the one modeled for us by the apostle Paul who wrote:

> For Christ's love compels us, because we are convinced that one died for all, and therefore all died. And he died for all, that those who live should no longer live for themselves but for him who died for them and was raised again. (2 Cor 5:14-15)

This, I contend, is the ground of our commitment to mission. It is God's prior faithfulness to us that makes possible a missional response to him in return that is both faithful and hopeful.

I hope my sharing this very personal story will help others better understand why I am willing to do my best to trust and obey the promptings I occasionally sense from the Spirit to communicate to others the grace and mercy of God. More than that, I hope that this story, as well as the others included in these pages, will motivate evangelical Christians to open their hearts toward an embrace of the missional pneumatology and the possibility of Ananias-like experiences with the Spirit of mission.

I began this book with a story of some ministry conversations I have been having with a neighborhood friend. While out walking just this morning (at the time of this writing) I stopped and chatted with this dear lady. In the course of our conversation she indicated that the physical ailment that I had promised to pray for had suddenly disappeared. She said to me, "Isn't that funny?" With a smile I responded that since I had been praying for her, maybe a better word for this development was "wonderful." She smiled in return.

So the conversation and the relationship continue. And all the while I keep praying, "Holy Spirit, what are you up to in my friend's life? How might I cooperate with you in achieving God's purposes for her?"

Where will all this lead? That is not my responsibility. It is my responsibility to obey any promptings that come from the Spirit of mission to speak and act toward her in a way that manifests the reality that the risen Christ is Lord, and that he longs to restore her to union with God and communion with others, in the context of a community, for the good of others and the world. A missional faithfulness through prophetic speech and action: this is our only responsibility—and great privilege.

> If you then, though you are evil, know how to give good gifts to your children, how much more will your Father in heaven give the Holy Spirit to those who ask him! (Lk 11:13)

> But you will receive power when the Holy Spirit comes on you; and you will be my witnesses in Jerusalem, and in all Judea and Samaria, and to the ends of the earth. (Acts 1:8)

Name Index

Subject Index

Scripture Index